High Performance Computing

High Performance Computing

Kevin Dowd

O'Reilly & Associates, Inc.
103 Morris Street, Suite A
Sebastopol, CA 95472

High Performance Computing
by Kevin Dowd

Editor: Mike Loukides
Production Editor: Leslie Chalmers
Book Designer: Jennifer Niederst

Printing History:

June 1993:   First Edition.

ISBN: 1-56592-032-5

Table of Contents

Figures

16: *Shared-Memory Multiprocessors*   *325*

B: *How to Tell When Loops Can Be Interchanged*   *351*

Examples

Tables

Preface

It's hard to keep track of an industry that changes as quickly as ours. The supercomputer and minisupercomputer markets are being dissolved from below by a handful of microprocessor families. The computers at the high end are peculiar collections of hundreds or thousands of processing elements, and generally very difficult to program. Gone are the days of the "garage" outfits; it takes many tens of millions of dollars to bring a competitive computer design to market. They may appear to be faster versions of computers that you already know, but the workstations of today are much faster and *very* different from those of just a year or two ago.

Where does the performance come from? Some of it comes from increased clock rates. But more significantly, both CISC and RISC architectures are borrowing and innovating with techniques formerly unique to supercomputers and large mainframes. They can execute two or more instructions at a time, and are being combined to form very powerful multiprocessors. Much of this performance is available just for moving your code to a new machine. Sometimes though, they can be fickle performers, and require your help.

For instance, did you know that the peak performance for matrix multiplication doubles on the IBM RS6000 if structured correctly? Or what a good compiler can do to help the Motorola 88100 processor handle branches at run time? Why is the Intel i860XP such an elusive target for compiler designers? What can be done to increase the performance of an application on a MIPS processor or SPARC?

Knowing how to judge the marketplace may be even more important than understanding how the new processors work. If you are faced with the task of interpreting benchmarks to support a purchase decision, it's good to feel confident about them. Industry benchmarks measure different things, some of which may apply to you and some of which may not. If you decide to run your own benchmarks, these will be your best barometer, provided that you administer them with care.

You can also tune your home-grown applications to squeeze more performance from the hardware you already own. But just as you can't tell what string to tune by banging all of a piano's keys at once, you can't tune a program based on a single performance measure. You need a profile that tells you how individual parts of your program behave. This will tell you where to focus your tuning efforts. Different flavors of applications exhibit characteristic execution profiles, revealing much about what can be done. For instance, simple source code transformations can make a big difference in numerically intensive applications. Ordering data access patterns or object files in the load module can ease troublesome cache behavior, and structuring critical branches correctly can lead to big performance gains.

Looking to the future, some applications will be good candidates for parallel computers. However, to run on a parallel machine, or to write code for a parallel machine, you need to think about how the program can be split up into pieces. For some applications, parallel computers are a natural, but others will benefit very little.

Who Should Buy This Book?

This book is written for people who are interested in computer performance or who need to understand it for their job. Those faced with purchase decisions will find clear explanations of industry benchmarks and the benchmark process, as well as a few pointers on what to watch out for. People writing or tuning code will learn techniques for getting the best performance from their workstations, plus an appreciation for how their programs play to the compiler and the hardware. And, for those who enjoy tracking computer performance developments, this book can serve as a reference to answer some of the how and why questions as the statistics come in.

What's in This Book

The book is divided into four sections. **Section I** describes computer architecture and compilers for those who want to know how the new processors get their performance.

Chapter 1, *What is High Performance Computing*, prepares the stage for the rest of the book.

Chapter 2, *RISC Computers*, briefly describes developments in computer architecture that lead to the design of Reduced Instruction Set Computers (RISC), and explains how they work.

Chapter 3, *Memory*, explains how computer memory systems are organized and why a good memory system is crucial for performance.

Chapter 4, *What an Optimizing Compiler Does*, gives a tour of an optimizing compiler and describes the techniques employed by most.

Section II is a hands-on guide for porting, profiling, benchmarking, and tuning, with some time out to consider what benchmarks mean, and what the compiler is looking for from the programmer.

Chapter 5, *Clarity*, gives you some tips for writing understandable code, an especially important topic in this book because optimizations can bruise the surrounding code. The clearer the author's intent, the easier it will be for others to maintain the code.

Chapter 6, *Finding Porting Problems*, explains some of the pitfalls you may face when moving programs between machines—particularly when migrating code from a VAX or IBM mainframe to a RISC platform.

Chapter 7, *Timing and Profiling*, tells you how you can measure the performance of a program, subroutine, or loop. This is important if you will be benchmarking or tuning your code.

Chapter 8, *Understanding Parallelism*, takes a break from the hands-on to explain what parallelism is. This chapter is good background for the tuning tips in the proceeding chapters, but it can also be read by itself, or as a follow-on to chapter 3.

Chapter 9, *Eliminating Clutter*, discusses optimization techniques for eliminating those parts of code that add to run time, but don't contribute to the answer.

Chapter 10, *Loop Optimizations*, explains how the parallelism in loops can be exposed so that an optimizing compiler can take advantage of it.

Chapter 11, *Memory Reference Optimizations*, describes techniques for improving the way programs make use of the memory system. As processors get faster, good memory access patterns become increasingly important.

Chapter 12, *Language Support for Performance*, talks about other ways to get more performance from programs, aside from hand tuning. Preprocessors, subroutine libraries, and explicitly parallel languages and environments are discussed.

Section III is about evaluating performance.

Chapter 13, *Industry Benchmarks*, describes the meaning of MIPs, Megaflops, Whetstones, Dhrystones and other commonly quoted measures of performance. This chapter can be read independently of the others.

Chapter 14, *Running Your Own Benchmarks*, discusses benchmarking strategies at a high level. This chapter is a good guide when you are planning a workstation acquisition and want to be sure that your benchmarks are comprehensive.

Section IV describes parallel and massively parallel computers and gives some examples of how you could structure your code to run on them.

Chapter 15, *Large Scale Parallel Computing*, talks about dividing an application so that it can be spread across multiple processors. It discusses two classes of distributed memory computers, and the challenges of programming them.

Chapter 16, *Multiprocessors*, describes shared memory computers, such as the multiprocessing workstations being offered by several vendors. These are programmed differently from distributed memory machines.

Most chapters are followed by a short set of exercises. Unlike the exercises in most engineering texts, these are mostly thought experiments, without well-defined answers. They are designed to get you thinking about the hardware on your desk. Most of the answers depend on the particular hardware you have, and will certainly change over time. I've written up some answers for a few common architectures; they are available via anonymous FTP.

Some related subjects fall outside the scope of this book, particularly algorithms, graphics, and I/O performance. However, this book gives you a good foundation for understanding these topics, as it will help you recognize the potential for performance in an algorithm or method.

Conventions

The following conventions are used in this book:

`Constant Width`	is used for source code samples, and for quotations from source code within the text, including variable and function names. Constant width is also used for output printed by a computer, and for the contents of files.

Constant
Bold   is used for commands typed verbatim by the user.

Italic   is used for command names, directory names, and filenames. It is also used for terms that are being defined.

Bold   is used for vectors (in the mathematical sense) and for command options. I admit that the difference between a mathematical vector and an array in a program is miniscule.

Acknowledgments

The key to writing is learning to organize thoughts, to tell a story, to see things the way others see them. I'd like to thank Mike Loukides, my editor, for helping me understand this. Mike has an unassuming manner that conceals a great talent for finding the simple truth in things and stating it plainly.

I'd also like to thank the staff at O'Reilly and Associates, particularly Leslie Chalmers, Stephen Spainhour, Clairemarie Fisher O'Leary, Chris Reilly, Edie Freedman, Ellie Cutler, Donna Woonteiler, Linda Walsh, Tim O'Reilly, and everyone whose behind the scenes efforts went into the finished product. A personal thanks to Leslie for copyediting the text several times, preening and polishing my English. Chris quickly and professionally created enough illustrations for a dozen books this size.

Thanks also to the reviewers, Philip Koopman Jr., Keith Bierman, Harold Dolan, Marshall Presser, Mike Frisch, Darryl Parsely, Andy Oram, and Eric Pearce for keeping me honest.

Thanks to my parents, Don and Carol, for making me what I am. And thanks to my wife Paula for making this possible, and for the time we sacrificed getting here.

I

Modern Computer Architecture

1

What is High Performance Computing?

Why Worry About Performance?

The dizzying rate at which computers are changing has one undeniable consequence: everyone is confused. The programmer is asking, "How do I optimize my code for this new machine?" The manager or buyer asks, "How do I make purchase decisions that I won't regret in two months?" The programmer needs to know how to structure code to "play to" a number of new architectures—something that's particularly hard since, in the past decade, we've gotten a bit lazy; C and FORTRAN do a good (but not perfect) job of shielding us from the difficulties of the hardware. The manager needs to know how to evaluate claims made by different vendors, and how to compare computers that may completely different, structurally, from each other.

In either case, though, you've got to start with a basic understanding of what goes into computer performance: aside from faster cycle times (which only tell part of the story), one computer will deliver better results than another. One may excel on floating point programs, but deliver mediocre results when you connect a dozen terminals for word-processing use—or vice versa. Understanding something about computer architecture is crucial to understanding computer performance—whether you're developing software or managing a purchasing organization.

By saying that you need to understand something about computer architecture, we're admittedly running against the current religion. Not terribly long ago any programmer worth his or her salary could write assembly code as fluently as high-level code (C, FORTRAN, PL/1, BASIC). When performance was really important to you, you'd code a few critical routines in assembly language. You'd write the rest of the program (90%, maybe even 99.9% of it) in a high-level language, like FORTRAN.

Well, that's the distant past—though for many of us, it's not all that distant. As compiler technology improved, and as computer cycle times got faster, assembly language programming gradually fell from style. Assembly language programming isn't chic, and will probably never be fashionable again. And we're not suggesting that you take it up as a hobby—far from it. But it *is* worth taking stock and figuring out what we gave up when we started to write code exclusively in C and FORTRAN. Admittedly, we gained a lot: code portability and quicker development cycles are nothing to sneeze at. But we did lose the ability to squeeze the last few cycles out of a program's execution time.

As long as we were only talking about a few cycles, the trouble of tweaking code for the best performance wasn't really worth the effort. The few people who really needed to worry about performance—those who had access to vector supercomputers—knew how to get it. In the last few years, the issues have changed a bit. The CISC processors of the early and middle 1980s were good, reliable workhorses: hand-tuning a few loops wouldn't yield much. However, computers of the 1990s have suddenly become more finicky. While they're better performers overall, a bit of extra attention paid to a few key loops here and there can pay off with a huge increase in performance.

Here's a quick example. I once was able to improve a program's performance by a factor of 100 by taking out some apparently harmless debugging code. Harmless? Well, yes: on an 80386-based personal computer, or a 68000-based workstation, the debugging code would have had a negligible effect on performance. On the workstation in question, though, a stray "if" statement happened to be just what was needed to prevent the compiler from making some crucial optimizations. This example may be extreme, but the problem itself (together with the thought that went into detecting and solving it) isn't unusual by any means.

Modern workstations are finicky for several reasons—in a nutshell:

- Processors incorporate pipelining (and other parallel techniques) to a much greater degree than they used to. When "pipelining" meant million dollar Cray supercomputers, the average software developer didn't have to think about this very much. But now that many common desktop computers are pipelined, including the HP 700 series, the IBM RS/6000, the DEC Alpha/AXP, and the next generation of Intel microprocessors, the average user has inherited the performance issues that formerly belonged to heavily funded research centers.

- Processors have become much, much faster in the past decade, but memory speeds haven't kept pace. In the hardware, a lot of fancy tricks are now used to help memory keep up with the CPU. But a bad memory access pattern in a crucial loop might defeat all this wonderful hardware—in which case, your 100 MHz processor isn't doing you a lot of good.

Fortunately, the task of hand-tuning code isn't as arduous as it was a few decades ago. You really don't need to know assembly language—though the ability to read an assembly listing won't hurt. A good modern compiler can do most of the work. Many tuning problems can be solved just by giving the compiler more information about your code: telling it explicitly what kinds of optimizations are legal. In the worst case, you'll need to rearrange some loops to improve memory reference patterns or to expose some parallelism that the compiler can take advantage of.

The most recent generation of processors is so fast that you may not notice you're only getting 40% or 50% of the performance you deserve. And you may not care. Faster processors running at 50% of capacity might be more cost-effective than several weeks of time spent hand-tuning code—but then again, they may not. If you don't understand what you're leaving "on the table," you're not in a position to judge whether the tradeoff is worthwhile or not. And you certainly don't know whether your investment in a "high-performance" workstation has paid off.

Measuring Performance

Once you've decided that you can't sit back and passively accept whatever performance your code and hardware give you, you need to know something about measuring performance: did the changes you made actually bring about an improvement? Is the new, 100 MHz GZMO-80 workstation really better than your old Sun 3?

Measuring performance can seem like an art—and, if you've ever sat in a conference room while a salesperson has filled it with a blue haze of benchmark numbers, it can seem like black art, indeed. But there aren't any real mysteries here. It isn't difficult to understand and interpret standard industry benchmarks. It's also easy to take the next step: to package your own benchmark, something that's representative of the work you actually do.

The difficulty of benchmarking is that most programs only stress one or two aspects of a computer: for example, a program that fits entirely into the computer's instruction cache may not test memory at all, though it may be a great measure of raw CPU speed. There is no single, completely representative test of a computer's behavior. Even your own code, while it may accurately reflect your workload today, may not reflect your workload next week or next year: add a fancier graphical interface, a better solver, and an interest in handling larger problems, and you may have a completely different game. To avoid surprises, you need to be acquainted with computer architecture, which will help you decide what the benchmarks are really measuring. It also helps to understand how a benchmarking group will tweak a program to get the best performance—even if you never do the job yourself.

The Next Step

Quite aside from economics, computer performance is a fascinating, challenging subject. Computer architecture is interesting in its own right, and a topic that any computer professional should be comfortable with. Getting the last bit of performance out of an important application can be a stimulating game, in addition to an economic necessity. And, while I won't vouch for it, there are probably a few people who enjoy matching wits with a clever vendor.

What do you need to get into the game? We've already touched on the topics:

- A basic understanding of modern computer architecture. You don't need an advanced degree in computer engineering, but you do need to understand the "lay of the land."
- A basic understanding of why some codes run well, and others don't—or, to look at it the other way, how to adapt code so that it will run well on a particular machine.
- A basic understanding of benchmarking, or performance measurement, so you can quantify your own successes and failures and cut through the fog that surrounds so many performance claims.

It seems to be an axiom that the need for computing power expands to fill the computing power available. If, in ten years, computers are ten or a hundred times faster than they are now, we'll still want more, and we'll still be worrying about performance. We'll want to solve even bigger problems and run even more complex programs. However, another fact is also likely to be true. Barring some real breakthroughs in compiler technology, the computers of the 2000's will be even more finicky than the computers of the 1990's. The next factor of ten in computer power probably won't come from huge increases in clock speed; sooner or later, physical laws limit what you can put on a chip. The next major gains will probably come from increasingly complex computers: massively parallel processors, and so on. As the future becomes the present, it will become even more important to understand computer performance.

That's what this book is all about. If you're interested, read on.

2
RISC Computers

Nobody knew that the transmission in their car was standard until the family down the street drove up in an automatic. The same sort of thing happened with *Complex Instruction Set Computers* (CISC), such as VAXes and PCs. We used them for years before learning that they were different somehow. They have been reclassified to make room for the corresponding new thing: *Reduced Instruction Set Computers* (RISC).

As you can see, there is some disagreement in instruction set philosophy: a CISC instruction set is made up of powerful primitives, close in functionality to the primitives of high level languages like C or FORTRAN. It captures the sense of "don't do in software what you can do in hardware." RISC, on the other hand, emphasizes low level primitives, far below the complexity of a high level language. You can compute anything you want using either approach, though it will probably take more machine instructions if you're using RISC. The important difference is that with RISC you can trade instruction set complexity for speed.

To be fair, RISC isn't really all that new. There were some important early machines that pioneered RISC philosophies, such as the CDC 6600 (1964) and the IBM 801 project (1975). It was in the mid 1980s, however, that RISC machines first posed a direct challenge to the CISC installed base. Heated debate broke out—RISC versus CISC—and even lingers today, though perhaps with less emotion; late generation CISC machines are looking more RISC-like, and some very old families of CISC, such as the DEC VAX, are being retired.

This chapter is about CISC and RISC instruction set architectures and the differences between them. I'll also describe newer processors with the ability to execute more than one instruction at a time.

Why CISC?

You might ask "If RISC is faster, why did people bother with CISC designs in the first place?" The short answer is that in the beginning, CISC *was* the right way to go; RISC wasn't always both feasible and affordable. Every kind of design incorporates trade-offs, and over time, the best systems will make them differently. In the past, the design variables favored CISC.

Space and Time

To start, let me ask you how well you know the assembly language for your workstation. The answer is probably that you haven't even seen it. Why bother? Compilers and development tools are very good, and if you have a problem, you can debug it at the source level. But thirty years ago, respectable programmers understood the machine's instruction set. High level language compilers were commonly available, but they didn't generate the speediest code, and they weren't terribly thrifty with memory. When programming, you needed to save both space and time, which meant you knew how to code in assembly language. Accordingly, you could develop an opinion about the machine's instruction set. A good instruction set was both easy to use and powerful. In many ways these qualities were the same: "powerful" instructions accomplished a lot, and saved the programmer from specifying many little steps—which, in turn, made them easy to use. But they had other, less apparent (though perhaps more important) features as well: powerful instructions saved memory and time.

Computers had very little storage by today's standards. An instruction that could roll all the steps of a complex operation, such as a do-loop, into single opcode* was a plus, because memory was precious. To put some stakes in the ground, consider the last vacuum tube computer that IBM built, the model 704 (1956). It had hardware floating point, including a division operation, index registers, and instructions which could operate directly on memory locations. For instance, you could add two numbers together and store the result back into memory with a single command. The Philco 2000, an early transistorized machine (1959), had an operation

---

*Opcode = operation code = instruction.

that could repeat a sequence of instructions until the contents of a counter was decremented to zero—very much like a do-loop. These were pretty complex operations, even by today's standards. But both machines had a limited amount of memory—32K words. The less memory your program took up, the more you had available for data, and the less likely you were to have to resort to overlaying portions of the program on top of one another.

Complex instructions saved time, too. Almost every large computer following the 704 had a memory system that was slower than its central processing unit (CPU). If a single instruction could encapsulate several primitive operations, such as incrementing a register and testing its value, there was the benefit of buying in bulk; time spent retrieving instructions from memory was reduced. This was particularly important because, with few exceptions, the machines of the late 1950s were very sequential; not until the current instruction was completed did the computer initiate the process of going out to memory to get the next instruction.* By contrast, modern machines form something of a bucket brigade—passing instructions in from memory and figuring out what they do on the way—so there are fewer gaps in processing.

If the designers of early machines had very fast and abundant instruction memory, sophisticated compilers, and the wherewithal to build the instruction "bucket brigade"—cheaply—they might have chosen to create machines with simple instruction sets. At the time, however, technology choices indicated that instructions should be powerful and thrifty with memory. Several sections ahead we will see how they built complexity into the instruction set using a technique called *microprogramming*.

Beliefs About Complex Instruction Sets

So, given that the lot was cast in favor of complex instruction sets, computer architects had license to experiment with matching them to the intended purposes of the machines. For instance, the do-loop instruction on the Philco 2000 looked like a good companion for procedural languages like FORTRAN. Machine designers assumed that compiler writers could

---

*In 1955, IBM began constructing a machine known as *Stretch*. It was the first computer to process several instructions at a time in stages, so that they streamed in, rather than being fetched in a piecemeal fashion. The goal was to make it 25 times faster than the then brand-new 704. It was six years before the first Stretch was delivered to Los Alamos National Laboratory. It was indeed faster, but it was expensive to build. Eight were sold for a loss of $20 million.

generate object programs using these powerful machine instructions, or possibly that the compiler could be eliminated, and that the machine could execute source code directly in hardware.

You can imagine how these ideas set the tone for product marketing. Up until the early 1980s it was common practice to equate a bigger instruction set with a more powerful computer. And in days when clock speeds were increasing by multiples, no increase in instruction set complexity could fetter a new model of computer enough so that there wasn't still a tremendous net increase in speed. CISC machines kept getting faster, in spite of the increased operation complexity.

As it turned out, assembly language programmers used the complicated machine instructions, but compilers generally did not. It was difficult enough to get a compiler to recognize when a complicated instruction could be used, but the real problem was one of optimizations: verbatim translation of source constructs isn't very efficient. An optimizing compiler works by simplifying and eliminating redundant computations. After a pass through an optimizing compiler, opportunities to use the complicated instructions disappear.

Memory Addressing Modes

The greatest strength of high level languages, such as FORTRAN and C, may be that they give programmers the freedom to organize data however it pleases them. Two dimensional data can be grouped into two dimensional arrays, or repeated patterns of dissimilar data can be grouped into C structures. One gets the impression that memory takes on the shape of the data, and that all variables are present all of the time. Of course they're not, but the details of dealing with the memory system are mercifully hidden from view.

For the assembly language programmer or a compiler, on the other hand, memory is no more than a sequence of storage locations.* The illusion that it has some other quality, like the multi-dimensionality of an array, has to

---

*This is true for machines with a central memory system. Later in the book we will look at computers with distributed memory systems, for which it is not true.

be provided in software, by the compiler, or in hardware. For instance, the array A appears to be part of the following FORTRAN subroutine:

```
        SUBROUTINE FOO (A,N)
        REAL A(*)
        DO 10 I=1,N
          A(I) = 0.0
  10    CONTINUE
```

In reality, A is passed in by a pointer, so upon entry we don't actually have A, *per se*, but a pointer to the start of the array. If we want to find the location of a particular element A(I), we have to calculate an offset from that pointer. The calculation needs to take into account the size of the elements of A as well:

```
address(A(I)) = address(A) + (I-1)*sizeof_datatype(A)
```

This is called an *address calculation*. It is a translation from the way the programmer views memory to the way the machine views it. Notice that there is more than one way to address the same location. We could have also found A(I) by stepping though the array from the start, as naturally happens when iterating in a loop, in which case the address of A(I) would be a function of the address of A(I-1):

```
address(A(I)) = address(A(I-1)) + sizeof_datatype(A)
```

For the compiler or assembly language programmer, it is not always necessary (or useful) to explicitly calculate the address of a piece of data. This is because all processors provide some capability for embedding address calculations into the instructions that reference memory. The components of the calculations, such as the pointer to A, come from registers or reserved fields within the instructions.

Hardware support for a particular kind of address calculation is called an *addressing mode*. Addressing modes are described by the sorts of functions they perform. For example, the term *indexed addressing mode* implies that an index register is involved, as might be needed when referencing data in an array via a subscript. Another example is *base register offset addressing mode*, in which a register holds the address of the start of a data area. Every processor, whether CISC or RISC, features some number of addressing modes. However, CISC processors generally support a wider variety. Again, the intent is that these will reflect the kinds of address calculations that are likely to be made from high level languages.

The number and complexity of the addressing modes is important because it is one of the features that the RISC approach to instruction set design tries to simplify. Sophisticated addressing modes complicate the instruction set just as much as sophisticated operations do.

Microcode

You might guess that a machine featuring a range of sophisticated addressing modes and instructions could be very complicated. Say, for instance, that a processor provides 200 different instructions, 100 of which can address memory. Of the instructions which can address memory, say that each can choose from five different addressing modes. That means that there are 100+100*5=600 legal instruction/address combinations. Additionally, some of them could be very involved, requiring several memory accesses. An example would be an operation that indirectly addresses* one of its operands. The length of the instruction might vary too, depending on the complexity or the number of auxiliary fields included. This is going to make the whole processor very complicated, especially the portion that decodes instructions and sequences the machine.

To get a feeling for what a CPU designer is up against, picture the inside of the processor as a collection of black box components (adders, shifters, and registers) connected together by *data paths* (wiring). To make it all work like a computer, you have to be able to selectively allow the black boxes to share data.

Figure 2-1 depicts a simple machine, and how it might execute a simple operation: adding the contents of two registers and returning the sum to a third. This takes three steps; in each step, the processor activates a pair of control points to move information across the data path. First it activates control points **a** and **f**, moving the contents of register 1; then **b** and **e**; then finally **c** and **d**, to move the result back to register 3. If we had two more data paths, we could perform the addition in a single step—the operands and result could be transferred almost simultaneously.

The choreography needed to activate the control points in the proper order comes from the CPU's *control section*. On a hardwired design, the control section is a tangle of dedicated sequential and combinatorial logic gates that converts the instructions from your program into control signals. For instance, an instruction that says "add register 1 to register 2 and leave the result in register 3" will be logically reduced to electrical signals that

---

*Indirect address: the address given in the instruction contains the address of the data, not the data itself.

activate control points. Although the above example is trivial, it helps to illustrate how much logic would be involved in building the control section for our hypothetical machine with 600 instruction/address combinations. On many older machines the control section, like the rest of the computer, was designed completely by hand. This was a difficult task in the first place, and was no easier to update and debug.

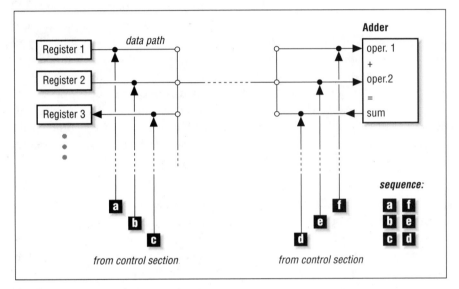

Figure 2-1: Registers, a single common data path, and an adder

In the early 1950s, a British scientist, Maurice V. Wilkes, introduced an easier method for controlling the machine: *microcoding.* He demonstrated that you could replace the hardwired control section with a set of *microinstructions* and a simple sequencer to dish them out, turning data paths and functional units on and off in the proper order. Each machine instruction—the lowest level that you would normally be able to see—was represented by a yet finer level of instructions called a *microprogram.* The sequencer was like a machine within a machine, interpreting your instructions with microcode, and giving the computer its personality.

The immediate benefit of microcoding versus hardwiring the control section was that it made it easier to build and maintain the instruction set; essentially, the instructions were being simulated, rather than being acted upon directly in hardware.* But microcoding also had two more powerful, secondary effects. Now nearly any instruction set could be emulated by any machine with a microcoded control section. Furthermore, extremely complicated operations—more complicated than anything you would want to hardwire—could be thrown into the instruction repertoire without additional hardware.

For the sake of argument, say that you want your instruction set to include an operation that converts lowercase letters to uppercase; you give the computer an "a" and the appropriate opcode, and out pops an "A." If you were implementing a non-microcoded design, you would have to build custom hardware to recognize the instruction and sequence the machine. If, on the other hand, your architecture was microcoded, the steps for converting lowercase letters to uppercase could be written into the microcode. Either way, it would appear to the user that there was a conversion instruction, but in the second case, it would be considerably easier for you to implement; you would essentially write a program to do it.

Since microcode allowed any machine to be emulated, it became possible to create an *architecture family*: a whole range of computers sharing a common instruction set. The first such architecture family was the S/360 series, introduced by IBM in 1964. From the programmer's point of view, the hardware looked the same for each machine in the family. Executable modules were portable between computers even though the processors might be based on completely different underlying hardware. The tremendous benefit (and marketing value) of the common instruction set architecture quickly became apparent. Incompatible computers, non-existent upgrade paths, recompilation, and recoding are discomforts people just don't want to deal with. A single microcoded architecture, on the other hand, can survive long enough to grow a large base of software and customers.

Microcode started as an engineering convenience, but as I mentioned previously, microcode (actually, complex instructions) also served to reduce traffic between the CPU and the memory system. An arbitrarily complex instruction could trigger a control sequence that would have taken a long

---

*The design and maintenance of hardwired processors is not as big a problem as it once was. Computers now take a big part in creating other computers. Silicon compilers, and more recently Logic Synthesis and VHDL—methods that turn design specifications into semiconductor layouts—have made it possible to hardwire fairly complex designs, yet retain the ability to debug or change them if necessary. They don't make the problem of complexity in hardwired designs disappear, but they go a long way to making it manageable. (VHDL stands for *V*ery *H*igh Speed Integrated Circuit *H*ardware *D*esign *L*anguage.)

time had it been written in more primitive steps and retrieved from memory in pieces. Furthermore, complex instructions freed up the (only) route between memory and the CPU so that data could move across it.

In short, microprogramming diminished traffic between the main memory system and the processor. We'll see shortly how developments in semiconductors, compilers, and computer architecture created alternatives to microcode. High speed caches, described in Chapter 3, pipelined instruction processing (next section), and advanced compiler technology made it attractive to replace the microcode with a compiler generated sequence of simple instructions.*

As I said before, with clock speeds increasing by leaps and bounds, it would have been hard to argue against using microcode until RISC machines arrived in the mid 1980s. More complex computers went faster anyway, just by virtue of increased hardware performance. But what was once essential has become a liability: all of these architectures—the VAX, the Intel 80x86 in PCs, the 680x0 family of processors, IBM's mainframes—have accumulated the baggage of many years of very complex and specialized instructions. It is not easy for new, microcoded CISC implementations to retain support for old instructions, yet stay competitive with RISC in terms of performance.

Making the Most of a Clock Tick

Everything within a digital computer (RISC or CISC) happens in step with a *clock:* a signal that paces the computer's circuitry. The rate of the clock, or *clock speed,* determines the overall speed of the processor. Like dancers doing the alley cat, the faster the music, the faster they dance. But just as you can't expect dancers to do the alley cat infinitely fast, there is an upper limit to how fast you can clock a computer.†

A number of parameters places an upper limit on the clock speed, including the semiconductor technology, packaging, and the length of wires tying the pieces together. Although it may be possible to reach blazing speed by optimizing all of the parameters, the cost can be prohibitive. Furthermore, exotic computers don't make good office mates; they can require too much power, produce too much noise and heat, or be too large. Anyway, there's incentive for manufacturer's to stick with manufacturable and marketable

---

*Not to imply that you can't use caches and microcode together...

†The alley cat falls apart somewhere below 1 MHz.

technologies. They have to look for other ways to get a performance advantage, which means making the best use of each clock tick.

Pipelines

Reducing the number of ticks it takes to execute an individual instruction would be a good idea, though cost and practicality become issues beyond a certain point. A greater benefit comes from overlapping instructions so that more than one can be in progress simultaneously. For instance, if you have two additions to perform, it would be nice to execute them both at the same time. How do you do that? The first, and perhaps most obvious approach, would be to start them simultaneously or side-by-side. Two additions would execute together and complete together in the amount of time it takes to perform one. As a result, the throughput would be effectively doubled. The downside is that you would need hardware for two adders in a situation where space is usually at a premium.

Other approaches for overlapping execution are more cost-effective than side-by-side execution. Imagine what it would be like if, after launching one operation, you could immediately launch another without waiting for the first to complete. Perhaps you could start another of the same type right behind the first one—like the two additions. This would give you nearly the performance of side-by-side execution without duplicated hardware. Such a mechanism does exist to varying degrees in all computers—CISC and RISC. It's called a *pipeline*. A pipeline takes advantage of the fact that many operations are divided into stages that can proceed concurrently.*

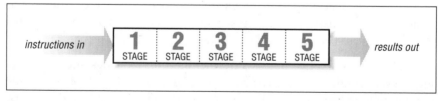

Figure 2-2: A pipeline

Figure 2-2 shows a conceptual diagram of a pipeline. An operation entering at the left proceeds on its own for five clock ticks before emerging at the right. Given that the pipeline stages are independent of one another,

---

*Here is a simple analogy: Imagine a group of kids crawling through a sewer pipe. They will all get through a lot faster if they pile in one after another than if they take turns.

up to five operations can be in-flight at a time. Consider how powerful this mechanism is: where before it would have taken five clock ticks to get a single result, a pipeline produces as much as one result every clock tick.

There are three primary areas where pipelining can be applied:

- Instruction Processing
- Memory References
- Floating Point Arithmetic Operations

We will look at instruction pipelining now, and return to the others later.

Instruction Pipelining

Pipelining is useful when a procedure can be divided into stages. Instruction processing fits into that category. The job of retrieving an instruction from memory, figuring out what it does, and doing it are separate steps we usually lump together when we talk about executing an instruction. The number of steps varies, depending on whose processor you are using, but for illustration, let's say there are five:

Instruction Fetch	The processor fetches an instruction from memory.
Instruction Decode	The instruction is recognized or decoded.
Operand Fetch	The processor fetches operands the instruction needs. These operands may be in registers or in memory.
Execute	The instruction gets executed.
Writeback	The processor *writes* the results *back* to wherever they are supposed to go—possibly registers, possibly memory.

Ideally, instruction 0 will be entering the operand fetch stage as instruction 1 enters instruction decode stage and instruction 2 starts instruction fetch, and so on. Our pipeline is five stages deep, so it should be possible to get five instructions in flight, all at once. If we could keep it up, we would see throughput of one instruction per clock cycle.

Simple as this illustration seems, instruction pipelining is complicated in real life. Each step must be able to occur on different instructions simultaneously, and delays in any stage have to be coordinated with all those that follow. For instance, if a complicated memory access occurs in stage three, the instruction needs to be delayed before going on to stage four because it will take some time to calculate the operand's address and retrieve it from memory. All the while, the rest of the pipeline will be stalled. A simpler instruction, sitting in one of the earlier stages, won't be able to continue until the traffic ahead clears up.

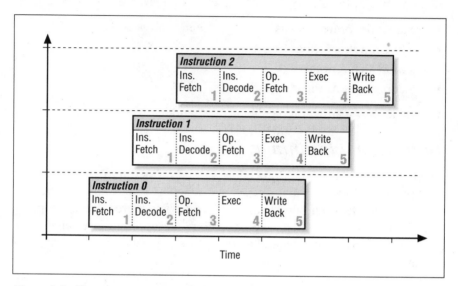

Figure 2-3: Three instructions in flight through one pipeline

Now imagine how a jump to a new program address, perhaps caused by an if-statement, could disrupt the pipeline flow. The processor draws instructions from memory sequentially. Discovering a jump in one of the stages means that everything else in the preceding stages suddenly comes from the wrong part of the program; new instructions have to be fetched from the place where the program was supposed to branch to, yet the pipeline will be full of instructions following the one that caused the branch. Somehow the processor either has to be able to clear out and restart the pipeline when a branch occurs, or it needs to be very clever about how branches are handled.

Anyway, you need optimal conditions to keep the pipeline moving. Even so, instruction pipelining is a big win—especially for RISC processors, as we'll see shortly. Interestingly, the idea dates back to the late 1950s and early 1960s with the UNIVAC LARC and the IBM Stretch. Instruction pipelining became mainstreamed in 1964, when the CDC 6600 and the IBM S/360 families were introduced with pipelined instruction units—on machines that represented RISC-ish and CISC designs respectively. To this day, ever more sophisticated techniques are being applied to instruction pipelining, as machines that can overlap instruction execution become commonplace.

Why RISC?

You could have built a RISC machine in 1960. (In fact, Seymour Cray built one in 1964—the CDC 6600.) However, given the same costs of components, technical barriers, and even expectations for how computers would be used, you would probably still have chosen a CISC design—even with the benefit of hindsight. A number of subsequent major (and some minor) developments have since made it possible to build RISC machines cheaply, including:

- Caches to speed instruction fetches
- Dramatic memory size increases/cost decreases
- Better Pipelining
- Advanced Optimizing Compilers

The belief that compilers would make use of sophisticated instructions and addressing modes didn't pan out. In fact, it was the other way around: experience with compilers showed that low level instructions could be shuffled about and optimized more easily. Compilers preferred simple instructions. Furthermore, humans were spending less time hand-coding, so the incentive to make the assembly language "beautiful" disappeared. It became acceptable to design machine code for the machine's sake, rather than the programmer's.

Caches and instruction pipelines reduced the apparent time it took to get instructions from memory. The cache could replace the function of the microcode control store because of its close integration with the processor. And because main memory was no longer the scarce resource it had once been, the code expansion that is characteristic of a program cast into RISC instructions became manageable. The requirement for program compactness vanished; it became possible to trade instruction set complexity for program size.

A number of the features of CISC processors, such as complex addressing modes and heavily microcoded instructions, made it difficult to design instruction pipelines that were resistant to stalls. This wasn't a problem 30 years ago, because there were practically no pipelined machines, but it made a big difference in the early 1980s. With more logic gates available, and better design tools, vendors looked for ways to increase the instruction overlap in their old designs. It became apparent that the biggest problem was that the CISC instruction sets included too many special cases. Pipelining is better suited to a simple instruction set architecture, as we'll see in the following section.

Characterizing RISC

RISC is more of a design philosophy than a set of goals. And of course every RISC processor has its own personality. However, there are a number of features commonly found in machines people consider to be RISC:

- Uniform Instruction Length
- Streamlined Instruction Set
- Simple Addressing Modes
- Load/Store Architecture
- Many Registers
- Delayed Branches

This list highlights the differences between RISC and CISC processors. Naturally, the two types of instruction set architectures have much in common—each uses registers, memory, etc. And many of the enablers of RISC are being employed in CISC machines too, such as caches and instruction pipelines. But it's the fundamental differences that give RISC its speed advantage. A smaller set of less powerful instructions makes it possible to build a faster computer.

However, the notion that RISC machines are generally simpler than CISC machines isn't correct. Other features, such as functional pipelines, sophisticated memory systems, and the ability to issue two or more instructions per clock (more later) make the latest RISC processors the most complicated ever built. Furthermore, much of the complexity that has been lifted from the instruction set has been driven into the compilers, making a good optimizing compiler a prerequisite for machine performance.

Let's put ourselves in the role of computer architect again and look at each item in the list above to understand why it's important.

Uniform instruction length

Our sample instruction pipeline had five stages: Instruction Fetch, Instruction Decode, Operand Fetch, Execution, and Writeback. As I said before, we want this pipeline to be able to process five instructions in various stages without stalling. That's challenging enough, but for a designer working with a CISC instruction set it would be especially difficult because CISC instructions come in varying lengths. A simple "return from subroutine" instruction might be one byte long, for instance, whereas it would take a longer instruction to say "add register such-and-such to memory location so-and-so and leave the result in the accumulator."

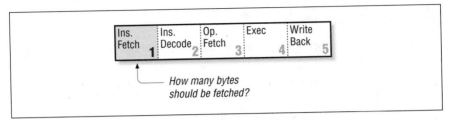

Figure 2-4: Variable length instructions make pipelining difficult

To understand why variable length instructions are a challenge, consider the following question: How does the processor know how many bytes to retrieve from memory during the instruction fetch stage? The next instruction could be one byte long, or it could be as many as six bytes long. The answer is that the processor has no way of knowing how long an instruction will be until it reaches the decode stage and determines what it is. If it turns out to be a long instruction, the processor may have to go back to memory and get the portion left behind; this will stall the pipeline.

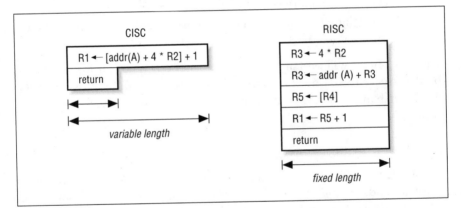

Figure 2-5: Variable length CISC versus fixed length RISC instructions

We could eliminate the problem by requiring that all instructions be the same length, and that there be a limited number of instruction formats. This way, every instruction entering the pipeline is known *a priori* to be complete—not needing another memory access. It would also be easier for the processor to locate the instruction fields that specify registers or constants. Altogether the pipeline would flow much more smoothly.

Streamlined instruction set

Taking a scientific approach to instruction set design, you might monitor an existing machine while it runs some interesting workloads. That would give you a clear picture of the variety of instructions executed, and their relative frequencies. From those observations, you could make choices about what kind of instructions are important before you begin crafting a new instruction set. This would be a departure from the earlier practice of choosing instructions that mimicked high level languages, or instructions that looked interesting. Streamlining the instruction set into a collection of simple operations will get us to the point where we don't have to depend on microcode—for the most part. We could implement the instruction set architecture in three ways:

- Eliminate the microcode altogether and hardwire every instruction.
- Keep a mix of microcoded and hardwired instructions and trap to microcode whenever a complex instruction comes down the pipe. This, of course, stalls the processor, but it does allow for some complex instructions to be intermixed with purely RISC operations.
- Trap to machine code to emulate a complex instruction. This is like calling a subroutine.

The first option will probably result in a faster machine. However, if complex instructions have to be supported, microcode is still a possibility. On the other hand, a series of RISC instructions may get the job done just as well.

Simple addressing modes

Just as we want to simplify the instruction set, we also want a simple set of hardware addressing modes. The reasons are the same: complicated address calculations, or those that require multiple memory references, will take too much time and stall the pipeline. This doesn't mean that your program won't be able use elegant data structures; the compiler can explicitly generate the extra address arithmetic when it needs it, as long as it can count on a few fundamental addressing modes in hardware. In fact, the extra address arithmetic is often easier for the compiler to optimize into faster forms (see the section entitled "Induction Variable Simplification," Chapter 4).

Of course, cutting back the number of addressing modes means that some memory references will take more real instructions than they might have taken on a CISC machine. However, because everything executes more quickly, it will still be a performance win.

Load/Store architecture

In a load/store instruction set architecture, memory references are limited to explicit load and store instructions. This is different from CISC, where arithmetic and logical instructions can include embedded memory references. There are three reasons why limiting loads and stores to their own instructions is a win.

First, we want all instructions to be the same length, for the reasons given above. However, fixed lengths impose a budget limit when it comes to describing what the operation does and what registers it uses. An instruction that both referenced memory and performed some calculation wouldn't fit within one instruction word.

Second, giving every instruction the option to reference memory would complicate the pipeline because there would be two computations to perform—the address calculation plus whatever the instruction is supposed to do—but there is only one execution stage. We could throw more hardware at it, but by restricting memory references to explicit loads and stores, we can avoid the problem entirely. Any instruction can perform an address calculation or some other operation, but no instruction can do both.

The third reason for limiting memory references to explicit loads and stores is that they can take more time than other instructions—sometimes two or three clock cycles more. A general instruction with an embedded memory reference would get hung up in the operand fetch stage for those extra cycles, waiting for the reference to complete. Again we would be faced with an instruction pipeline stall.

Explicit load and store instructions can kick off memory references in the pipeline's execute stage, to be completed at a later time (they might complete immediately—it depends on the processor and the cache). An operation downstream may require the result of the reference, but that's all right, as long as it is far enough downstream that the reference has had time to complete.

Many registers

Memory references are not cheap; they take up time and space. Anything the compiler can do to minimize them will help the performance.

One possibility is to try to keep frequently used variables in registers, rather than ferrying them back and forth from memory. Better that they hang around in registers where it will cost nothing to reuse them. Of course, in order to keep a fair number of variables in registers you are going to need a fair number of registers. This is one of the reasons why RISC processors usually have at least 16 and some times as many as 64.

Delayed branches

Studies show that branches, conditional and unconditional, generally occur every five to ten machine instructions (for RISC) in compiled programs. This means it is important to handle branches efficiently, otherwise they cut too deeply into the performance. Look at the picture of the instruction pipeline again to understand the challenges.

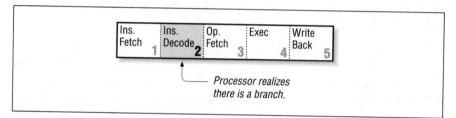

Figure 2-6: Processor encounters a branch

Assume that the processor is executing a piece of code that contains a branch. The earliest it will recognize the branch is in the decode stage, by which time it will have already fetched the instruction immediately following the branch. This could be a disaster, because the fetched instruction may be intended for some other path in the program, and now it has made its way into the pipeline. What do we do?

A straightforward approach would be to cancel any instructions in the pipeline following the one that caused the branch. The trouble is that if the program has a branch every seven instructions or so, this will result in a large number of canceled operations and wasted cycles. Furthermore, the instruction in the pipeline might actually be the correct one to execute next, as would be the case if a conditional branch fell through.

Rather than take a penalty for cleaning out the pipeline, many RISC designs ask the compiler to place an instruction after the branch. This instruction, in what is called the *branch delay slot,* is executed whichever way the branch goes. An instruction in this position should be useful, or at least harmless, whichever way the branch proceeds. That is, you expect the processor to execute the instruction following the branch in either case, and plan for it. In a pinch, a no-op can be used. A slight variation would be to give the processor the ability to *annul* (or squash) the instruction appearing in the branch delay slot if it turns out that it shouldn't have been issued after all.

	ADD	R1,R2,R1	*Add r1 to r2 and store in r1*
	SUB	R3,R1,R3	*Subtract r1 from r3, store in r3*
	BRA	SOMEWHERE	*Branch somewhere else*
LABEL1	ZERO	R3	*Put a 0 into r3 (branch delay slot)*
	...	...	

Figure 2-7: The Branch Delay Slot—ZERO R3 executes either way

In practice, delayed branches aren't enough of a solution for the processor designs coming out today. At times, it can be difficult to fill a branch delay slot. And if the processor is able to execute multiple instructions per clock (jumping ahead a little), then the penalty for branching may be much higher. Finding one instruction for the delay slot may be hard enough; now, how do you find several? We'll look into these questions in a little while.

A Few More Words About Pipelining

Floating point arithmetic and memory references have their own special pipelines. The goal is the same: free up the processor to go off and do other things while an operation works its way through. Conceptually, you can picture a memory pipeline or a floating point pipeline as an extension of the instruction execute stage or as being located off to the side, by itself.

Memory References

Memory reference pipelines come in two forms. The first is "invisible" pipelines used by typical load and store instructions. After the processor executes a load, it usually takes one or two extra cycles before the memory system (cache) can return the requested data.* You don't want to delay the instruction pipeline with extra steps, so you let the memory reference continue on its own.

---

*A notable exception is the SuperSPARC processor from Texas Instruments. Memory references are recognized and started very early in the instruction pipeline. Provided cache access goes OK, a memory reference takes no longer than any other instruction.

The extra cycles influence the way the compiler schedules instructions that use data from memory. Because loads take some time to complete, the compiler has to find something else to do for a while. Picture a program using data from memory on a processor that requires one extra cycle for memory loads. Figure 2-8 shows an efficient way to schedule memory references.

	LD	R10, R2(R0)	*Load of R10 from memory starts*
	LD	R11, R3(R0)	*Load of R11 from memory starts*
	ADD	R4,R10,R5	*First load completed (R10 available), R4 ◄—— R10 + R5*
LABEL1	SUB	R4,R11,R4	*Second load completed (R11 available), R4 ◄— R11 - R4*
	...	...	

Figure 2-8: Memory references scheduled early to account for pipeline depth

If instruction 1 says "load register 10 from memory location such and such," the next instruction cannot expect register 10 to contain the datum because the load operation will still be in progress. The value won't appear in register 10 until another clock tick passes. What happens if you try to use the data too soon depends on the brand of computer you own. In some cases you will get a "garbage" value (MIPS R3000, for example); in others you will stall the instruction pipeline for one cycle (SPARC, for example).

A handful of processors (the Intel i860 is one) also have "visible" memory pipelines under tight control by the compiler. References through visible pipelines bypass parts of the memory system (particularly the cache) and take a predictable, though longer, amount of time to complete. These compiler controlled, visible memory references are good in situations where you are processing large amounts of data arranged in a regular pattern, as is common in vector operations. I will have much more to say about memory references in the chapters ahead.

Floating Point Pipelines

Floating point computations can be pipelined, too. Generally, this includes floating point addition, subtraction, multiplication, comparisons, and conversions, though it might not include square roots and division. Once a pipelined floating point operation is started, calculations continue through the several stages without delaying the rest of the processor. The result will appear in a register at some point in the future.

Some processors are limited in the amount of overlap their floating point pipelines can support. Internal components of the pipelines may be shared (for adding, multiplying, normalizing, and rounding intermediate results), forcing restrictions on when and how often you can begin new operations. In other cases, new operations can be started without regard for what went before. We say that such operations are *fully pipelined*.

To take a few examples, the TI SuperSPARC can start a double precision addition, followed by a multiplication in the next cycle, but you have to let another cycle go by before you can do it over again. Other processors, such as the RS/6000 and the Intel i860, can accept new floating point additions or multiplications with few restrictions, giving them higher quoted peak floating point rates for the equal clock rates.

The "depth" of floating point pipelines for affordable computers has decreased over the last ten years. More transistors and newer algorithms make it possible to perform a double precision addition or multiplication in just two or three cycles. Floating point hardware used to be optional—you needed a coprocessor—but today it is almost universally integrated into the processor.

Classes of Processors

The Holy Grail for RISC machines was to achieve one instruction per clock. The idealized RISC computer running at, say 50 MHz, would be able to issue 50 million instructions per second. As we have seen, a single instruction will take five or more clock ticks to get through the instruction pipeline, but if the pipeline can be kept full, the aggregate rate will, in fact, be one instruction per clock. We are in an interesting transition now. Most of the players either have, or are about to release, architectures that can deliver more.

The way you get two or more instructions per clock is by starting several operations side-by-side, possibly in separate pipelines. For instance, if you have a floating point addition and a multiplication to perform, it should be possible to begin them simultaneously, provided they are independent of each other (as long as the multiplication does not need the output of the addition as one of its operands and vice versa). You could also execute multiple fixed-point instructions—compares, integer additions, etc.—at the same time, provided that they, too, are independent. Machines that can do this are called *multiple instruction issue* processors.

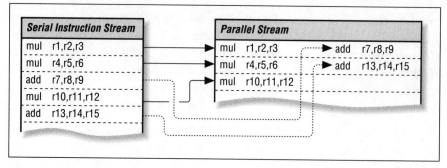

Figure 2-9: Decomposing a serial stream

The number and variety of operations that can be run in parallel depends on both the program and the processor. The program has to have enough usable parallelism so that there are multiple things to do, and the processor has to have an appropriate assortment of functional units and the ability to keep them busy. The idea is conceptually simple, but it can be a challenge for both hardware designers and compiler writers. Every opportunity to do several things in parallel exposes the danger of violating some precedence (i.e., performing computations in the wrong order). And how you go about managing parallel execution isn't written in stone either. Research and experimentation continues even as the products come to market.

There are three fundamentally different approaches to parallel RISC, and some hybrids—each of which will be shaking themselves out in the next couple of years:

- Superscalar
- Superpipelined
- Long Instruction Word

Let's look at each type and a few representative examples. (Appendix A has a more comprehensive list.)

Superscalar Processors

A *superscalar* processor can schedule operations for side-by-side, pipelined execution on-the-fly, at run time. When it is supported by a compiler that can generate an instruction stream with an even mix of relatively independent integer, floating point, memory, and branch operations, a superscalar processor is easily coaxed for performance. Most are capable of peak rates of three or four operations per clock cycle, and, given the right conditions, can average close to 2.0 operations per clock or beyond.

Examples of processors that fit into this category are the IBM RS/6000, TI's SuperSPARC, the Motorola 88110, the HP Precision Architecture 7100, DEC AXP, and the recently announced MIPS SSR, a follow-on to the R4000. The oldest of them, the RS/6000, can start up to four operations per cycle:

- One floating point instruction
- One fixed point instruction (or memory reference)
- One condition code manipulation
- A branch

The RS/6000 is a remarkable achievement made possible by observing RISC philosophy on instruction length and variety, and by providing very sophisticated control hardware and multiple internal instruction streams. You program it serially—one instruction after another—but the processor fetches several instructions at a time and starts them in parallel. Additionally, there is a floating point multiply-add, dual operation, which (sort of) pushes the count to five operations per clock.

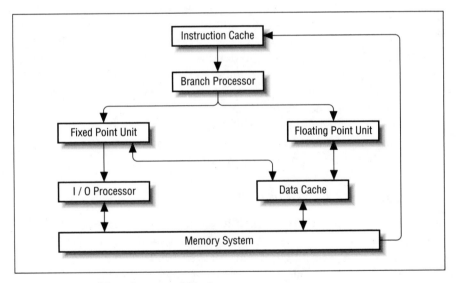

Figure 2-10: RS/6000 functional blocks

Processing in the fixed and floating point units is coordinated, yet independent, in separate instruction pipelines. Both have queues that can buffer instructions up to twelve deep. Best of all, they don't have to remain completely in sync. The fixed point unit can get up to two instructions ahead of the floating point unit, or the floating point unit can get up to six instructions ahead of the fixed point unit, before a delay in one pipeline effects the other. This gives the processor the exceptional ability to even its own load, and keep the functional units busy.

The whole show is overseen by the branch processor, which is like a captain on the bridge; it makes decisions about where the ship will go next, and hands instructions down to the fixed and floating point units. If a branch can be initiated sufficiently far in advance, it will cause no apparent processing delay. In the worst case, there will be a three cycle penalty, and the fixed and floating point units will have to cancel some of their instructions (more about this shortly).

The description of the RS/6000 gives you an idea how a superscalar processor works. Other superscalar designs can initiate two to four operations per clock.* But be careful: it's not a straightforward comparison. Superscalar processors run at different clock rates and have different instruction mixes, issue rules, and restrictions.

Interestingly, the Intel Pentium (the 80586) also fits in the superscalar category, marking the start of a trend that is going to blur RISC/CISC differences. Pentium has both a RISC "core" and extensive support for the 80x86 instruction set (probably supported by traps to microcode). Intel claims it will be capable of 160 MIPS at maturity. To put this in proportion, industry analysts estimate that IBM PC clones number around 100 million worldwide (nobody really knows), and the number of SPARC machines is around 650,000. Of course, not all of those clones will be traded up to Pentium processors, but with a ratio of 154:1 between clones and the installed base of the leading vendor of RISC workstations, the Intel Pentium certainly appears to figure prominently in the marketplace.

Superpipelined Processors

Roughly stated, simpler circuitry can run at higher clock speeds. Put yourself in the role of a CPU designer again. Looking at the instruction pipeline of your processor, you might decide that the reason you can't get more speed out of it is that some of the stages are too complicated or have too much going on, and they are placing limits on how fast the whole pipeline can go. Because the stages are clocked in unison, the slowest of them forms a weak link in the chain.

---

*Four operations for SSR; three operations per cycle on the SuperSPARC; two on the 88110, 7100, and DEC AXP.

If you divide the complicated stages into less complicated portions, you can increase the overall speed of the pipeline. This is called *superpipelining.* More instruction pipeline stages with less complexity per stage will do the same work as a pipelined processor, but with higher throughput.

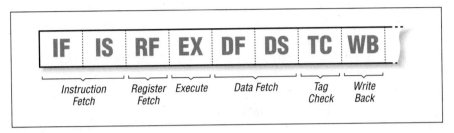

Figure 2-11: MIPS R4000 Instruction Pipeline

Theoretically, if the reduced complexity allows the processor to clock faster, you can achieve nearly the same initial performance as superscalar processors, yet without instruction mix preferences. For illustration, picture a superscalar processor with two units—fixed and floating point—executing a program that is composed solely of fixed point calculations; the floating point unit will go unused. This will reduce the superscalar performance by one half. A superpipelined processor, on the other hand, will be perfectly happy to handle an unbalanced instruction mix at full speed.

Superpipelines are not new; deep pipelines have been employed in the past, notably on the CDC 6600. The label is a marketing creation to draw contrast to superscalar processing, and other forms of efficient, high speed computing. An example of a current processor that relies solely on deep pipelines for higher throughput is the R4000 from MIPS (now part of Silicon Graphics), incorporated in Silicon Graphics workstations and some DEC workstations. I have heard the R4000 called a multiple instruction issue processor, but this is largely semantics. The instruction fetch stage is divided into two parts—Instruction Fetch First Half and Instruction Fetch Second Half—you could stretch it to say that it is "fetching two operations per clock." Really, the R4000 is a very fast single stream processor.

Superpipelining can be combined with other approaches. You could have a superscalar machine with deep pipelines (DEC AXP and MIPS SSR are examples). In fact, you should probably expect that faster pipelines with more stages will become so commonplace that nobody will remember to call them superpipelines after a while. The technique is already creeping into other processors—even CISC; Intel's 80486DX2, a modified 80486, is a CISC processor incorporating some superpipelining.

Long Instruction Word (LIW)

Machines in the third parallel RISC category, *Long Instruction Word*, get their speed from side-by-side execution, like superscalar processors. However, there is one basic difference: whereas superscalar machines can make parallel the instruction stream at run time, an LIW depends on the compiler to do it, at compile time. In some respects, the sophisticated hardware that's missing from the processor has been moved into the compiler (which makes for slow compilers, by the way).

Each parallel instruction is actually two or more regular RISC instructions cemented together into a single long instruction word. Every clock tick, one of these long instructions is fetched and fed into separate pipelines controlling different parts of the processor.

The Intel i860 is an example of an LIW processor. It has two operating modes. The first, *single instruction mode*, makes the processor look very much like a classic RISC machine. There is pipelined instruction overlap, but only one new operation can be initiated with each clock cycle.

The other, *dual mode*, starts two instructions per clock cycle—one floating point and one of a choice of fixed point instruction, memory reference, or branch (a "core" operation, in Intel parlance).* You can switch the processor from one mode to the other during operation, and perhaps frequently within a given program.

Very Long Instruction Word (VLIW) machines are LIWs with "wider" instructions (even more operations per clock). There might be several floating point, integer, branch, and memory operations initiated each clock cycle. The potential for VLIW processors is great, but they require very sophisticated compilers; the instruction stream decomposition that happens at run time in a superscalar machine has to be done off-line for a VLIW. You might guess that this would make things easier because it gives the processor less to worry about at run time. However, everything that might go wrong has to be accounted for when compiling—conflicting memory references, instructions that depend on the results of previous instructions, out of order

---

*Think of the dual-mode instructions for the Intel i860 like a wedding party making its way up the aisle: the order and relationship of the participants is fixed and determined well ahead of time.

execution, etc. Instruction scheduling problems that might be self-correcting on a superscalar processor have to be carefully prepared in advance by a VLIW compiler.

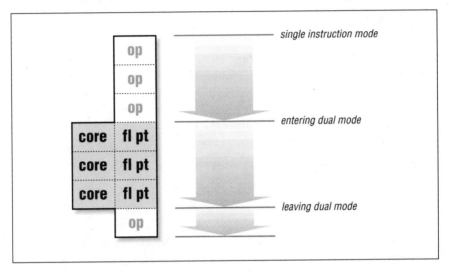

Figure 2-12: Intel i860 transition between modes

Still, the potential is great. Although it might be difficult to scale up a superscalar design to handle ten or more operations per clock, a company called Multiflow Computer has already proven that it is possible to build a very long instruction word machine and compilers that could schedule up to twenty-eight instructions per clock. When plodding through "junk" code, Multiflow's compiler could only schedule three or four instructions at a time, but for numerically intensive codes it was possible to achieve tens of instructions per clock. The processor had eight floating point pipelines and four memory pipelines—all scheduled at compile time. Multiflow has since gone out of business, but I'd hate to let that fact water down my endorsement—it was a nifty idea.

Other Advanced Features

Now you have a feel for the kinds of spinning plate acts these parallel RISC processors perform. When they can keep the pipelines full, the performance is tremendous. The problem is that it takes a lot of coordination to execute many instructions at once, whether it be done in the compiler, in the hardware, or both. If one portion of the instruction stream spends too much time waiting for a resource or another result, the rest of the instructions eventually get caught up in it too. There can be some loose interplay between, say, integer and floating point parts of the instruction stream—particularly on superscalar processors. This allows instructions to creep past one another a bit. However, they can only get so far apart. It's like pulling a fish net through a hole: you may be able to get the knots through in a slightly different order, but they're still tied together.

I am going to briefly introduce some clever additional devices for keeping the pipelines running smoothly. These are not present in all processors, though the reasons for having them apply to basically all computers, RISC, CISC, parallel, and non-parallel. I've catalogued them along with some RISC processors in Appendix A.

Register Bypass

A RISC instruction gets its operands from registers and returns its results to registers. This takes only a few clock cycles. Sometimes, however, a subsequent instruction needs the result of an earlier one right away. Rather than wait for that result to migrate all the way back to the destination register just to be picked up again, a few processors feature what is called *register bypass*: values written back from one instruction can be "shorted" to others that need them. It's like handing someone the keys to the washroom when you pass them in the hallway: "Here you go, Joe." Register bypass helps to reduce delays in code sequences where results depend upon others to proceed—particularly where parallelism is in short supply.

Register Renaming

Other kinds of slowdowns don't reflect defects in the program, but in the way the instruction stream makes use of the machine's resources. For instance, if the processor encounters instructions that reuse registers too soon—before other instructions have finished with them—the pipeline can suffer a delay. The compiler can try to guard against these artificial delays by assigning registers in rotation, but it isn't always easy to do. At certain points in the program, registers may be scarce. Furthermore, two uses of a register that might have appeared safely separated in the object code could actually bunch up on one another as instructions jockey for position at run time.

To guard against artificial register delays, some processors—the RS/6000 is one—provide a hardware *register renaming* capability. The processor detects that a register is being oversubscribed (for independent uses) and substitutes another in its place, on-the-fly.

Register renaming also makes it easy for a vendor to support multiple versions of the same processor with differing numbers of registers. An application only has to be compiled once; at run time it will expand to use all of the registers available. By comparison, applications for processors without register renaming have to be compiled with a minimum fixed number of registers in mind, and may need to be recompiled to take advantage of an increased set of registers.

Reducing Branch Penalties

As we saw above, branches are one of the biggest pipeline hazards. Flushing the pipeline every time a branch is encountered would cost far too much time. We need some mechanisms to reduce the penalty or, if possible, eliminate it altogether. The generic, delayed branch approach is OK when the compiler can guess which way the branches will go at run time, and when there's enough spare work so that the compiler can fill the branch delay slot with a useful instruction. However, it gets more difficult when parallelism is scarce, or when the processor is capable of multiple instructions per clock. Branch delay slots of more than two instructions are generally a performance liability.

Annulled operations

The first incremental improvement to the delayed branch is a branch with a cancel option. If the compiler can't find an instruction that will be useful following a branch, it can fill the delay slot with an instruction it thinks will be useful, but one that can be *annulled* (or squashed) if the branch happens to take the other path. This is a "toes testing the water" form of speculative execution. A few extra instructions may creep their way into the pipeline for an anticipated payoff, but get canceled before reaching the execution stage.

In superscalar processors, the notion of a delayed branch disappears altogether. There is no requirement that the compiler hold its breath and choose an instruction to follow a branch because if the processor determines early enough that a branch is coming, it can start fetching instructions from the new location. The ability to annul instructions is still useful though. A superscalar processor may not have enough advance warning about a branch and have to cancel several operations already in the queues. Branching with ability to annul operations is a feature of SPARC, SuperSPARC, RS/6000, and the HP 7100.

While we're at it, you can imagine that any instruction could fill in behind a branch—useful or not—as long as it didn't have a permanent side effect. For instance, if an integer addition fills the branch delay slot, and if it turns out that it shouldn't have been executed, the final answer won't be affected if the results of the addition are discarded. There are limits, however. What if the instruction that shouldn't have been executed is a floating point operation or a memory reference, and it causes an exception? Then you have a problem. The exception handler will be invoked to process an error that essentially didn't happen.

Expect to see more speculative execution in processors around the corner. Several companies are already addressing challenges in operation scheduling and exception handling. For instance, Metaflow is working on a SPARC implementation they call *Thunder.* This processor will get its performance by allowing operations to creep ahead and execute "speculatively." If it turns out that they shouldn't have happened, it's up to the processor to wind back the clock and undo (or discard) whatever they did, including exceptions.

Conditional assignments

Another hardware mechanism for reducing branch penalties is the *conditional assignment.* These are instructions that look like branches in source code, but turn out to be a special type of assignment instruction in the object code. They are very useful because they replace test and branch sequences altogether. The following line of C code captures the sense of a conditional branch:

```
a = b < c ? d : e;
```

Based on some test (b < c in the example), a destination register (a) is assigned the value of one of two other registers (one of which may be itself). There is a comparison, but no branch. Floating point conditional assignments are part of some supercomputer class instruction sets (like vector processors), and are appearing in other processors too, such as DEC AXP and SuperSPARC.

Branch target buffers

Processors also include other mechanisms to lessen branch impact. Instructions being fed from memory (cache) flow pretty smoothly when they follow one right after another. In fact, the processor anticipates that more instructions are going to be needed and prefetches them into a device called a *prefetch buffer,* which in turn feeds the instruction pipeline. The problems start when there are branches in the instruction stream. The pre-fetch buffer is probably not going to be holding the branch target when the branch occurs, so without some special preparations the pipeline will stall until prefetching begins at the new location.*

To avoid starving the processor for things to do, we need a device that anticipates the branch target as well. One possibility is that the processor could prefetch along two (or more) paths, though this would require very complicated hardware, and is not something you will see in current works-tations. A less drastic approach is to provide a small cache called a *branch target buffer* that contains information pairs describing previous branches and the instructions found at their target addresses. If a branch occurs, the processor can quickly substitute one or two instructions from the branch target buffer while prefetching begins from the new location. Of course, the branch target buffer has to have instructions from the branch target address, or it can't provide them. For instructions to be contained in the branch target buffer, there has to have been a recent branch to the same address. The difference is that the first time through, the branch target buffer wouldn't have contained the needed instructions, and the pipeline would have stalled while they were fetched from memory. Branch target buffers are features of the Motorola 88110 and DEC AXP.

Hardware branch prediction

On some machines, the compiler gets to choose an opcode that says which way it believes a branch is likely to go. It's an improvement over the typi-cal scheme—prefetch as if the branch won't be taken—because some kinds of conditionals usually branch. An example would be a do-loop exit test. Because most do-loops go around more than twice, the probability of falling through at the bottom, as opposed to branching back to the top, is less than 50%.

Another simple way to predict where a branch will go is to look at the branch displacement. A branch backward could be taken as unlikely, whereas a forward branch could be called likely. This way the processor could start prefetching from either the fall-through path or the branched path merely based on where the branch would land.

---

*If the instructions from the branch target address aren't in the instruction cache (covered in Chapter 3), the penalty can be very significant— much greater than that of flushing the pipe-line. This is because it will take a number of cycles for the processor to go out to main memo-ry and restock (part of) the cache with new instructions, and restart the instruction pipeline.

Though not included in current workstation processors, it is also possible to have dynamic branch prediction mechanisms. The CPU could keep a little chalkboard that records which way each branch went the last few times through, and use this as a predictor for how they will go in the future. The question is whether this would buy you much. Static branch prediction, or information fed back by profilers, can correctly characterize most branches most of the time for most codes.

Closing Notes

Congratulations for reaching the end of a long chapter! I have talked a little bit about old computers, CISC, RISC, and mentioned supercomputers in passing. I think it's interesting to observe that RISC processors are not a branch off a long established tree. Many of the ideas that have gone into RISC designs are borrowed from other types of computers, but none of them evolved into RISC—RISC started at a discontinuity. There were hints of a RISC revolution (the CDC 6600 and the IBM 801 project) but it really was forced on the world (for its own good) by CPU designers at Berkeley and Stanford in the early 1980s.

It will be very interesting to see what becomes of RISC as semiconductor density doubles and quadruples, giving designers more and more transistors to work with. How complex will RISC designs become, and what kinds of new innovations will we see? Will you be able to get a single chip multiprocessor—two or more CPUs on a chip?* How high will clock rates go?† And how will designers tackle some of the fundamental architectural problems, perhaps the largest being memory systems? It is hard to design a memory system that can keep up with a very fast processor. We'll look at that next.

Exercises

1. Imagine a *multiway branch*—one instruction that can choose from multiple branch targets. Why would a multiway branch be important in a machine that can execute many instructions per clock cycle?

---

*Intel says you will have a 250 MHz, four processor (with vector units), 386 compatible, notebook sized computer by the end of the decade.

†Processors operating at high clock rates require a lot of power and produce a lot of heat. Expect to see operating voltages drop over the next few years; dropping the voltage reduces power and cooling requirements.

2. Speculative execution is safe for certain types of instructions; results can be discarded if it turns out that the instruction shouldn't have executed. Floating point instructions and memory operations are two classes of instructions for which speculative execution is trickier, particularly because of the chance of generating exceptions. For instance, dividing by zero or taking the square root of a negative number will cause an exception. Under what circumstances will a speculative memory reference cause an exception?

3. Consider this loop:

    ```
    while (a > b)
        a = a - b;
    ```

    What difficulties does this present to the instruction pipeline? Assume that a and b are floating point numbers. What do you expect will happen in the floating point pipelines?

4. Picture a machine with floating point pipelines that are 100 stages deep (that's ridiculously deep), each of which can deliver a new result every nanosecond. That would give each pipeline a peak throughput rate of 1 Gflop, and a worst case throughput rate of 10 Mflops. What characteristics would a code need to have to take advantage of such a pipeline?

3

Memory

Let's say that I offer you an upgrade for your workstation: For one dollar I will trade your CPU for another that clocks at 250 MHz. For five dollars I'll give you a 500 MHz CPU. It sounds like a great deal, doesn't it? Assume that the machine you have now clocks at 50 MHz and runs the 100×100 Linpack benchmark* at 22 MFlops. A straightforward projection suggests that your new Linpack number will be 220 MFlops. Right? Well, the reason I hesitate is that we haven't accounted for your memory system. The same CPU running at 500 MHz would have a voracious appetite for memory, an average of 2.6 gigabytes per second while running Linpack—a data rate that only the memory systems of high-end supercomputers can provide. So if we can rework the deal a little: I will be happy to sell you a 500 MHz CPU for five dollars, but the memory system will cost you an extra two million. Sold?

The above proposal isn't just academic. There is an increasing disparity between the speed of CPU chips and memory. And because computers are getting faster, the amount of data they can crunch in a given interval is going up too. The trouble is that when you want to process lots of data at high speeds you need a memory system that is large, yet at the same time fast—a big challenge. Possible approaches are:

- Every memory system component can be made individually fast enough to respond to every memory access request.
- Slow memory can be accessed in a round-robin fashion (hopefully) to give the effect of a faster memory system.
- The memory system design can be made "wide" so that each transfer contains many bytes of information.
- The system can be divided into faster and slower portions and arranged so that the fast portion is used more often than the slow one.

---

*The Linpack benchmark performs Gaussian Elimination. See Chapter 13.

- The instructions and data could be segregated so that demand for instructions is decoupled from demand for data.

Again, economics are the dominant force in the computer business. A cheap, statistically optimized memory system will be a better seller than a prohibitively expensive, blazingly fast one, so the first choice is not much of a choice at all. But the last three or four choices, used in combination, can attain a good fraction of the performance you would get if every component was fast. Chances are very good that your workstation incorporates several or all of them.

Once the memory system has been decided upon, there are things people can do in software to see that it is used efficiently. A compiler that has some knowledge of the way memory is arranged and the details of the caches can optimize their use to some extent. The other place for optimizations is in user applications, as we'll see later in the book. A good pattern of memory access will work with, rather than against, the components of the system.

In this chapter I will discuss how the pieces of a memory system work. We'll look at how patterns of data and instruction access will factor into your overall run time, especially as CPU speeds increase. I'll also talk a little bit about the performance implications of running in a virtual memory environment.

Memory Technology

Theoretically, any system that can alternate between two or more static states can be used as memory for a computer. You just have to instrument it so that you can inquire about its state, or change it remotely. For example, a room full of vacuum cleaners, some running and some not, is a collection of two-state devices that could be used to store information. A running vacuum cleaner could be a logical "1," and an idle vacuum could be a "0." After a little bit of experience, you might decide that the access time was too slow, and the cost per bit too high. Eventually, you would find a method for storing data that optimized the cost against the access time.

To date there have been no commercially successful designs incorporating vacuum cleaner memory. But the idea is sound: look for a physical system that can be cheaply exploited for data storage. In the past, production memory systems have used magnetic drums, disks, dot patterns on CRTs, and vibrations in mercury and magnetic cores. It's not that there weren't faster or more elegant memory devices available; at the time these things offered the best price/performance. Keep in mind that even if the differential cost of one technology versus another is as low as 1/1000th cent per bit, the figure becomes significant when you talk about a large memory system. For instance, a computer with 32 million bits of memory (4 MB) will cost $320 more on an increase of 1/1000th cent per bit.

Random Access Memory

Almost all fast memories used today are semiconductor based.* They come in two main flavors: *dynamic random access memory* (DRAM) and *static random access memory* (SRAM). The term random means that you can address memory locations in any order. This is to distinguish random access from serial memories, where you have to step through all intervening locations to get to the particular one you are interested in. The terms dynamic and static have to do with the design of the memory cells. DRAMs are charge-based devices, where each bit is represented by a stored electrical charge. The charge can leak away in a very short amount of time, so the system has to be continually refreshed to prevent data from being lost. Static memories retain their data as long as they have power, without the need for any form of data refresh.

DRAM offers the best price/performance, as well as highest density of memory cells per chip. This means lower cost and less board space. On the other hand, some applications such as cache and video memory require higher speed, to which static RAM is better suited. You can choose between static and dynamic RAMs at higher speeds—down to about 60 nanoseconds (ns). For shorter times, the price of dynamic RAM increases sharply and the utility decreases, making static RAM the only possible choice. Today you would pay about .0004 cents per bit for 70 ns dynamic RAM and .0015 cents per bit for static RAM at 20 ns.

Random access memory chips store data in a matrix. Your computer accesses a particular bit by giving row and column addresses that describe an intersection in the matrix where the bit is stored (see Figure 3-1). It's sort of like a Manhattan address, i.e., 9th Avenue and 42nd Street. The choices for row and column addresses can be derived from the high and low order bits of a memory address. For instance, a 1 MB DRAM needs 20 address bits in order to locate all of its 1,048,576 memory locations. A

---

*Magnetic core memory is still used in applications where radiation "hardness"—resistance to changes caused by ionizing radiation—is important.

straightforward way to map memory addresses to row and column addresses is to decompose the address into two pieces—row and column.

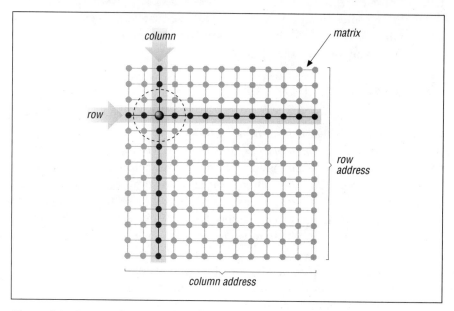

Figure 3-1: Row - Column memory address

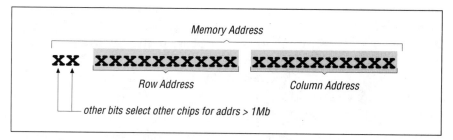

Figure 3-2: Direct mapping of memory address to RAM

If you want to address a full MB of memory you will need lots of pins on the memory chips: 20 pins for address bits (2^{20} = 1 MB), two for power, one for data, one to indicate whether data is being written or read, one for the data itself, another to select the chip, and possibly more—at least 26 pins. However, DRAMS are usually designed with less pins. Instead of presenting the whole address at once, the two parts of the address—row and column—are clocked in separately. There are two reasons for this.

The first is that accessing a bit is actually a two step process:

1. A row of bits is fetched.
2. A bit is selected from the row.

The selected bit is then made available on the output. The other reason has more to do with economics. If address lines can be shared for column and row addresses, the board design will be less complicated and the cost and size will be reduced.

For accesses that share the same row or column address, dynamic RAMS can operate in what is called *page mode*. Rather than repeat the whole address for each cell referenced, the memory system can present the first half of the address just once (fetch a row of bits), and then vary the other portion by itself. This is a big win because the first step is the one that takes the most time; bit selection happens quickly.

Access Time

The amount of time it takes to read or write a memory location is called the *memory access time*. It takes into account the steps that go into locating data in the memory chips:

- Present Row Address.
- Present Column Address.
- Exchange Data.

As I mentioned above, if you are using the same row or column address repeatedly, you can sometimes skip one of the steps.

A related quantity is the *memory cycle time*. Whereas the access time says how quickly you can reference a memory location, cycle time describes how often you can make references. They sound like the same thing, but they're not. For instance, if you ask for data from memory chips with a 70 ns access time, it may be 200 ns before you can ask for more data from the same chips. This is because the chips must internally recover from the previous access.

Access and cycle times for commodity DRAMs are shorter than they were just a few years ago, meaning that it is possible to build faster memory systems. But CPU clock speeds have increased too. The home computer market makes a good study. In the early 1980s, the access time of commodity DRAM was shorter than the clock cycle of the IBM PC XT. This meant that DRAM could be connected directly to the CPU without worrying about overrunning the memory system. Faster XT and AT models were introduced in the mid 1980s with CPUs that clocked more quickly than the access times of available commodity memory. Faster memory was available for a price, but vendors punted by selling computers with *wait states* added to the memory access cycle. Wait states are artificial delays that slow down references so that memory will appear to match the speed of a faster CPU—at a penalty. Today, CPU speeds are even farther ahead of DRAM speeds. The clock time for commodity home computers has gone from 250 ns for the XT to around 30 ns for a 386/33 MHz, but the access time for commodity DRAM has decreased disproportionately less—from 200 ns to around 70 ns.

The CPU/memory speed gap is even larger in workstations. Some models clock at intervals as short as 10 ns. How do vendors make up the difference between CPU speeds and memory speeds? Memory chips with 10 ns access times are available, but it is too expensive to build a complete memory system from them. The solution to the problem is a combination of caches and wide memory systems. In some cases, multiple memory banks play a part too.

Caches

Have you ever eaten in an airport at one of those chest high tables with no seat? For those who have not, the table I'm talking about has the dimensions of a trash can lid placed atop a sawed-off lolly column. Imagine what it would be like to hold Thanksgiving dinner at one. There would be the traditional foods: turkey, mashed potatoes, gravy, baked beans, french fries, onion rings, clam strips, and cigars. And your whole family would be there. But the table surface would be far too small to hold all of your plates plus all of the food. You would have to institute a policy of bringing the one or two dishes that were in highest demand to the table, and setting the rest down on the floor until they were needed. For instance, the onion rings and cigars might be set on the table top as people helped themselves. Everything else would be down on the floor behind you. When another dish was brought to the table, the least popular of the ones on the table top would be rotated out.

In effect, you would be doing for the Thanksgiving feast what a cache does for a computer's memory system. Those items that are needed most are brought to a place where they can be accessed quickly, and the rest are placed into a larger storage area with longer access times. Analogous optimizations apply too. For instance, when Uncle Elmo asks for the potatoes, you could fetch the gravy on the assumption that he will immediately ask for that as well.

Uncle Elmo will tell you that a cache is a small amount of very fast, expensive memory that acts as a proxy for the main memory system. It is divided into a number of equal sized slots known as *lines*. Each line contains a handful of sequential main memory locations, generally four to eight integers or real numbers. Whereas the data within a line comes from the same part of memory, neighboring lines can contain data that is far separated within your program, or perhaps data from somebody else's program, as in Figure 3-3. When you ask for something from memory, the computer checks to see if the data is available within one of these cache lines. If it is, the data is returned with a minimal delay. If it is not, then your program may be delayed while a new line is fetched from main memory. Of course, if a new line is brought in, then another one has to be thrown out. If you're lucky, it won't be the one containing the data that you are just about to need.

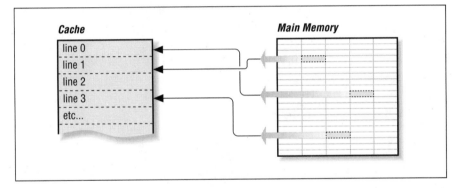

Figure 3-3: Cache lines can come from different parts of memory

When every reference can be found in a cache, you say that you have a 100% hit rate. Generally, a hit rate of 95% or better is considered OK. Below that, application performance drops off steeply.

Caches are not only good for data which is being read, they are good for writes too. In a simple uniprocessor system, data written into cache generally stays in the cache until the cache line is replaced, at which point it is written out into main memory. On multi-processors (computers with several CPUs) written data must be returned to main memory so the rest of the processors can see it, or all other processors must be made aware of local cache activity. Perhaps they need to be told to invalidate old lines containing the previous value of the written variable so that they don't accidentally use stale data. This is known as maintaining *coherency* between the different caches. The problem can become very complex in a multi-processor system.*

Caches are effective because programs naturally exhibit characteristics which help keep the hit rate high. These characteristics are called spatial and temporal *locality of reference*; programs often make use of instructions and data which are near to other instructions and data, both in space and time. When a cache line is retrieved from main memory, it contains not only the information that caused the cache miss, but also some neighboring information. Chances are good that the next time your program needs data, it will be in the cache line just fetched or another one recently fetched. (This is like getting Uncle Elmo the gravy when he asks for the potatoes.)

The caches in your computer may be as small as 4 KB or as large as 2 MB. As I said before, the whole memory system would be made of cache speed memory except that it would be prohibitively expensive. But generally, the larger the cache, the better off you are. Much of your program and data will fit in the cache, very little of it being bounced out, so after some initial misses you can obtain a very high hit rate. Caches come in several flavors: direct mapped, set-associative, and fully-associative.

Direct Mapped Cache

The process of pairing memory locations with cache locations is called *mapping*. Of course, if a cache is smaller than main memory then you have to share the same cache lines for different memory locations. The way memory locations are mapped to cache lines can have a great effect on the way your program runs, because if two heavily used memory locations map onto the same cache line then the miss rate will be higher than you would like it to be.

Direct mapping is the simplest algorithm for deciding how memory maps onto the cache. Say, for example, that your computer has a 4 KB cache. In a direct mapped scheme, memory location 0 will map into cache location 0, as will memory locations 4K, 8K, 12K, etc. In other words, memory maps onto the cache size. Another way to think about it is to imagine a metal spring with a chalk line marked down the side. Every time around the spring, you encounter the chalk line at the same place modulo the circumference of the spring. If the spring is very long, then the chalk line crosses

---

*Chapter 16 describes cache coherency in more detail.

many coils— the analog being a large memory with many locations mapping into the same cache line.

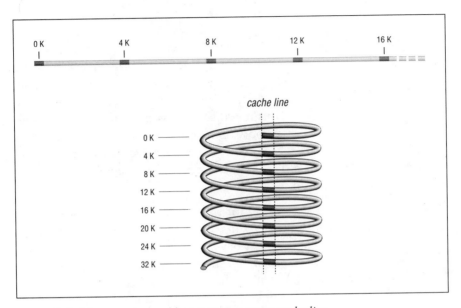

Figure 3-4: Many memory addresses map to same cache line

Problems occur when alternating run time memory references in a direct mapped cache point to the same cache line. Each reference will cause a cache miss and replace the entry just replaced, causing a lot of overhead. The popular word for this is *thrashing*. When there is lots of opportunity for thrashing, a cache can be more of a liability than an asset because each cache miss requires that a cache line be refilled—an operation that moves more data than merely satisfying the reference directly from main memory. It is easy to construct a pathological case that causes thrashing in a direct mapped cache:

```
      REAL*4 A(1024), B(1024)
      COMMON /STUFF/ A,B
      DO 10 I=1,1024
        A(I) = A(I) * B(I)
  10  CONTINUE
      END
```

The arrays **A** and **B** both take up exactly 4 KB of storage, and their inclusion together in COMMON assures that they both start 4 KB apart in memory. In a 4 KB direct mapped cache, the same line that is reserved for A(1) will be reserved for B(1), and likewise for A(2) and B(2), etc., so alternating references cause repeated cache misses. To fix it, you could either adjust the size of the array **A**, or put some other variables into COMMON, between them.

Fully Associative Cache

At the other extreme from a direct mapped cache is a *fully associative cache*, where any memory location can be mapped into any cache line, regardless of memory address. Fully associative caches get their name from the type of memory used to construct them—associative memory. Associative memory is like regular memory, except that each memory cell knows something about the data it contains. In an associative cache, for instance, each cache line has a record of the memory address it represents, and perhaps when it was last used.

When the processor goes looking for a piece of data, the cache lines are asked all at once whether any of them has it. The cache line containing the data holds up its hand and says "I have it"; if none of them do there is a cache miss. It then becomes a question of which cache line will be replaced with the new data. Rather than map memory locations to cache lines via an algorithm, like a direct mapped cache, the memory system can ask the fully associative cache lines to choose among themselves which memory locations they will represent. Usually the least recently used line is the one that gets overwritten with new data. The assumption is that if the data hasn't been used in quite a while then it may not be used in the future.

Fully associative caches have superior performance to direct mapped caches. It is very difficult to find real world examples of programs which will cause thrashing in a fully associative cache. However, the expense is very high, both in terms of size and price, so the associative caches that do exist tend to be small.

Set Associative Cache

Now imagine that you have two direct mapped caches sitting side-by-side in a single cache unit. Each memory location corresponds to a particular cache line in each of the two direct mapped caches. The one you will choose to replace during a cache miss is subject to a decision about whose line was used last—the same way the decision was made in a fully associative cache except that now there are only two choices. This is called a *set associative cache*. Set associative caches generally come in two and four-way designs.

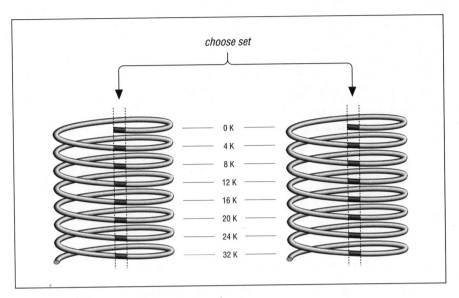

Figure 3-5: Two-way set associative cache

Of course, there are benefits and drawbacks to each type of cache. A set associative cache is much more immune to cache thrashing than a direct mapped cache of the same size, because for each mapping of a memory address into a cache line there are two or more choices for where it can go. The beauty of a direct cache, however, is that it is easy to implement and, if made large enough, will perform roughly as well as a set-associative design. Your machine may contain several caches of several different types for several different purposes. Here's a little program for causing thrashing in a two-way set associative cache:

```
      REAL*4 A(1024), B(1024), C(1024)
      COMMON /STUFF/ A,B,C
      DO 10 I=1,1024
        A(I) = A(I) * B(I) + C(I)
10    CONTINUE
      END
```

Like the previous cache thrasher program, it forces repeated accesses to the same cache lines, except that now there are three variables contending for the same mapping instead of two. Again, the way to fix it would be to change the size of the arrays or sandwich something in between them, in COMMON. By the way, if you accidentally arranged a program to thrash like this, it would be very hard for you to detect it—aside from a feeling that the program runs a little slow. Very few vendors provide tools for measuring cache misses.

Uses of Cache

So far I have glossed over the two kinds of information you would expect to find in a cache between main memory and the CPU: instructions and data. But if you think about it, the demand for data is separate from the demand for instructions. In superscalar processors, for example, it is possible to execute an instruction that will cause a data cache miss alongside other instructions that require no data from cache at all, i.e., they operate on registers. It doesn't seem fair that a cache miss on a data reference in one instruction should keep you from fetching other instructions because the cache is tied up. Furthermore, a cache depends on locality of reference between bits of data and other bits of data or instructions and other instructions, but what kind of interplay is there between instructions and data? It would seem possible for instructions to bump perfectly useful data from cache, or vice versa, with complete disregard for locality of reference.

Many CISC designs use a single cache for both instructions and data. If you have a high-end 80486 PC it will also use a single cache. But newer designs are employing what is known as *Harvard Memory Architecture*, where the demand for data is somewhat segregated from the demand for instructions. Main memory is a still a single large pool, but these machines have separate data and instruction caches, possibly of different designs. For instance, the IBM RS/6000 uses a two-way set associative cache for instruction memory, but a four-way set associative cache for data. By providing two independent sources for data and instructions, the aggregate rate of information coming from memory is increased and interference between the two types of memory references is minimized. You can expect both higher performance and higher cost from a machine using a Harvard Memory Architecture.

Virtual Memory

Virtual Memory machines, such as your UNIX workstation, translate the logical memory addresses your program generates into physical addresses in the memory system. Whereas your program sees its address space starting at 0 and working its way up to some large number, the actual physical addresses assigned can be very different. It gives a degree of flexibility by allowing all processes to believe that they have all of the memory system to themselves. Another trait of virtual memory systems is that they divide your program's memory up into *pages*—chunks. Page sizes vary from 512 bytes to 16 KB, depending on the machine. Pages don't have to be contiguous, though your program sees them that way. By being separated into pages, programs are easier to fit together in memory, or move out to disk in portions.

Page Tables

Say that your program asks for a variable stored at location 1000. In a virtual memory machine, there is no direct correspondence between your program's idea of where location 1000 is and the physical memory systems' idea. To find where your variable is actually stored, the location has to be translated from a virtual address to a physical address. The map containing such translations is called a *page table*. Each process has a several page tables associated with it, corresponding to different regions, such as program text and data segments.

To understand how address translation works, imagine the following scenario: at some point, your program asks for data from location 1000. By choosing location 1000, you have identified which region the memory reference falls in, and this identifies which page table is involved. 1000 then helps the processor choose an entry within the table. For instance, if the page size is 512 bytes, then location 1000 will fall within the second page (pages range from addresses 0-511, 512-1023, 1024-1535, etc). Therefore, the second table entry should hold the address of the page housing the value at location 1000. Are you with me so far?

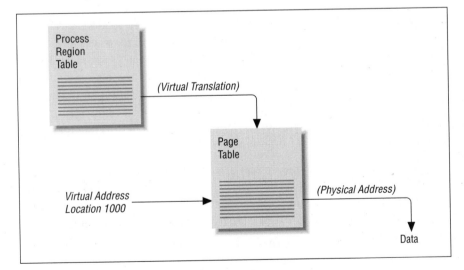

Figure 3-6: Virtual to physical address mapping

The operating system stores the page table addresses virtually, so it's going to take a virtual to physical translation to locate the table in memory. One more virtual to physical translation, and we finally have the true address of location 1000. The memory reference can complete and the processor can return to executing your program.

Translation Lookaside Buffer

As you can see, address translation through a page table is pretty complicated. It required two table lookups (maybe three) to locate our data. If every memory reference was that complicated, virtual memory computers would be horrible performers. Fortunately, locality of reference causes virtual address translations to group together; a program may repeat the same virtual page mapping millions of times a second. And where we have repeated use of the same data, we can apply a cache.

All modern virtual memory machines have a special cache called a *translation lookaside buffer* or TLB for virtual to physical memory address translation. The two inputs to the TLB are an integer that identifies the program making the memory request and the virtual page requested. From the output pops a pointer to the physical page number. Virtual address in—physical address out. TLB lookups occur in parallel with instruction execution, so if the address data is in the TLB, memory references will proceed quickly.

Like other kinds of caches, the TLB is limited in size. It doesn't contain enough entries to handle all of the possible virtual to physical address translations for all the programs that might run on your computer. Larger pools of address translations are kept out in memory, in the page tables. If your program asks for a virtual to physical address translation, and the entry doesn't exist in the TLB, then you suffer a *TLB miss*. The information needed may have to be generated (a new page may need to be created) or it may have to be retrieved from the page table.

The TLB is good for the same reason that other types of caches are good: it reduces the cost of memory references. But like other caches, there are pathological cases where the TLB can fail to deliver value. The easiest case to construct is one where every memory reference your program makes causes a TLB miss:

```
REAL X(10000000)
COMMON X,Y
```

```
        DO 10 I=0,1000
           DO 20 J=1,10000000,10000
              Y = X(J+I)
   20      CONTINUE
   10    CONTINUE
```

Assume that the memory page size for your computer is less than 40 KB (fair assumption). Every time through the inner loop in the above example code, the program asks for data that is 4 bytes*10,000 = 40,000 bytes away from the last reference. That is, each reference falls on a different memory page. This causes 1000 TLB misses in the inner loop, taken 1001 times, for a total of at least one million TLB misses. To add insult to injury, each reference is guaranteed to cause a data cache miss as well. Admittedly, no one would start out with a loop like the one above. But presuming that the loop was any good to you at all, the restructured version in the code below would cruise through memory like a warm knife through butter:

```
        REAL X(10000000)
        COMMON X,Y
        DO 10 I=1,10000000
           Y = X(I)
   10    CONTINUE
```

The reversed loop has good locality of reference and TLB misses occur only every so often.

Page Faults

A page table (or TLB) entry also contains other information about the page it represents, including flags to tell whether the translation is valid, whether the associated page can be modified, and some information describing how new pages should be initialized. References to pages that are not marked valid are called *page faults*.

Taking a worst case scenario, say that your program asks for a variable from a particular memory location. The processor goes to look for it in the cache and finds it isn't there (cache miss), which means it must be loaded from memory. Next it goes to the TLB to find the physical location of the data in memory and finds there is no TLB entry either (a TLB miss). Then it tries consulting the page table (and refilling the TLB), but finds that either there is no entry for your particular page, or that the memory page has been shipped to disk (both are page faults). Each step of the memory hierarchy has shrugged off your request. A new page will have to be created in memory and possibly, depending on the circumstances, refilled from disk.

A simple data access has been stretched into a trip to the Department of Motor Vehicles.

Although they take a lot of time, page faults aren't errors. Even under optimal conditions every program will suffer some number of page faults. Writing a variable for the first time or calling a subroutine that has never been called can cause a page fault. This may be surprising if you have never thought about it before. The illusion is that all of your program is present in memory from the start, but some portions may never be loaded. There is no reason to make space for a page whose data is never referenced or whose instructions are never executed. Only those pages that are required to run the job get created or pulled in from the disk.*

The pool of physical memory pages is limited because physical memory is limited, so on a machine where many programs are lobbying for space there will be a higher number of page faults. This is because physical memory pages are continually being recycled for other purposes. However, when you have the machine to yourself and memory is less in demand, allocated pages tend to stick around for a while. In short, you can expect less page faults on a quiet machine. One trick to remember if you ever end up working for a computer vendor: always run short benchmarks twice. The number of page faults will go down. This is because the second run will find the text pages left in memory by the first, and you won't have to pay for page faults again.†

Paging space (swap space) on the disk is the last and slowest piece of the memory hierarchy for most machines. In the worst case scenario we saw how a memory reference could be pushed down to slower and slower performance media before finally being satisfied. If you step back, you can view the disk paging space as having the same relationship to main memory as main memory has to cache. The same kinds of optimizations apply too, and locality of reference is important. You can run programs that are larger than the main memory system of your machine, but sometimes at greatly decreased performance. When we look at memory optimizations in Chapter 11, we will be concentrating on keeping the activity in the fastest parts of the memory system, and avoiding the slow parts.

---

*The term for this is *demand paging*.

†Text pages are identified by the disk device and block number they came from.

Improving Bandwidth

Peak memory bandwidth figures are an example of performance limits that you are guaranteed not to exceed. The term *bandwidth*, borrowed from radio, means the difference between the minimum and maximum frequency in a channel. For us, that is the difference between the slowest memory transfer rate, zero MB, and the fastest, *n* MB. In other words, as far as memory system transfer rates are concerned, the term bandwidth refers to peak speed.

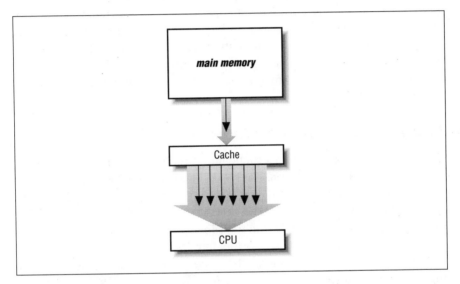

Figure 3-7: Simple memory system

Because memory systems are divided into pieces, there are different bandwidth figures between different components. The transfer rate between a cache and the CPU may be much higher than the bandwidth between main memory and the cache, for instance. There may be several caches and paths to memory as well. Usually, the peak memory bandwidth quoted by vendors is the speed between the data cache and the memory system. However, this is a peak transfer rate, which means that it generally cannot be sustained for very long. Peak rates are also subject to the presence of certain optimal conditions, such as the memory access patterns.

A related quantity is *latency*—the time between the points when a memory reference is initiated and when the first data bytes show up at the other end of the pipe. The bandwidth through a given path may be very high, but if the latency is high as well, the path will (probably) be unsuitable for small chunks of data. On the other hand, if you're moving a lot of data through a high bandwidth/high latency channel, the latency won't affect you so much; its significance will be lost in the volume of data moved.

Large Caches

As I said at the start of this chapter, the disparity between CPU speeds and memory is growing. If you look closely, you can see vendors innovating in several ways. Some workstations are being offered with 2 MB data caches! This is larger than the main memory systems of machines just a few years ago. With a large enough cache, a small (or even moderately large) program can fit completely inside, and get incredibly good performance. Watch out for this when you are testing new hardware. When your program grows too large for the cache, the performance may drop off considerably, perhaps by a factor of five or more, depending on the memory access patterns.

Interleaved Memory Systems

Consider what happens when a cache line is refilled from memory: consecutive memory locations fill consecutive locations within the cache line. The number of bytes transferred depends on how big the line is—anywhere from 16 bytes to 128 bytes or more. We want the refill to proceed quickly because an instruction is stalled in the pipeline, or perhaps the processor is waiting for more instructions. Fortunately, because the memory transfer comes from consecutive locations, the system can use page mode addressing (described previously) and benefit from the reduced DRAM access and cycle times. Of course, it's still preferable not to suffer too many cache misses, but at least the refills can proceed quickly.

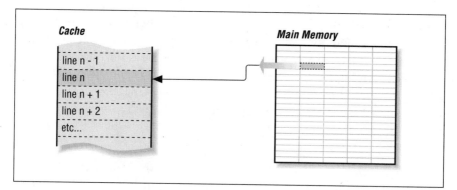

Figure 3-8: Page mode cache refill

A data cache, backed up by memory arranged in a single bank (or perhaps several banks covering different memory address segments) works acceptably well for general purpose computers. However, there are some kinds of computing—especially large scale numerical computing—for which a data cache can be a liability. This is because large numerical programs may address great amounts of data with little regard for locality of reference.* And recall that when a program's access pattern lacks locality of reference, a cache may actually hurt the run time; the cache miss rate will be high. For this reason, number crunching computers often have special instructions that bypass data cache memory; the data are transferred directly between the processor and the main memory system.† In fact, some numerical computers have no data cache at all.

How then does a memory system without a data cache (or one that is bypassing the data cache) produce data at a high enough rate to keep the processor busy? Clearly, a single memory bank can't keep up; the access and cycle times for commodity DRAM are too long. And we can't depend on page mode, as we did for cache refills, because memory references may not be sequential.

What if, instead of a single bank, the memory system was constructed from an interleaved collection of many banks, organized so that each consecutive data word falls on a different bank? Imagine how this would work: as your program steps sequentially through an array, it visits the banks in a round-robin fashion. The banks may share data and address lines, but their use is overlapped and staggered through time (memory references are pipelined); as one bank is being addressed, another is presenting its data. And as long as the pattern is repeated—bank0, bank1, bank2, ..., bank0—data will flow smoothly from memory.

You can imagine that other memory access patterns will work well too. For instance, references to every ninth data word will rotate through the banks in the same order as consecutive references. Or stepping backwards through an array also visits each bank in turn, though in reverse order—bank0, bank7, bank6 ...

---

*More correctly: "*Old* numerical programs may address ...." No matter what kind of machine you are writing for today, you should have locality of reference as one of your design goals. Locality of reference is important for effective programming of workstations and the newest wave of supercomputers, as we'll see in Chapters 11 and 15.

†By the way, most machines have uncached memory spaces for process synchronization and I/O device registers. However, memory references to these locations bypass the cache because of the address chosen, not necessarily because of the instruction chosen.

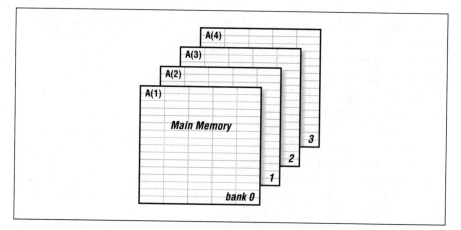

Figure 3-9: Multi-banked memory system

You have probably guessed, however, that we run into a problem when we go looking for every eighth data word. Because there are exactly eight banks, a single bank is being visited repeatedly—the round-robin scheme fails. Access time for the bank will be stretched to include the cycle time plus the access time of the memory chips within the bank. The program will be delayed for the time it takes the oversubscribed bank to recover from the last access and complete the current one. This is called a *bank stall.*

Different access patterns are subject to bank stalls of varying severity. For instance, accesses to every fourth word in an eight bank memory system would also be subject to bank stalls, though the recovery would occur sooner. References to every second word might not experience bank stalls at all; each bank may have recovered by the time its next reference comes around—it depends on the relative speeds of the processor and memory system. Irregular access patterns are sure to encounter some bank stalls.

In addition to the bank stall hazard, memory references made directly to a multi-banked memory system carry a greater latency than those of (successfully) cached memory accesses. This is because references are going out to memory that is slower than cache, and there may be additional address translation steps as well. However, banked memory references are pipelined. As long as references are started well enough in advance, several pipelined, multi-banked references can be in-flight at one time, giving you good throughput.

Vector supercomputers,* such as the CRAY Y/MP and the Convex C3, are machines that depend on multi-banked memory systems for performance. The C3, in particular, has a memory system with up to 256-way interleaving (it also has a cache, by the way). This helps to reduce the chances of repeated access to the same memory bank by providing a lot of banks to choose from. If you do hit the same bank twice in a row, however, the penalty is a delay of nearly 300 ns—a long time for a machine with a clock speed of 16 ns. So when things go well, they go very well. But when the access pattern isn't perfect, bank stalls slow the computations considerably.

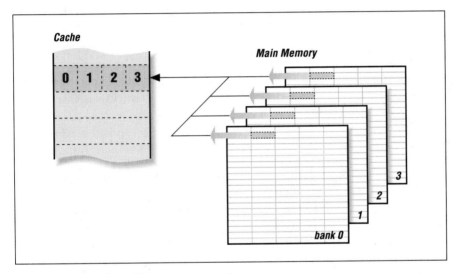

Figure 3-10: Cache refill from interleaved memory

As you can see, there are trade-offs between pipelined, multi-banked memory references and cached references. The two can coexist, though most computers depend on caches alone. Because this book is primarily concerned with RISC processors and workstations, the tuning techniques in later chapters will focus more closely on preserving cache entries than avoiding bank stalls. However, I will discuss non-cached memory references again when there are interesting differences to point out, particularly in Chapter 11.

I would be remiss, however, if I didn't mention that pipelined memory references to multi-banked memory systems do appear in some RISC processors. In fact, we can expect to see more support for non-cached memory

---

*Vector computing is explained in more detail in Chapter 8.

systems in the future. MIPS' new SSR and the Intel i860 feature pipelined memory reference instructions that bypass the data cache. In the case of SSR, multibanked references stream into their own special cache, apart from the data cache. This serves as a holding pen for data being fed to the floating point units. Both processors—the i860 and SSR—depend on bypassing instructions for number crunching, as their on-chip data caches are fairly small.

Software Managed Caches

Here's an interesting thought: sometimes the compiler has information about the way memory is being used. For instance, if your program steps through an array with a fixed stride, it may be possible for the compiler to anticipate where the next memory references will go. Given information like that (and appropriate hardware support), it seems like it should be possible for the compiler to "prime" the cache with data it is going to need in the near future. This could be better than the way we've talked about using the cache so far: issuing a memory reference and hoping that the data is in there. Instead, the cache could be managed, in part, by software.

Hardware support for *software managed caches* is something that several new processors feature, such as the Motorola 88110 and DEC Alpha/AXP. For instance, imagine a cache hint instruction that the compiler could issue to start the process of filling a cache entry in advance. It would look like a load instruction, except that it wouldn't delay processing if there happened to be a cache miss, and would (perhaps) have the "bit bucket" (they're discarded) as its destination. In a processor that could only issue one instruction per cycle, there might be no payback to a cache hint instruction; it would take up valuable time in the instruction stream in exchange for an uncertain benefit. On a superscalar processor, however, a cache hint could be mixed in with the rest of the instruction stream and issued alongside other, real instructions. If it saved your program from suffering extra cache misses, it would be worth having.

Memory Reference Reordering

One more mental exercise before we part. There is a lot of benefit to moving memory references around. The earlier memory loads are initiated, the sooner operands for other instructions will be available. Likewise, the later stores are made, the less the likelihood that they will have to wait for their data to become available. For this reason an optimizing compiler generally tries to move loads "up" in the instruction stream, and move stores "down."

When it is clear that two memory references go to different addresses, it is safe for them to move past one another. However, in the following code, we can't tell that the memory references go to different addresses:

```
X(K)  = B + C + D
A     = X(I)
```

If K and I are equal, data is stored to one location, X(K), then immediately loaded from the same location. If things got mixed up, so that X(I) was loaded before X(K) was stored, then the answers would be wrong. Naturally, a machine that gets the wrong answers won't be very useful. In the absence of hardware support or specific information about I and K, the compiler can only guarantee that the two suspicious memory accesses don't overlap by not letting them get too close to one another. This will maintain correctness in the program, but it may also leave large gaps in the instruction stream, which will reduce performance. In the example above, the load of X(I) *has to* follow the store of X(K), because I and K are unknown.

A piece of hardware called a *stunt box* can help in this situation. Originating with powerful CDC and IBM machines of the 1960s, it's used on a handful of processors today (the Motorola 88110 is one). Like a traffic cop, the stunt box monitors data movement in and out of the memory system (or cache). The rule it follows is simple (though the hardware is complicated): Don't let a store pass a load or another store to the same address. Other loads and stores can proceed as soon as their data are ready—even in a different order than they were issued.

The stunt box's ability to dynamically order references makes it possible for the compiler to issue loads and stores without putting a safety zone between them (although it is still limited in how much it can intermix them). For instance, all the instructions that take part in calculating X(K) could be issued, immediately followed by the reference to X(I), without worry. If, at run time, it turns out that they specify the same memory address, then the assignment A=X(I) will be held up while the first statement completes. Otherwise, it can proceed, perhaps even passing the reference to X(K).

Multiple References

I confess: I really brought up out-of-order memory references to lead into a different subject. If parallel RISC CPUs are ever going to be able to issue more instructions per clock, say seven or eight, something fundamental will have to change in the way they use memory. Future processors are going to have to be able to issue *multiple* memory references per cycle, otherwise they starve for data. What are some of the challenges?

A processor that could do two memory operations would need twice the address calculation hardware, and perhaps be equipped to handle two cache accesses at once. Or maybe each processor could have two data caches, one for each (nearly) concurrent memory reference. Perhaps caches wouldn't be used at all when multiple memory references are issued together. This would be a natural extension of the long instruction word architecture of the i860, given some fundamental support in the memory system.

In fact, RISC processors capable of issuing multiple memory references are already starting to appear. For instance, the MIPS SSR can feed two floating point memory references from a *streaming cache*—a holding pen for multi-banked memory references. The compiler issues instructions to a special (vector) address generator that fills the streaming cache sufficiently far in advance so that the floating point units can be kept busy. (See Chapter 8 for a description of vector processing).

Whatever the case, computers capable of multiple memory accesses will need to have particularly sophisticated policies regarding memory reference ordering. It will take an intelligent compiler, perhaps backed up by hardware such as a stunt box, to make sure that multiple references can execute safely side-by-side. I should also mention the challenges aren't exactly new. Memory reference ordering is already very important in vector processors or vector libraries and multiprocessors. It will become very important in the workstations around the corner, too—for scalar operations. In the upcoming chapters, I discuss the problems that accompany instruction and memory access reordering in more detail.

Closing Notes

They say that the computer of the future will be a good memory system that just happens to have a CPU attached. We've just seen some of the many challenges in delivering data to the CPU fast enough to keep it from getting cold. As CPUs get even faster, good memory systems are going to be more and more critical for performance. It's also important that programs be crafted with data access patterns in mind. In Chapter 11, I'll show you how to restructure memory accesses so that they "play to" your memory system strengths.

Exercises

1. The following code segment traverses a pointer chain. How will such a code interact with the cache if all the references fall within a small portion of memory? How will the code interact with the cache if references are stretched across many megabytes?

   ```
   while ((p = (char *) *p) != NULL);
   ```

2. How would the code in Exercise 1 behave on a multi-banked memory system that has no cache?

3. Many numerical applications access memory in regular, repeated patterns. Under what circumstances could a compiler take advantage of a software managed cache to reduce cache miss for a numerical application?

4. A long time ago, people regularly wrote self-modifying code—programs that wrote into instruction memory and changed their own behavior. What would be the implications of self-modifying code on a machine with a Harvard memory architecture?

4

What an Optimizing Compiler Does

A compiler's job is to take something written in a language you can understand and translate it into a language the computer understands. That might be enough, but as anyone who has ever listened to a child tell a story knows, there is no limit on how long it can take to say one thing. The goal of an *optimizing compiler* is the efficient translation of a higher level language. Optimal translation may be too much to ask for; in situations where optimal code is required, such as the inner sections of the operating system, or in mathematical subroutine libraries, there are always a few cycles to be saved by tuning or hand coding.

Of course, if an algorithm is poorly organized from the beginning, any expression of it will be less than perfect too. But within the limits of our ability to tell the compiler what it is we want to do, we would like to ask for the best machine language representation we can get. What makes a representation good is: it gives the correct answers, and it executes quickly.

Naturally, it makes no difference how fast a program runs if it doesn't produce the right answers* (although this never stopped a computer salesperson). But given an expression of a program that will execute correctly, an optimizing compiler looks for ways to streamline it. As a first cut, this usually means simplifying the code, throwing out extraneous instructions, and sharing intermediate results between statements. More advanced optimizations seek to restructure the program, and may actually make the code grow in size, though the number of instructions executed will (hopefully) shrink.

---

*However, you can sometimes trade accuracy for speed.

When it finally comes to generating machine language, the compiler has to know about the registers and rules for issuing instructions. For performance, it needs to understand the costs of those instructions and the latencies of machine resources, such as the pipelines. This is especially true for processors that can execute more than one instruction at a time. It takes a balanced instruction mix—the right proportion of floating point, fixed point, memory and branch operations, etc.—to keep the machine busy.

Lastly, the compiler has to be careful not to create its own logjams. For instance, careless reuse of a particular hardware resource, such as a register,* can cause a needless delay, waiting for that resource to be free for use by other instructions. We'd also like to ask the compiler to issue costly instructions as early as it can so others that depend on their results don't have to loiter.

Pick your battle: an optimizing compiler has work to do at all levels. I'll be talking about many different types of optimizations throughout the rest of the book. In this chapter, I want to focus on what are commonly called *classical optimizations.* These are well documented, have been in use for years, and can help performance on all types of computers. Nothing about them is specific to parallel RISC processors.

Optimizing Compiler Tour

We will start by taking a walk through an optimizing compiler to see one at work. I think it's interesting, and if you can empathize with the compiler, you will be a better programmer; you will know what the compiler wants from you, and what it can do on its own.

Intermediate Language Representation

The first duties of an optimizing compiler are to parse and translate a high level language, such as C or FORTRAN, into an *intermediate language* (IL) representation. The intermediate language expresses the same calculations that were in the original program, in a form that the compiler can manipulate more easily. Furthermore, instructions that aren't present in the source, such as address expressions for array references, become visible along with the rest of the program, making them subject to optimizations too.

---

*On a machine without register renaming, described in Chapter 2.

How would an intermediate language look? In terms of complexity, it is similar to assembly code but not so simple that the definitions* and uses of variables are lost. We will need definition and use information to analyze the flow of data through the program. Typically, calculations would be expressed as a stream of *quadruples*—statements with exactly one operator, (up to) two operands and a result.† Presuming that anything in the original source program can be recast in terms of quadruples, we have a usable intermediate language. To give you an idea of how this works, I'm going to rewrite the statement below as a series of four quadruplets:

```
A = -B + C * D / E
```

Taken all at once, this statement has four operators and four operands: /, *, +, and - (negate), and B, C, D, and E. This is clearly too much to fit into one quadruple. We need a form with exactly one operator and at most two operands per statement. The recast version below manages to do this, employing temporary variables to hold the intermediate results:

```
T1 = D / E
T2 = C * T1
T3 = -B
A  = T3 + T2
```

A workable intermediate language would, of course, need some other features, like pointers. I'm going to suggest that we create our own intermediate language so we can investigate how optimizations work. To begin, we need to establish a few rules:

- Instructions consist of one opcode, two operands, and a result. Depending on the instruction, the operands may be empty.

- Assignments are of the form X := Y op Z, meaning X gets the result of op applied to Y and Z.

- All memory references are explicit load from or store to "temporaries" tn.

- Logical values used in branches are calculated separately from the actual branch.

- Jumps go to absolute addresses.

---

*By "definitions," we mean the assignment of values. Not declarations.
†More generally, code can be cast as *n*-tuples. It depends on the level of the intermediate language.

If we were building a compiler, we would need to be a little more specific. For our purposes, this will do. Consider the following bit of C code:

```
while (j < n) {
    k = k + j * 2;
    m = j * 2;
    j++;
}
```

This loop translates into the intermediate language representation shown below.

Example 4-1: Intermediate Language for a Single Loop

```
A::  t1   := j
     t2   := n
     t3   := t1 < t2
     jmp (B) t3
     jmp (C) TRUE

B::  t4   := k
     t5   := j
     t6   := t5 * 2
     t7   := t4 + t6
     k    := t7

     t8   := j
     t9   := t8 * 2
     m    := t9
     t10  := j
     t11  := t10 + 1
     j    := t11
     jmp (A) TRUE
C::
```

Each C source line is represented by several IL statements. On many RISC processors, our IL code is so close to machine language that we could turn it into object code immediately. But would we want to? No, not yet. Just by looking at it you can see places to save a few instructions. For instance, j gets loaded into temporaries in four places; surely we can reduce that. We have to do some analysis and make some optimizations.

Basic Blocks

After generating our intermediate language, we want to cut it into *basic blocks*. These are code sequences that start with an instruction that either follows a branch or is itself a target for a branch. Put another way, each basic block has just one entrance (at the top) and one exit (at the bottom). Figure 4-1 represents our IL code as a group of three basic blocks.

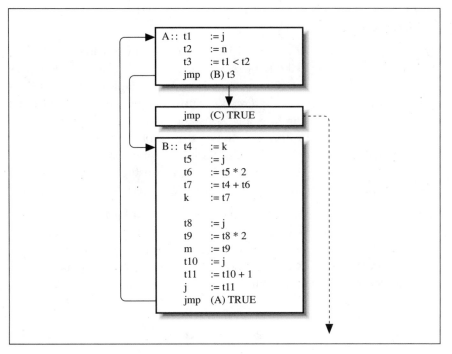

Figure 4-1: Example 4-1 divided into basic blocks

Basic blocks make code easier to analyze. If you have ever played chess and tried to envision what moves might be open to you several turns ahead, you have a feel for how branches can complicate the process; it may be impossible to tell where your pawn will be three moves hence. By restricting flow of control within a basic block from top to bottom and eliminating all the branches, we can be sure that if the first statement gets executed, then the second one does too, and so on. Of course, the branches haven't disappeared, but we have forced them outside the blocks in the form of the connecting arrows—the *flow graph*.

We are now free to extract information from the blocks themselves. For instance, we can say with certainty which variables a given block uses and which variables it defines (sets the value of). We might not be able to do that if the block contained a branch. We can also gather the same kind of information about the calculations it performs. After we have analyzed the blocks, so that we know what goes in and what comes out, we can paint them over so that the insides are no longer visible, and just worry about the interaction between blocks.

Forming a DAG

One method for analyzing a basic block is to organize it into a *Directed Acyclic Graph* (DAG).* Like the basic block it represents, a DAG describes all of the calculations and relationships between variables. The data flow within a DAG proceeds in one direction; most often a DAG is constructed from top to bottom. Identifiers and constants will be placed at the "leaf" nodes—the ones on the top. Operations, possibly with variable names attached, make up the internal nodes. Variables appear in their finals states at the bottom. The DAG's edges order the relationships between the variables and operations within it. All data flow proceeds from top to bottom.

To construct a DAG, the compiler takes each tuple and maps it onto one or more nodes. For instance, those tuples that represent binary operations, such as addition (a+b), will form a portion of the DAG with two inputs (a and b) bound together by an operation (+). The result of the operation may feed into yet other operations within the basic block (and the DAG).

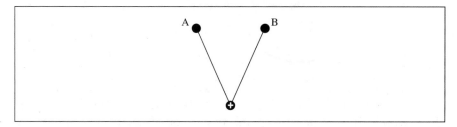

Figure 4-2: Tuple mapped into a DAG

The very process of building a DAG unearths and eliminates repeated subexpressions, or different variables that are serving redundant purposes. This is because repeated operations and temporary variables tend to map onto the same nodes. When finished, the DAG completely describes the activity throughout the basic block, though perhaps with fewer temporary variables and operations. The compiler can then regenerate a new, sleeker version of the basic block directly from the DAG.

---

*A *graph* is a collection of nodes connected by edges. By *directed*, we mean that the edges can only be traversed in specified directions. The word *acyclic* means that there are no cycles in the graph. That is, you can't loop anywhere within it.

To see how this works, we'll take a detailed look at Basic Block B from Figure 4-1. For reference, here's the basic block again.

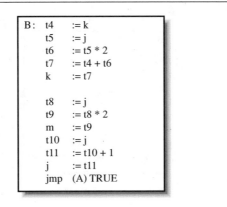

```
B:  t4    := k
    t5    := j
    t6    := t5 * 2
    t7    := t4 + t6
    k     := t7

    t8    := j
    t9    := t8 * 2
    m     := t9
    t10   := j
    t11   := t10 + 1
    j     := t11
    jmp   (A) TRUE
```

Figure 4-3: Basic Block B

Figure 4-4 shows the DAG corresponding to this basic block. Many of the temporaries are grouped together, and redundant calculations, such as t5*2 and t8*2, have been mapped onto the same nodes. Notice also that there is an extra edge between t6 and t11. This represents a *dependency* between the two nodes; the operations at the node representing t6 must occur before t11. Otherwise, j might become redefined before m is calculated from it.

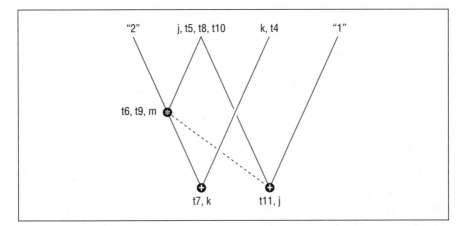

Figure 4-4: DAG for Block B

Now that we have constructed an efficient DAG for Block B, we can reconstruct the basic block. Notice that the new block, in Figure 4-5, has fewer operations than the original one.

```
B:  t4     := k
    t5     := j
    t6     := t5 * 2
    m      := t6
    t7     := t6 + t4
    k      := t7
    t11    := t5 + 1
    j      := t11
    jmp    (A) TRUE
```

Figure 4-5: Revised Basic Block B

You can see that some of the tuples and temporary variables have been eliminated. This will translate into a savings in both execution time and register assignments.

Uses and Definitions

As the DAG is constructed, the compiler can make lists of variable *uses* and *definitions*, as well as other information, and apply these to global optimizations across many basic blocks taken together. Looking at the DAG above, we can see that the variables defined are k,j, and m, and the variables used are k and j. Considering many basic blocks at once, we can say how far a particular variable definition reaches—where its value can be seen. From this we can recognize situations where calculations are being discarded, where two uses of a given variable are completely independent, or where we can overwrite register resident values without saving them back to memory. We call this investigation *data flow analysis*.

To illustrate, suppose that we have the flow graph in Figure 4-6. Beside each basic block I have listed the variables it uses and the variables it defines. What can data flow analysis tell us?

Notice that a value for A is defined in block X but only used in block Y. That means that A is dead upon exit from block Y or immediately upon taking the right hand branch leaving X—none of the other basic blocks uses the value of A. That tells us that any associated resources, such as a register, can be freed for other uses.

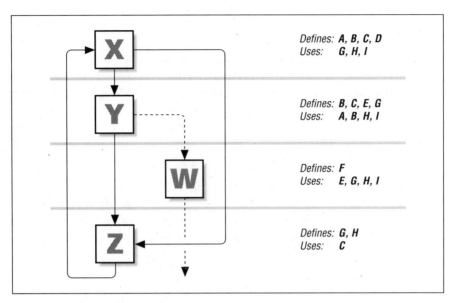

Defines: *A, B, C, D*
Uses: *G, H, I*

Defines: *B, C, E, G*
Uses: *A, B, H, I*

Defines: *F*
Uses: *E, G, H, I*

Defines: *G, H*
Uses: *C*

Figure 4-6: Flow graph for data flow analysis

We can see that D is defined in basic block X, but never used. This means that the calculations defining D can be discarded.

Something interesting is happening with the variable G. Blocks X and W both use it, but if you look closely you'll see that the two uses are distinct from one another, meaning that they can be treated as two independent variables.

A compiler featuring advanced instruction scheduling techniques might notice that W is the only block that uses the value for E, and so move the calculations defining E out of block Y and into W, where they are needed.

In addition to gathering data about variables, the compiler can also keep information about subexpressions. Examining both together, it can recognize cases where redundant calculations are being made (across basic blocks), and substitute previously computed values in their place. If, for instance, the expression H*I appears in blocks X, Y, and W, it could be calculated just once in block X and propagated to the others that use it.

Loops

Loops are the center of activity for many applications, so there is often a high payback for simplifying or moving calculations outside, into the computational suburbs. Forget the notion of a FORTRAN do-loop or a C for-loop for the moment. We will identify loops as a particular subset of nodes in the flow graph. The original source lines that generated them might not be loop constructs at all—they could be an if-statement and a goto. They will look the same to us as we crawl through the flow graph.

Once we have identified the loops, we can apply the same kinds of data-flow analysis that we applied above. Among the things we are looking for are calculations that are unchanging within the loop and variables that change in a predictable (linear) fashion from iteration to iteration.

How does the compiler identify a loop in the flow graph? Fundamentally, two conditions have to be met:

- A given node has to dominate all other nodes within the suspected loop. This means that all paths to any node in the loop have to pass through one particular node, the dominator. This node will form the header at the top of the loop.
- There has to be a cycle in the graph. Given a dominator, if we can find a path back to it from one of the nodes it dominates, we have a loop. This path back is known as the *back-edge* of the loop.

The flow graph in Figure 4-6 contains one loop and one red herring. You can see that node **B** dominates every node below it in the subset of the flow graph. That satisfies Condition 1 and makes it a candidate for a loop header. There is a path from **E** to **B**, and **B** dominates **E**, so that makes it a back-edge, satisfying Condition 2. Therefore, the nodes **B**, **C**, **D**, and **E** form a loop. The code segment below matches the flow diagram of Figure 4-6:

```
        . . . .
        NNODES = 0                    A
        DO 10 I=1,N                   B
            J = LIST (I)              B
            IF (J .EQ. 0) GO TO 30    B
   20       J = NEXT(J)               C
            NNODES = NNODES + 1       C
   30       IF (J .NE. 0) GO TO 20    D
   10   CONTINUE                      E
```

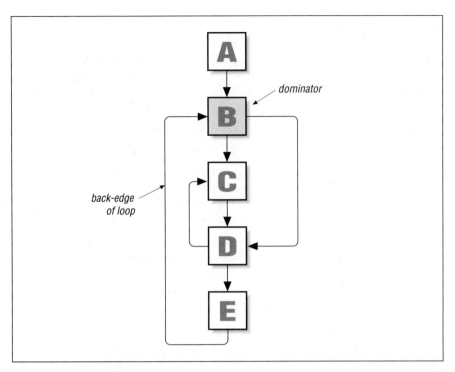

Figure 4-7: Flow graph with a loop in it

The loop goes through an array of linked list start pointers and traverses the lists to determine the total number of nodes in all lists. Letters to the extreme right correspond to the basic block numbers in the flow graph.

At first glance it appears that the nodes **C** and **D** form a loop too. The problem is that **C** doesn't dominate **D** (and vice versa), because entry to either can be made from **B**, so condition 1 isn't satisfied. Frankly, this second loop candidate in Example 4-1 is pretty contrived. Generally, the flow graphs that come from code segments written with even the weakest appreciation for a structured design will offer better loop candidates.

After identifying a loop, the compiler can concentrate on that portion of the flow graph, looking for instructions to remove or push to the outside. Certain types of subexpressions, such as those found in array index expressions, can be simplified if they change in a predictable fashion from one iteration to the next. I'll discuss some of these loop optimizations specifically below.

Object Code Generation

The last step of compilation is object code generation. While data flow analysis techniques are pretty standard for all computers and compilers, code generation is very specific to the target processor. And as we know, processors have become very sophisticated. I'm not going to go into the same detail with object code generation as I did with data flow analysis. I am going to talk about some of the challenges the compiler designer faces.

Anything that isn't handled in hardware has to be addressed in software. That means if the processor can't resolve resource conflicts, such as overuse of a register or pipeline, then the compiler is going to have to take care of it. This isn't necessarily a bad thing—it is a design decision. A smart compiler and dumb hardware might be cost effective for certain applications. Two processors at opposite ends of this spectrum are the Intel i860 and the IBM RS/6000. The first depends heavily on the compiler to schedule instructions and fairly distribute resources. The second manages both things at run time, though it still depends on the compiler to provide an even instruction mix.

In all computers, register selection is a challenge because, in spite of their numbers, registers are precious. You want to be sure that the most active variables become register resident at the expense of others. On machines without register renaming (Chapter 2), you have to be sure that the compiler doesn't try to recycle registers too quickly, otherwise the processor will have to delay computations as it waits for one to be freed.

Depending on the processor, the compiler may have to make some assumptions about which way conditional branches will go when the program runs. Processors using delayed branches will depend on the compiler guessing correctly and filling the branch delay slot with a useful instruction. Others with branch cache buffers or branch tables will be able to adapt to the run time branch pattern.

Some instructions in the repertoire will also save your compiler from having to issue others. Examples are auto-increment for registers being used as array indices or conditional assignments in lieu of branches. These both save the processor from extra calculations, and make the instruction stream more compact.

In addition to the IL optimizations we looked at above, there is room for more optimizations at code generation time. A second level intermediate language and more data flow analysis will eliminate more calculations—perhaps some introduced by the compiler itself. Less extensive, *peephole* optimizations can examine several instructions at a time, searching for opportunities to streamline register use, simplify computations, or eliminate useless instructions (such as a store followed by a load from the same address).

Lastly, there are opportunities for increased parallelism. Programmers generally think serially, specifying steps in logical succession. Unfortunately, serial source code makes serial object code. A compiler that hopes to efficiently use the parallelism of the processor will have to be able to move instructions around and find operations that can be issued side by side. This is one of the biggest new challenges for compiler writers today. As superscalar and VLIW designs become capable of executing more instructions per clock cycle, the compiler will have to dig deeper for operations that can execute at the same time.

Classical Optimizations

I hope that you now have a feeling for how an optimizing compiler works. Although it looks like a compiler does many things at once, the different optimization techniques generally take turns, trying to accomplish specific goals. Some are effective within basic blocks, while others are more global in nature, involving the whole routine taken altogether. Ordering the optimizations is a black art and usually requires that some passes be repeated. It is not uncommon for particular optimizations to create dead code or new copies of variables to be cleaned up by others. For compilers that use two levels of intermediate code, the whole suite may be repeated all over again.

In this section, I am going to list classical optimizations by name, and tell you what they are for. I'm not suggesting that *you* make the changes; your compiler should be able to handle it. As I said at the start of the chapter, if you understand what the compiler can (and can't) do, you will become a better programmer because you will be able to play to the compiler's strengths.

Copy Propagation

To start, let's look at a technique for untangling calculations. Take a look at the following segment of code—notice the two computations involving X.

```
X = Y
Z = 1. + X
```

As written, the second statement requires the results of the first before it can proceed—you need X to calculate Z. This could translate into a delay at run time.* With a little bit of rearrangement we can make the second statement independent of the first, by *propagating* a copy of Y. The new calculation for Z uses the value of Y directly:

```
X = Y
Z = 1. + Y
```

Notice that I left the first statement, X=Y, intact. You may ask, "Why keep it?" The problem is that we can't tell whether the value of X is needed elsewhere. That is something for flow analysis to decide. If it turns out that no other statement needs the new value of X, the assignment will be eliminated later by "dead code removal."

Copy propagation is an optimization that occurs both locally and globally. During construction of the DAG, assignments of one variable to a second within the block are handled by merely ganging two labels onto one node. Globally, data flow analysis identifies blocks where an assignment reaches without modification. If any are found, then the compiler may be able to perform copy propagation across the flow graph.

Constant Folding

A clever compiler can find constants throughout your program. Some of these are "obvious" constants like those defined in parameter statements. Others are less obvious like local variables which are never redefined. When you combine them in a calculation you get a *constant expression*. The little program below has two constants, I and K:

```
PROGRAM MAIN
INTEGER I,K
PARAMETER (I = 100)
K = 200
J = I + K
END
```

Because I and K are constant individually, the combination I+K is constant, which means that J is a constant too. The compiler reduces constant expressions like I+K into constants with a technique called *constant folding*.

---

*This is called a *flow dependence*. I describe dependencies in detail in Chapter 8.

How does constant folding work? Knowing what you know about data flow analysis, you can see that it is possible to examine every path along which a given variable could be defined en route to a particular basic block. If you discover that all paths lead back to the same value, which is a constant, you can replace all references to that variable with that constant. This replacement has a ripple-through effect. If the compiler finds itself looking at an expression which is made up solely of constants, it can evaluate the expression at compile time and replace it with a constant too. After several iterations, the compiler will have located most of the expressions that are candidates for constant folding.

Dead Code Removal

Programs often contain sections of "dead" code that have no effect on the answers, and can be removed. Occasionally, dead code is written into the program by the author, but a more common source is the compiler itself; many optimizations produce dead code that needs to be swept up afterwards.

Dead code comes in two types:

* Instructions that are unreachable
* Instructions that produce results which are never used

You can easily write some unreachable code into a program by directing the flow of control around it—permanently. If the compiler can tell that it is unreachable, it will eliminate it. For example, it is impossible to reach the statement I = 4 in the program below:

```
PROGRAM MAIN
I = 2
WRITE (*,*) I
STOP
I = 4
WRITE (*,*) I
END
```

The compiler will throw out everything after the STOP statement and probably give you a warning. Unreachable code produced by the compiler during optimization will be quietly whisked away.

Computations with local variables can produce results that are never used. By analyzing a variable's definitions and uses, the compiler can see whether any other part of the routine references it. Of course it can't tell the ultimate fate of variables that are external or common, so those computations will always be kept (as long as they are reachable). In the program below, computations involving k contribute nothing to the final answer, and are good candidates for dead code elimination.

```
main ()
{
  int i,k;
  i = k = 1;
  i += 1;
  k += 2;
  printf ("%d\n",i);
}
```

Strength Reduction

Operations or expressions have various time costs associated with them. Sometimes it is possible to replace a more expensive calculation with a cheaper one. We call this *strength reduction*. The following code fragment contains two expensive operations:

```
Y = X**2
J = K*2
```

For the exponentiation operation on the first line, the compiler will generally make an embedded mathematical subroutine library call. In the library routine, X is converted to a logarithm, multiplied, then converted back. Overall, squaring X will be very expensive—taking perhaps hundreds of machine cycles. The key is to notice that X is being raised to a small integer power. A much cheaper alternative would be to express it as X*X, and pay only the cost of multiplication. The second statement shows integer multiplication of a variable K by 2. Adding K+K yields the same answer, but takes less time.

There are many opportunities for compiler generated strength reductions—these are just a couple of them. We will see an important special case when we look at induction variable simplification. Strength reduction is also useful as a peephole optimization: when the compiler crawls through the intermediate code looking for cheap and easy stocking stuffer optimizations.

Variable Renaming

In Chapter 2, I talked about *register renaming*. Some processors can make run time decisions to replace all references to register 1 with register 2, for instance, to eliminate bottlenecks. Register renaming keeps instructions that are recycling the same registers for different purposes from having to wait until previous instructions have finished with them.

The same situation can occur in programs— the same variable (i.e., memory location) can be recycled for two unrelated purposes—as is the variable x in the fragment below:

```
x  = y * z;
q  = r + x + x;
x  = a + b;
```

When the compiler recognizes that a variable is being recycled, and that its current and former uses are independent, it can substitute a new variable to keep the calculations separate:

```
x0 = y * z;
q  = r + x0 + x0;
x  = a + b;
```

Variable renaming is an important technique because it clarifies that calculations are independent of each other, which increases the number of things that can be done in parallel. Variable renaming can take place both locally, at the basic block level, and globally, as a product of data flow analysis.

Common Subexpression Elimination

Subexpressions are pieces of expressions. For instance, A+B is a subexpression of C*(A+B). If A+B appears in several places, like it does below, we call it a *common subexpression:*

```
D = C * (A + B)
E = (A + B)/2.
```

Rather than calculate A and B twice, the compiler can generate a temporary variable and use it wherever A + B is required.

```
temp = A + B
D = C * temp
E = temp/2.
```

When we looked at basic blocks, we saw how subexpressions could be eliminated as a DAG was constructed. Common subexpression elimination occurs globally too.* Information about expressions can be collected during data flow analysis along with variable use/definition information. By examining both together, the compiler can detect which subexpressions reach which basic blocks, and whether any of the variables within them have been reassigned.

---

*Again, by "global," we mean throughout a subroutine, not between subroutines. Good inter-routine analysis is available from a few vendors.

Different compilers go to different lengths to find common subexpressions. Most pairs, such as A+B, will be recognized. Some can recognize reuse of intrinsics, such as SIN(X). Don't expect the compiler to go too far though. Subexpressions like A+B+C are not computationally equivalent to reassociated forms like B+C+A, even though they are algebraically the same. See Chapter 10 for more details.

Address calculations provide a particularly rich opportunity for common subexpression elimination. You don't see the calculations in the source code; they're generated by the compiler. For instance, a reference to an array element A(I,J) may translate into an intermediate language expression such as:

```
address(A) + (I-1)*sizeof_datatype(A)
+ (J-1)*sizeof_datatype(A) * column_dimension(A)
```

If A(I,J) is used more than once, we'll have multiple copies of the same address arithmetic. Common subexpression elimination will (hopefully) discover the redundant copies and group them together.

Loop Invariant Code Motion

Loops are where the action is. The compiler will look for every opportunity to move calculations out of a loop and into the surrounding code. Expressions that don't change after the loop is entered (*loop invariant expressions*) are prime targets. The following loop has two loop invariant expressions:

```
      DO 10 I=1,N
        A(I) = B(I) + C * D
        E = G(K)
10    CONTINUE
```

Below, I have modified the expressions to show how they can be moved to the outside.

```
      temp = C * D
      DO 10 I=1,N
        A(I) = B(I) + temp
10    CONTINUE
      E = G(K)
```

Recall that we are able to recognize the sections of the flow graph that formed loops. From use/definition information on the associated basic blocks, we can identify expressions containing variables that are unchanging. *Loop invariant code motion* is simply the act of moving the repeated, unchanging calculations to the outside.

As with common subexpression elimination, address arithmetic is a particularly important target for loop invariant code motion. Slowly changing portions of index calculations can be pushed into the suburbs, to be executed only when needed.

Induction Variable Simplification

Loops can contain what are called *induction variables*. Their value changes as a linear function of the loop iteration count. For example, K is an induction variable in the following loop. Its value is tied to the loop index:

```
      DO 10 I=1,N
         K = I*4 + M
   10 CONTINUE
```

Induction variable simplification replaces calculations for variables like K with simpler ones. Given a starting point and the expression's first derivative, you can arrive at K's value for the nth iteration by stepping through the n-1 intervening iterations:

```
      K = M
      DO 10 I=1,N
         K = K + 4
   10 CONTINUE
```

The two forms of the loop aren't equivalent—the second won't give you the value of K given any value of I. But because you can't jump into the middle of the loop on the nth iteration, K will always take on the same values as it would have had we kept the original expression.

Induction variable simplification probably wouldn't be a very important optimization, except that array address calculations look very much like the calculation for K in the example above. For instance, the address calculation for A(I) within a loop iterating on the variable I would look like this:

```
   address = base_address(A) + (I-1) * sizeof_datatype(A)
```

Performing all of that math is unnecessary. The compiler can create a new induction variable for references to A and simplify the address calculations:

```
   outside the loop...
   address = base_address(A) - (1 * sizeof_datatype(A))
   inside the loop...
   address = address + sizeof_datatype(A)
```

Induction variable simplification is especially useful on processors that can automatically increment a register each time it is used as a pointer for a memory reference. While stepping through a loop, the memory reference and the address arithmetic can both be squeezed into a single instruction—a great savings.

Register Variable Detection

On many older CISC processors there were few general purpose registers. Because many of the instruction formats could operate directly on memory locations, you could choose to leave the less critical variables out in main memory and bring the more important ones into registers. On RISC designs, there are often many more registers to choose from, and everything has to be brought into a register anyway. This means that, for at least a little while, all variables will be register resident.

The new challenge is to determine which variables should live the greater portion of their lives in registers. Variables that are needed once, and then returned to storage, certainly don't need an executive parking space. With others, you want to avoid repeatedly storing and reloading them because memory references take time and use up valuable bandwidth. To determine which variables should remain resident, the compiler has to examine how frequently each appears to be used, and whether the uses are independent of each other. This information comes from data flow analysis.

Closing Notes

We've seen just a portion of the work that goes into making programs run fast. It varies between vendors, but you can find different kinds of optimizations throughout the process. In the extreme case (if a vendor benchmarks your program), each of the following steps is possible:

- An analyst chooses the highest optimization level that will produce "plausible" results.
- A pre-compiler replaces portions of the program with subroutine library calls, or makes some in-place changes.
- The compiler performs the classical optimizations, plus a number of architecture-specific optimizations.
- The linker tries to place routines to minimize instruction cache miss.
- Post-linkage optimizer improves register usage or reorders the program's modules for better cache utilization.
- Run time (hardware) decisions override the compiler's register selections or branch probability guesses.
- Somebody ignores the results :-).

Throughout the book, we will be looking at more advanced optimizations. I'll be showing you how you would code them by hand, as well as discussing automatic preprocessors. Whenever we come across something that is important to a parallelizing compiler, I'll point that out too. Again, the idea is that if you know what the compiler prefers, you will be able to get the most from it.

Exercises

1. Does your compiler recognize dead code in the program below? How can you be sure? Does the compiler give you a warning?

   ```
   main()
   {
       int k=1;
       if (k == 0)
           printf ("This is never executed.\n");
   }
   ```

2. Compile the following (or the same function translated into C) with and without optimization. Does the size of the code change appreciably (look at the *.o* file)?

   ```
   INTEGER FUNCTION NTEST(N)
   INTEGER I,J,K,L,M,N
   PARAMETER (I=1,J=1,K=1,L=1,M=1)
   NTEST  = I+3*K-2+J*L-I+M-1*I*K+M-L*J*M-3+5*K
   +          + I+3*M-2+K*L-I+M-1*I*N+M-L*K*M-3+5*J
   END
   ```

3. How would you design a source code profiler to count the number of times each statement is executed? What do you know about basic blocks that would simplify the job?

II

Porting and Tuning
Software

5

Clarity

A chapter about coding style may seem out of place to you, but it is as important as any other chapter in the book. When coding or making changes, you are creating a legacy for two completely different audiences: humans and compilers. They don't frequent the same restaurants, but they do have this in common: they both benefit from a clear expression of your intentions. The human needs to understand how data flows through the program, and where to find the functional divisions. The compiler needs to know the same things so it can optimize your code.

Clarity also has a compounded benefit because your program is likely to run on a variety of different computers over the years. Depending on the application, there is a chance that you or someone else will be going through it in search of parallel constructs to be spread across multiple processors. Furthermore (I'm a little embarrassed to admit this), this book will look at some loop optimizations and parallelizing constructs that help performance but are a little bit ugly, and only marginally portable. If the surrounding code is more attractive, it will lessen the sense that we went through it with a chainsaw. Good comments will also help someone "back out" the changes at such time as they are no longer useful.

As a style guide, this chapter isn't very rigorous. I have faith in your judgement, and I don't think that you have to code things the way I do for your programs to be understandable. Even so, I'd like to lend you a few broad tips for the benefit of the compilers and programmers that follow (I may be among them). And I'd like to thank all of those whose nicely written code I've ported or tuned over the years.

Under Construction

When you first write an application, or are replacing an algorithm or tuning, you want the correct answer. Perhaps you don't care how the code looks. You might say "I can worry about that later." You just want it to work. But unless your efforts are a total failure, there will come a time when the appearance will be important.

A little bit of care during the initial development goes a long way toward the longevity of programs or modifications. In my experience, you only have to be careful about how you sculpt the first few hundred lines, after which point you will have set a standard for yourself, and for the rest of the development effort. People who maintain your programs will tend to stick with your style, especially if it's good.

Later, when you are reworking a code, clarity is important too. As I said before, some of the optimizations I'll suggest are at odds with coding for beauty. This isn't to say that everything we do will leave a scar. Most of the beauty will survive optimization. Modern compilers are very good at simplifying expressions and moving redundant calculations out of the way, which is a lifesaver when you want to write understandable code without paying for it in performance.

Comments

All around the world, there are people who love programming so much they do it for a hobby. Even if you are not one of them, you may have shared the experience that makes programming an attractive pastime—the excitement of taking an abstract mental process, and expressing it symbolically. After you've got it working, you are free to experiment and improve upon it as you like.

Maybe you've shared the following experiences too. The weekend comes around, you put your work down and go do something else for a couple of days. When you return on Monday, you pick up the listing on your desk, and like magic, the whole mental girder-works underlying your program reappears! For anyone else, it is just a listing, but for you it is a blueprint for an intricate machine that makes data.

Now suppose that two years go by and someone comes to see you with a question about a subroutine you wrote. You look at it and you see ... nothing, just a flat, two dimensional listing. The mental picture of the intricate workings of your program has long since vanished. Between the two of you, you can't figure out what it was supposed to do (frustrating, if not embarrassing). This is the time when you wish you had taken more care to comment the code. No one will call on you to explain something you've plainly commented, and they will be much less likely to scrap the code because they can't understand it.

People who are kind enough to comment their code seem to fall into one of two categories: those who explain what blocks of code are for, and those who explain what lines of code are for. It's a good habit to be in the first group, and comment blocks rather than lines. A sentence or two before each significant step of the program helps your reader much more than a continuous narrative. If you keep comments in blocks you will be forced to describe, at a higher level, what the following chunk of code is supposed to do. People writing scattered comments often fall into a trap where comments are merely line-by-line translations of the code into English, like this painfully obvious example:

```
C   I will now increment X.
    X = X + 1
```

Clues in the Landscape

Whereas comments say something about what the code is doing, "pretty printing" tells something about the flow of control. There are automatic tools for pretty printing, but you can easily do it yourself by merely indenting two or four characters every time you enter the body of a control structure, such as a loop. It will give your program a shape—a contour so revealing that you can tell where to find the innermost structures from all the way across the room. Pretty-printed code is also much easier to modify, debug, and explain.

Example 5-1: Comments, asterisks, and pretty printing

```
C***********************************************************
C   L S T S R C H
C***********************************************************
C
        INTEGER FUNCTION LSTSRCH (LIST, NLIST, LTARGT)
C
C This routine searches the list LIST for the element
C LTARGET.  NLIST tells the number of list elements
C
C LSTSRCH returns the index number of the element if found,
C -1 if LTARGT is not an element of LIST.
C
```

Example 5-1: Comments, asterisks, and pretty printing (continued)

```
      INTEGER LIST(NLIST)
      INTEGER NLIST
      INTEGER LTARGT
      INTEGER NOTFOUND
      PARAMETER (NOTFOUND = -1)
C
C**********************************************************
C
      DO 10 I=1, NLIST
        IF (LIST(I) .EQ. LTARGT) THEN
          LSTSRCH = I
          RETURN
        ENDIF
  10    CONTINUE
C
C If the element wasn't found return -1.
C
      LSTSRCH = NOTFOUND
      END
```

It helps to make functionally distinct areas visually distinct too. I prefer separating sections with a lines of asterisks, though you may prefer blanks or dashes. Visual borders make it easy for somebody reading the code to see where one major step ends, and another one starts. It's also a good method for policing yourself—you'll be more likely to treat sections of the program modularly if you mark them off.

Variable Names

If you were trying to become the world's largest manufacturer of auto-mobiles, what name would you choose for your company? How do the names "TEMP," "N3," or "Q" grab you? Obviously, none of them would be a good choice; they say nothing about your business. It's a similar situation with variables—people expect the name to represent the thing. They will trust that you have chosen labels with meaning. So, if I could offer only one piece of advice on variable names, it would be this: be predictable. An association between the purpose of the variable and the name is important.

Consider the two subroutines below. Which is clearer? There's nothing wrong with the first subroutine, but I think you'll agree that the second one tells more about its purpose and what it is doing. In fact, the variable names make the code so clear that you would know how to fix it if it were broken.

Example 5-2: Variable names count

```
double q(n,x,y)
  int n;
  double x[],y[];
  {
    int i;
    double s=0.;
    for (i=0 ; i<n ; i++)
        s += x[i] * y[i];
    return(s);
  }

double areasum(n,width,height)
  int n;
  double width[],height[];
  {
    int i;
    double area=0.;
    for (i=0 ; i<n ; i++)
        area += width[i] * height[i];
    return(area);
  }
```

The length and complexity of a variable name should be proportional to its scope. For instance, loop index variable names should never be more than one or two characters long because they are generally local in scope, and easily recognized when used within the context of the loop. A long index variable name gives the false impression that the variable has another life outside the loop.

Strike a balance with the length of the rest of the identifiers. Overly descriptive names force the use of continuation lines and can make C or FORTRAN look like COBOL. On the other hand, terse identifiers tell you nothing about what is being calculated, and make programs difficult to debug. You have probably had to search through a program for a variable named something simple like E, only to find that 30% of the lines have an E in them somewhere.

Programmers sometimes reuse variables they have already defined in the interest of saving space or wear and tear on the compiler.* As far as programmers reading through your code are concerned, recycling variables named I, J, K, or TEMP are harmless enough, but if you reuse something named OUTLET_TEMPERATURE, no one will be able to follow what you're doing. In general, you don't have to be stingy with local variables. You

---

*On the contrary, variable reuse complicates data flow analysis!

can define new ones whenever you need them. Chances are that they will not require any additional storage. The compiler often keeps local variables in registers.

Variable Types

Just as people expect the name to represent the thing, they also expect certain types of names to represent certain types of things. For instance, it's conventional for integers to begin with the letters I through N, even in C programs. Likewise, they won't expect variable names that start with other letters to represent integers. Other, perhaps weaker, conventions concern the naming of pointer variables in C (names end with a "p"), or complex variables in FORTRAN (start with "Z"). But whatever you choose for a convention, do your reader a favor and stick with it. Imagine the confusion if all of your pointer variables end with a "p" except for one. Anyone trying to follow your code would ask "What's so special about *that* variable?"

When you are coding in C, you are required to explicitly declare and *type* each variable you plan to use. At the very least, you have an opportunity to choose incorrectly. In FORTRAN, on the other hand, variables can have *implicit* declarations. That means that you can make up new ones as you go along, without explicitly declaring any storage to go with them. By default, identifiers beginning with A though H, and O through Z are default-typed as real values. Everything starting with I through N is typed as an integer. Unfortunately, implicit declarations can be made by mistake because typos don't trigger any messages or warnings from the compiler.

Many FORTRAN compilers allow you to turn off implicit variable declarations with a command line flag, or by placing IMPLICIT NONE just after the program statement. With implicit typing turned off, you get an error message when you try to use an undeclared variable. This a nice feature, and you should use it if you have it.* Not only will it be a great aid for finding typos during development, but it guards against accidental changes in type, such as might occur if a declaration is mistakenly deleted.

---

*IMPLICIT NONE is part of ISO 1539:1991, Fortran 90. It was not part of FORTRAN 77, though many compilers support it.

Named Constants

As far as numerical constants are concerned, consider declaring variables for them too, rather than entering them directly. For instance, NDECK may be clearer than 52, or EPSILON might be preferable to 1.0E-38. Some common sense is necessary here of course. If you declare variables for all the natural numbers and use them where a numerical value would be perfectly understandable, you will be making the code harder to understand. For example, DO 10 I=IONE,ITWO,IONE is a little ridiculous.

Don't be squeamish about creating extra variables to hold the values of numerical constants. The compiler will recognize them as constants and the resulting code will be much the same as if you typed the value in verbatim. If you want to make it abundantly clear that a variable specifies a constant, define it using PARAMETER or #define statements. This will have the added benefit of making it easier to change later.*

Be aware that numerical constants such as 1, 1. and 1.0d0, have types too. As an illustration, say you have a real variable X, defined as:

```
X = 1/3
```

From the above statement you would expect the value of X to be set to 0.0. Because 1/3 is a constant integer expression, it evaluates to integer 0 before the assignment is made. People frequently forget that the same kind of process takes place between single precision numerical constants and double precision variables. For instance, if A is defined as double precision, and you are looking for a good approximation to the value 1/3, then you should use double precision numerical constants in the assignment:

```
A = 1.0d0/3.0d0
```

rather than single precision:

```
A = 1./3.
```

The first result will be accurate to over 15 decimal places. The second is only good to about 7 decimal places.

---

*Sometimes people define named constants with intrinsics. A common example is an assignment of the form PI = 4.0D0 * DATAN(1.0D0), which generally gives a better approximation to PI than you can get if you explicitly type it in.

INCLUDE Statements

The syntax for INCLUDE statements is not guaranteed by the FORTRAN standard,* but they do so much to safeguard your program from local changes in COMMON block sizes, parameters, etc., that it is a good idea to use them. The most prevalent form is INCLUDE 'filename', where the targeted file name is enclosed in single quotes.

As is often done with C, you should consider placing all your parameter definitions in an INCLUDE file which is separate from variable declarations. That way the file with the parameter statements won't reserve any storage, and can be included in every subroutine in your application. Example 5-3 and Example 5-4 show a couple of INCLUDE files; Example 5-5 shows a subroutine that would use them.

Example 5-3: Parameter statements

```
C**************************************************************
C    defs.inc
C**************************************************************
C
C This file contains parameter definitions
C
      IMPLICIT NONE
      INTEGER MAXPTS
      PARAMETER (MAXPTS = 1000)
```

Example 5-4: Declarations

```
C**************************************************************
C    points.inc
C**************************************************************
C
C This file contains declarations for data storage for data points
C read in from the input file.
C
      REAL X(MAXPTS), Y(MAXPTS)
      COMMON /POINTS/ X,Y
```

Example 5-5: Routine using both INCLUDE files

```
C**************************************************************
C    readpts
C**************************************************************
C
```

---

* INCLUDE statements are part of Fortran 90.

Example 5-5: Routine using both INCLUDE *files* (continued)

```
      SUBROUTINE READPTS (LU)
C
C Read points from logical unit LU into common X and Y.
C
      INTEGER LU
      INCLUDE 'defs.inc'
      INCLUDE 'points.inc'
      INTEGER I
C*************************************************************
C
      DO 10 I=1,MAXPTS
        READ (LU,'(2F10.0)') X(I), Y(I)
   10 CONTINUE
      END
```

By the way, notice that I have made declarations first for the arguments, then included the COMMON variables, and finally the local variables. By ordering them in this fashion you can make it easy for a reader to understand the scope of the declarations.

Use of COMMON

If you look at an older program, you may see COMMON areas used as general scratch space. One routine may use a COMMON block for integers, for instance. Another may use it for real variables, and some parts may be declared differently in different routines. Additionally, large tracts of COMMON may be equivalenced to other variables so they can be reused for different purposes within a single routine.

People coded this way on older machines because memory was limited, and when it came down to sacrificing readability in order to get the program to fit into core, they did what they had to do.

Naturally, reusing COMMON for different purposes in different parts of the program effects the clarity of the code. For instance, imagine that you found that something was wrong with the value of A in the subroutine FOO:

```
      SUBROUTINE FOO
      COMMON /STUFF/ A,B,C
      ...
      IF (some_event) A = B * C
      CALL BAR
      WRITE (*,*) A
      END
      SUBROUTINE BAR
      COMMON /STUFF/ I,J,K
      ...
```

```
      IF (some_event) I = 1
      END
```

Where would you look for a bug? Because the COMMON block is used for different things in different places, it opens up many possibilities for what might have gone wrong, thus complicating the search.

There are other reasons to be judicious with COMMON. Although it may be clear to the author what parts of COMMON are being used for what purposes, to other people—and to optimizing compilers—it may be impossible to follow.

With new, multiple-CPU machines coming on the market, it is probable that your code will run on one soon. Using COMMON for input and output to a subroutine is nearly as manageable as passing data through subroutine arguments. But when COMMON is used as scratch space—especially intermixed with subroutine calls—it will be very difficult to tell whether the code can be parallelized. In the upcoming chapters we will see some other reasons why using COMMON for scratch is not a good practice; it can have an effect on performance—even on single processor machines. Again, it is a question of the compiler being able to "see" what the COMMON area is being used for.

The Shape of Data

A traditional computer has a *linear memory model*—memory addresses start at zero and work their way up. Elements of a one-dimensional array sit neatly in a row. Multidimensional arrays are mapped onto linear memory according to well understood rules (in FORTRAN and C). Programmers who understand the rules can safely reshape data structures across subroutine boundaries by declaring the arrays differently in different routines. For instance, the two routines below use the same array C, but declare its shape differently:

Example 5-6: Changing the Shape of an Array

```
      PROGRAM MAIN
      INTEGER M,N
      PARAMETER (N=3, M=4)
      DOUBLE PRECISION C(N,M)
      CALL FAZ(C,N*M)
      END
C
      SUBROUTINE FAZ(C,K)
      DOUBLE PRECISION C(K)
```

Example 5-6: Changing the Shape of an Array (continued)

```
      DO 10 I=1,K
        C(K) = 0.0D0
 10   CONTINUE
```

The upper `main` routine reserves a three by four array for **C**. The lower routine, `FAZ`, declares **C** as a single-dimensioned array. Same memory locations, different shape. On a computer with a linear memory model, the routine `FAZ` will work as expected; the twelve elements of array **C** will be initialized to zero.* But imagine what would happen if the computer *didn't* have a linear memory layout. Say it had a two-dimensional memory system, four by eight elements in size (small, for illustration). The array **C** might get mapped as in the figure below.

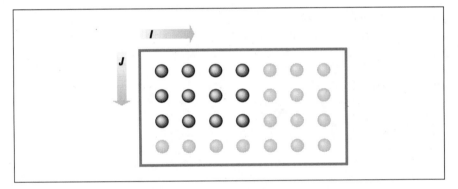

Figure 5-1: Array C in two-dimensional memory

What will happen when subroutine `FAZ` is called? `FAZ` is coded with the assumption that the elements of **C** are arranged linearly on memory, but they're not. If we step down the rows (or across the columns), we'll soon wander outside **C**, into no-man's land; `FAZ` will fail. We mistakenly assumed a particular memory model, and implicitly reshaped the array **C** across subroutine boundaries.

C and FORTRAN do not restrict the programmer from assuming something about the memory system, and reshaping arrays. In fact, the compiler often can't tell that data is being reshaped, if routines are compiled separately. However, there are computers—particularly some parallel supercomputers—whose memory model is non-linear. For the best performance (or

---

*If it's not clear why this is so, see Chapter 11 for a description of how FORTRAN and C map arrays into memory.

correctness) these machines require you to fully declare arrays, and retain their shape across subroutine boundaries. Data can be reshaped, but it's done explicitly with directives provided as part of the parallel programming environment.

Closing Notes

There is plenty more to be said about coding style; whole books have been written on the subject. Again, my reason for writing a chapter like this was not to try to convince you that I have all the answers. Rather, I'd simply like to say that careful coding matters. Unless your program is a total failure, people and compilers will be trying to understand it for years to come.

6

Finding Porting Problems

Anyone who has moved code from one brand of computer to another has a war story to tell. As often as not, it's "so-and-so's machine doesn't do something-or-other correctly." However, there are times when the problem doesn't belong to so-and-so's machine at all, but is instead the result of a dormant coding error or standards violation* exposed by the right (or wrong) combination of compiler and computer. Something that ran forever on your VAX may not run correctly on a RISC workstation, and it may not be obvious why.

Sleeping bugs are aggravated by the software development environment for RISC workstations. RISC compilers take full advantage of the flexibility in the language standards in the interest of generating code that runs quickly. They can be unforgiving when the programmer forgets to specify that a variable is supposed to be saved or static, or assumes that variables will be zero-initialized by default. Other times, especially when coming from a mainframe environment, basic differences in the way the machine represents data can expose a bug.

Nonportable constructs that cause syntax error messages at compile time are easy enough to find. It's those that make it through the compiler, yet foul up the answer that are the worst to deal with. If the nature of your troubles is that your program "dumps core" when it runs, you are actually very fortunate. At least you will be able to determine the routine in which the problem occurs.† But if your program runs for twelve hours and completes with a bad answer, then you have a real puzzle. Where do you look?

---

*This applies to *other* people's code, of course. Not yours.

†People run into this often enough for it to bear mentioning: In a UNIX environment, you want to run the code under a debugger (*adb*, *sdb*, *dbx*, *gdb*...) until it breaks. Then find out what routine you are in with a stack backtrace.

Before you ship the machine back, you might want to examine the code to see if it contains some nonportable constructs—like those we are going to discuss in this chapter. These could be the reason your answers are wrong or "kinda" wrong.* Also, see Chapter 10 if the results seem to change with compiler optimization levels. You may have a program that is sensitive to floating point optimizations. There is a completely separate set of issues involving operating system interfaces—especially for "systems" codes and C programs—that I am not going to discuss. For more general information about writing portable C programs, see *Practical C Programming*, by Steve Oualline, *Posix Programmer's Guide*, by Donald Lewine (O'Reilly & Associates, Inc.), or *C: A Reference Manual*, by Harbison and Steele (Prentice-Hall).

Problems in Argument Lists

Modules are often compiled separately, preventing the compiler from examining callers and callees together. Mistakes made at subroutine boundaries (arguments accidentally omitted, argument type mismatches, etc.) can escape unnoticed for years. But what slips through on one machine may fail on another, giving the appearance of a compiler bug. You might wonder how a mistake in an argument list can ever have worked correctly. Let's answer the question by looking at a few cases.

Aliasing

When two subroutine arguments, or a COMMON or external variable and an argument, refer to the same storage location, we say that the variables are *aliases* of one another. For instance, if I pass two pointers to a subroutine (or two variables are copied in), and they ultimately refer back to the same location, then they are aliases:

```
REAL A,B,C
INTEGER I
EQUIVALENCE (A,I)
B = A
CALL FOO (A,A)      <--- aliases
CALL BAR (A,B)      <--- Not aliases
CALL BAZ (A,I)      <--- aliases
```

---

*Many of the FORTRAN problems described here can be unearthed by a tool called *FTNCHEK*, available via anonymous ftp from research.att.com. Go to directory */netlib/fortran* and *get ftnchek.Z*. C problems can often be found by *lint*, bundled with your software development tools.

Aliasing of arguments or COMMON is permitted as long as none of the variables are assigned a new value (per the ANSI FORTRAN Standard X3.9-1978). However, if one aliased variable is changed, the final value is not guaranteed for any of them.

The following code shows what can happen when two arguments are aliased:

```
PROGRAM MAIN
INTEGER IX
IX = 1
CALL ADD1 (IX, IX)
WRITE (*,*) IX
END

SUBROUTINE ADD1 (IA,IB)
INTEGER IA, IB
...        ...
IF (IA .EQ. 1)  IB = IA + 1
IF (IB .EQ. 2)  IA = 1
END
```

Argument IX is passed into the subroutine ADD1 twice—once as the argument IA, and once as the argument IB. Since IA and IB both refer back to the same location, the value that IX takes when ADD1 returns depends on which of the two the compiler chooses to write back into memory first. On a machine with a strictly sequential compiler, the last calculations made would correspond closely to the last source statements, so you might expect that the final answer would be 1. But there is no requirement that the value of IA be returned to its storage location before IB, and you, the writer of the program, can't say which it will be.

Aliasing is generally more problematic with RISC machines than with CISC, because of RISC's many registers. Values tend to remain loaded in registers for the life of the subroutine, or until the register is desperately needed for something else. There is no telling when a register-resident variable will make its way back into main memory storage.

Aliasing problems can be difficult to find because of the way variables change names across subroutine boundaries. Beware of pieces of COMMON passed as arguments. If the routine being called shares the same COMMON block as the calling routine, it should raise a red flag in your search. It may be that the same storage location is being written as both a COMMON variable, and as an argument.

Aliasing is not prohibited for C programs—and you might even be able to imagine cases where it would be desirable. But the possibility that arguments (pointer arguments, naturally) could be aliases of one another forces the compiler to be more conservative than a FORTRAN compiler would be. A C compiler can't optimize the equivalent (pointer intensive) code as well as a FORTRAN compiler might.

Argument Type Mismatch

Another argument handling pitfall involves data type mismatches between arguments passed by a calling routine and dummy variables that accept them in the callee. In certain instances, programs that pass single precision arguments to double precision dummy variables, or vice versa, may appear to work perfectly well on a VAX or IBM mainframe, only to die horribly when ported to a RISC machine. The failure is due to a different internal representation of floating point numbers.

To understand better, let's briefly examine how floating point values are represented. All computers store floating point numbers stored in pieces: a sign, an exponent, and a mantissa. If you are unfamiliar with this concept in connection with computers, think of it in terms of scientific notation. Take Avogadro's number, `3.02e+26`. If you pick it apart, you'll find the sign is positive, you have an exponent of `26` and a mantissa of `3.02`.

Within a computer, there are only a finite number of bits set aside for each component, and this limits the accuracy and range of the floating point representation. On most machines, *single precision* numbers are stored within 32 bits, and *double precision* numbers are stored within 64 bits. The number of bits dedicated to each component can be different, depending on the precision of the number and the manufacturer of the computer. However, vendors bringing new products to market today have generally settled on one set of floating point representations for both single and double precision numbers. The formats are part of ANSI/IEEE 754-1985, a standard which describes how floating point numbers are stored and used in computer hardware. You will find that you can trade unformatted binary data files between machines of different makes if they are both using IEEE 754 representation.*

---

*This is often, but not always the case. Byte ordering is not standard between manufacturers.

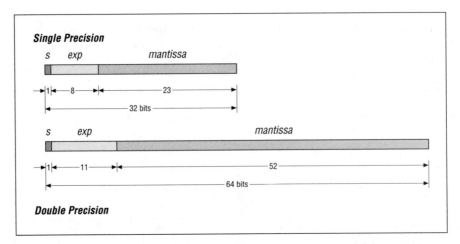

Figure 6-1: IEEE 754 floating point formats

IEEE 754 single and double precision representations, shown in Figure 6-1, differ from one another in both the number of bits dedicated to the exponents and to the mantissas. Because the field lengths are different, it is impossible to mistake a single precision value for a double precision value. For instance, if you pass a single precision value into a subroutine expecting a double precision argument, or vice versa, the value you receive will look nothing like the one you thought was passed. You will probably notice the bug the first time you run the code.

On the other hand, IBM mainframes, large CDC machines, and VAXes use a variety of floating point formats predating the IEEE 754 standard, one of which is illustrated in Figure 6-2. Within some of their formats, the only difference between a single and a double precision number is the length of the mantissa—the exponent stays the same from one precision to another. As a consequence, if you pass a single precision argument into a subroutine expecting a double precision value, or vice versa, the number you'll receive will look sort of like the one you passed—often close enough so that you won't notice there is a coding error.

Programs can run on a VAX or a mainframe for years with a concealed bug of this sort. But because the formats for single and double precision are very different on IEEE 754-based machines, the bug will rear its ugly head and cause bad results and anguish when ported. The quickest way to eliminate the possibility of such a bug is to go through all of the subroutines and turn every floating point number into double precision. You could do this by adjusting all the declarations, of course, but there is often an easier way. Many vendors' compilers have "autodouble" flags for promoting all floating point variables to higher precision. The advice comes with a caveat, however: sometimes there are equivalences or other gotchas which make "autodoubling" impossible, as we'll see next.

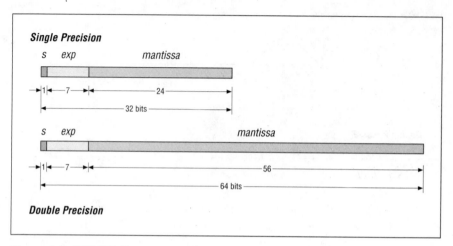

Figure 6-2: IBM 370 floating point formats

Storage Issues

Memory is more plentiful and much cheaper than it used to be (back when life was hard, and you ate lichens because you wanted to). However, the temptation to reuse arrays for several different purposes, even when it's not necessary, has deep roots in the souls of many programmers. The trouble is that re-using storage effects portability and, in many cases, performance. Compilers can't see through your declarations to understand your reasons for reusing memory, so they have to be conservative, and assume that every declaration is sacred.

Memory systems are also becoming more elaborate. Designers are making trade-offs in favor of performance, some of which have implications for C or FORTRAN programmers. We'll see an example shortly, when we look at memory reference alignment restrictions.

Equivalenced Storage

As I mentioned earlier, people sometimes equivalence large tracts of COM-MON to local variables for use as general scratch space. This is often done to conserve memory (and often at a cost in performance). However, there is a potential portability hazard when integers and reals are equivalenced; there is no guarantee that the two types will be the same length on different types of machines, or that the equivalence relationship will be useful on all machines. On most, single precision numbers and integers are both four bytes long, as shown in Figure 6-3. But on Cray machines, for instance, reals and integers are each eight bytes in length.*

Let's look at a not-so-hypothetical example in which equivalencing integers and reals could get you into trouble. Say you wrote a program in which you regularly equivalenced arrays of reals and arrays of integers, one for one. Additionally, say that you intend to run it both on the Cray and on your workstation.

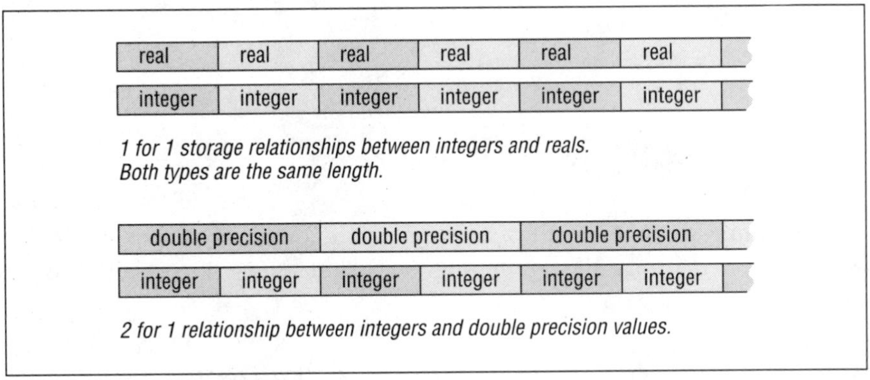

real	real	real	real	real	real

integer	integer	integer	integer	integer	integer

*1 for 1 storage relationships between integers and reals.
Both types are the same length.*

double precision	double precision	double precision

integer	integer	integer	integer	integer	integer

2 for 1 relationship between integers and double precision values.

Figure 6-3: Equivalence storage relationship on most computers

If you wish to keep the same storage relationship between the equivalenced integers and reals, then you will have to settle for single precision real values on the workstation. These may not give you the accuracy you are counting on and getting from the Cray. If, on the other hand, you choose to promote all of the real numbers to double precision, you will then be equivalencing storage 2 for 1, and will have to rework your

---

*Furthermore, integers and floating point numbers often have separate register banks. Switching between integer and floating point references can generate extra memory operations in order to support explicit equivalencing.

program so that other data in the scratch space isn't overwritten. Either way, your code will be unportable. The best approach would be to determine whether the equivalence is actually necessary, and eliminate it if possible.

In the future, the inconsistency between lengths of reals and integers will probably show up in other places. The MIPS R4000 and DEC Alpha/AXP, for instance, are microprocessor architectures with support for native 64 bit integers. In theory, the same storage relationship the CRAY allows between 8 byte integers and reals will be possible on these machines too. But another opportunity opens up as well—the ability to equivalence two reals to every integer.

C programmers can equivalence storage locations too, using unions, though use of unions usually has nothing to do with saving memory. In the following code, `foo.x` and the array `foo.i` share the same locations:

```
main ()
{
    union {
        int i[2];
        double x;
    } foo;

    foo.x = 1.0;
    printf ("%8.8x%8.8x\n",foo.i[1],foo.i[0]);
}
```

C programmers (and even a few FORTRAN programmers) can use automatic and dynamic memory allocation, so there is little sense in pre-allocating a large scratch pool.

Memory Reference Alignment Restrictions

There are a number of devices that increase memory system performance, such as caches, interleaved memory banks, etc. Vendors also make data paths "wide," so that many bytes are fetched or stored each time you go out to memory. This makes it possible to transfer, say, four bytes at a time in one operation, rather than one at a time in four operations. You can see why this would help with performance.

However, wide data paths are often accompanied by data alignment rules that specify the preferred alignment boundaries for different data types. Ignoring those restrictions can cause a time penalty or even a core dump when your program runs. The alignment rules specified in the following table will satisfy nearly every computer.

Table 6-1: Preferred Alignment Boundaries on Most Computers

Data Type	Alignment
Double Precision	8 Bytes (address: multiple of 8)
Integer, Real, Logical	4 Bytes (address: multiple of 4)
Integer*2	2 Bytes (address: multiple of 2)
Byte, Character	1 Byte (any address)

Trouble occurs when a wide data type, such as a double precision variable, is referenced at a memory location that straddles an alignment boundary. Instead of a single memory access, it takes two, and the pieces have to be cemented together or split apart, depending on whether a load or store is in progress. A compiler will assure that local variables are never misaligned, but it is possible to force misalignment of arguments and COMMON variables in your source code, as in the following example:

```
BLOCKDATA FOO
REAL*4 A,B
REAL*8 R
COMMON /BAR/ A,R,B
END
```

You may always assume that the first member of a COMMON block is correctly aligned for every possible data type. But you can force other variables to be misaligned by carefully (or perhaps carelessly) placing together variables of different widths. For instance, the variable A is aligned with the beginning of the COMMON block, but its presence forces R to be misaligned because R does not reside on a double precision boundary—an address that is equal to zero modulo the size of the data type. The variable B, on the other hand, will not be misaligned because it still falls on a single precision boundary.

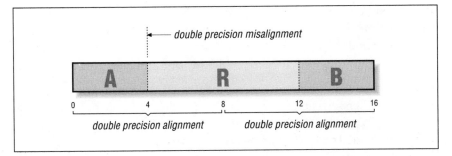

Figure 6-4: Misaligned variables

The problem in Figure 6-4 is easy to fix because you can see the misalignment by looking at the source code. A compiler will see it too, and will give you a warning. But there is another kind of opportunity for misaligned accesses where you won't get a warning, because it is not visible at compile time. It occurs when you pass subroutine arguments that are misaligned for the receiving variables. For example, if you allocate a large integer array, and pass out pieces for use as scratch, you can create alignment problems that won't be apparent to the compiler.

In Example 6-1 I have declared an integer array of 100,000 elements, and placed it in a COMMON block.

Example 6-1: Program for creating misaligned references

```
      PROGRAM BAR
      INTEGER IARRAY(100000)
      COMMON /STUFF/ IARRAY
C
C PASS A MISALIGNED POINTER TO 49999 D.P. VALUES
C
      CALL FOO(IARRAY(2),49999)
      END
C
      SUBROUTINE FOO (DPVAL,N)
      DOUBLE PRECISION DPVAL(*)
C
C 49999 MISALIGNED REFERENCES IN A ROW.
C
      DO 10 I = 1,N
         DPVAL(I) = 1.0D0
  10  CONTINUE
      END
```

You can be confident that the COMMON block will start at a location which is aligned with all possible data types. But passing the second integer from the array to a routine expecting a double precision variable will cause misaligned references. When subroutine FOO runs it will make 49,999 misaligned memory references. All N values of DPVAL follow one immediately after another in memory. If the first reference is misaligned, which it is, then all remaining N-1 references will be too.

There are plenty of opportunities for misaligned references in C programs. Situations where dynamic storage is being allocated and passed out are analogous to the FORTRAN example in Example 6-1. The memory allocation routine `malloc()` is guaranteed to return a pointer to a memory location that is aligned on a double precision boundary. But with a little care, you can still issue a misaligned memory reference, as I do in Example 6-2.

Example 6-2: Misaligned reference in C

```
main ()
{
      int    *p;
      double *q;
      int i;

      p = (int *) malloc (sizeof(int) * 3);
      q = (double *) (p + 1);

      for (i=0; i<1000000; i++)
            *q = (double) 1.0;        /* misaligned */
}
```

It might be interesting to run this code on your machine and see if it fails. If it succeeds, you might want to see how it compares to a reference which is aligned correctly, as would be the case if you replaced q with p inside the loop. Chances are very good that the aligned reference will execute 30% faster, or better.

If you are a C programmer, you might look at the example of the FORTRAN COMMON block misalignment (at the top of this section) and wonder why the same thing doesn't happen when you define a structure with mixed type variables as its members. Below we have a structure definition for a double precision sandwich—a double surrounded by two ints:

```
struct {
     int    i;
     double x;
     int    j;
} stuff;
```

The stuff struct won't cause a problem because C compilers have more leeway for allocating memory for structures than FORTRAN compilers have for laying out a COMMON block. The struct members can be padded left or right with unused storage so that every element is correctly aligned.

Closing Notes

We have seen some of the problems you might encounter when moving engineering and numerical codes to RISC platforms. There are other mistakes you might look for too, such as mismatched argument lists, or incorrect assumptions about the way data is stored. And be sure to look at the discussion about associative transformations in Chapter 10.

Let me close with a little advice. Having worked for a couple of computer companies, I can state with confidence that the last compiler and development features debugged are those that "nobody uses." The list includes things like *assigned gotos* and *alternate returns*. For C programs it is features such as *comma valued expressions*, and *bit fields*. Naturally, language components pass the compiler test suite back at the vendor's home office. But they don't get the use that dull and boring parts of the language, such as the end statement, get. It may be that you use them all the time, but if the folks around you don't, you are at risk; some kinds of constructs just seem to have an affinity for bugs.

So, if you're making use of a new compiler, or if there is any chance that your code will be ported to other platforms, code defensively—be dull and boring.* There is nothing more frustrating than a day looking for a bug in your code only to find one in the compiler.

Exercises

1. Here is a piece of code taken from the chapter. The value of K is not explicitly saved between invocations of the subroutine INCR. What output does the program give you for both optimized and unoptimized runs?

   ```
           PROGRAM MAIN
           INTEGER I
           DO 10 I=1,100
             CALL INCR(I)
   10      CONTINUE
           END

           SUBROUTINE INCR(I)
           INTEGER I,K
           IF (I .EQ. 1) K = 0
           K = K + 1
           WRITE (*,*) K
           RETURN
           END
   ```

2. Run the following program to see how the double precision argument is modified by a subroutine expecting a single precision value. Did the compiler find the mistake?

---

*New compilers accompany each new CPU generation—every two or three years. Therefore almost all compilers are new.

```
PROGRAM MAIN
DOUBLE PRECISION A
A = 1234.D10
CALL FOO(A)
END
SUBROUTINE (A)
REAL A
WRITE (*,*) A
END
```

3. How does your computer handle misaligned references? Here's a program from the chapter. Run it twice, once with q set to p+1, and once with q set to p. Don't use compiler optimization. Do you notice a difference in the run times? Do both versions execute correctly?

```
main ()
{
        int    *p;
        double *q;
        int i;

        p = (int *) malloc (sizeof(int) * 3);
        q = (double *) (p + 1);

        for (i=0; i<1000000; i++)
            *q = (double) 1.0;        /* misaligned */
}
```

7
Timing and Profiling

Perhaps getting your code to produce the right answers is enough. After all, if you only plan to use the program once in a while, or if it only takes a few minutes to run, execution time isn't going to matter that much. But it might not always be that way. Typically, people start taking interest in the run time of their programs for two reasons:

- The workload has increased.
- They are considering a new machine.

It's clear why you might care about the performance of your program if the workload increases. Trying to cram 25 hours of computing time into a 24 hour day is an administrative nightmare. But why should people who are considering a new machine care about the run time? After all, the new machine will presumably be faster than the old one, so everything should take less time. The reason is that when people are evaluating new machines, they need a basis of comparison—a benchmark. People often use familiar programs as benchmarks. It makes sense: you want a benchmark to be representative of the kind of work you do, and nothing is more representative of the work you do than the work you do!

Benchmarking sounds easy enough, provided you have timing tools. And you already know the meaning of time.* You will just want to be sure that what those tools are reporting is the same as what you think you're getting—especially if you have never used them before. To illustrate, imagine if someone took your watch from you one day and replaced it with another that expressed time in some funny units or three overlapping sets of hands. It would be very confusing; you might have a problem reading it at all. You would also be justifiably nervous about conducting your affairs by a watch you don't understand.

---
*Time is money.

UNIX timing tools are like the six-handed watch, reporting three different kinds of time measurements. They aren't giving conflicting information; they just present more information than you can jam into a single number. Again, the trick is learning to read the watch. That's what the first part of this chapter is about. We'll investigate the different types of measurements you can take to determine how a program is doing. In Chapter 14 we'll apply what we've learned when we talk about how to conduct a formal benchmark.

If you are planning to tune a program, you will need more than timing information. Where is time being spent—in a single loop, a subroutine call overhead, or with memory problems? For tuners, the latter sections of this chapter discuss how to profile code at the procedural and statement levels. I'll also discuss what profiles mean and how they predict the approach you will have to take when, and if, you decide to tweak the code for performance, and what your chances for success will be.

Timing

I'll assume that your program runs correctly. It would be rather ridiculous to time a program that's not running right, though this doesn't mean it doesn't happen. Depending on what you are doing, you may be interested in knowing how much time is spent overall, or you may be looking at just a portion of the program. I'll show you how to time the whole program first, and then talk about timing individual loops or subroutines.

Timing a Whole Program

You can time program execution by placing the *time* command before everything else you normally type on the command line. When the program finishes, a timing summary will be produced. For instance, if your program is called *foo*, you can time its execution by typing `time foo`. If you are using the C shell or Korn shell, *time* is one of the shell's built-in commands. With a Bourne shell, *time* is a separate command executable in */bin*. In any case, the following information will appear at the end of the run:

- User time
- System time
- Elapsed time

These timing figures will be easier to understand with a little background. As your program runs, it switches back and forth between two fundamentally different modes: *user mode* and *kernel mode*. The normal operating state is user mode. It is in user mode that the instructions the compiler generated on your behalf get executed, in addition to any subroutine library calls linked with your program.* It might be enough to run in user mode forever, except that programs generally need other services, such as I/O, and these require the intervention of the operating system—the kernel. A kernel service request made by your program, or perhaps an event from outside your program, causes a switch from user mode into kernel mode.

Time spent executing in the two modes is accounted for separately. The *user time* figure describes time spent in user mode. Similarly, *system time* is a measure of the time spent in kernel mode. As far as user time goes, each program on the machine is accounted for separately. That is, you won't be charged for activity in somebody else's application. System time accounting works the same way, for the most part; however, you can, in some instances, be charged for some system services performed on other people's behalf, in addition to your own. This is because your program may be executing at the moment some outside activity causes an interrupt. This seems unfair, but take consolation in the fact that it works both ways: other users may be charged for your system activity too, for the same reason.

Taken together, user time and system time are called *CPU time*.

```
CPU time = user time + system time
```

Generally, the user time will be far greater than the system time. You would expect this because most applications only occasionally ask for system services. In fact, a disproportionately large system time probably indicates some trouble. For instance, programs that are repeatedly generating exception conditions, such as page faults, misaligned memory references, or floating point exceptions, will use an inordinate amount of system time. Time spent doing things like seeking on a disk, rewinding a tape, or waiting for characters at the terminal don't show up in CPU time. That's because these activities do not require involvement of the CPU; the CPU is free to go off and execute other programs.

---

*Cache miss time is buried in here too.

The third piece of information (corresponding to the third set of hands on the watch), *elapsed time*, is a measure of the actual (wallclock) time that has passed since the program was started. For programs that spend most of their time computing, the elapsed time should be very close to the CPU time. Reasons why elapsed time might be greater are:

- You are timesharing the machine with other active programs.*
- Your application performs a lot of I/O.
- Your application requires more memory bandwidth than is available on the machine (applies to multiprocessors).
- Your program was paging or swapped.

People often record the CPU time and use it as an estimate for elapsed time. This is okay on a single CPU machine, provided that you have seen the program run when the machine was quiet and noticed the two numbers were very close together. But for multiprocessors, the total CPU time can be far different from the elapsed time. Whenever there is a doubt, wait until you have the machine to yourself and time your program then, using elapsed time.

If you are running on a Berkeley UNIX derivative, the C shell's built-in *time* command can report a number of other useful statistics. The default form of the output is shown in Figure 7-1. Check with your *csh* manual page for more possibilities.

In addition to figures for CPU and elapsed time, *csh* time command produces information about CPU utilization, page faults, swaps, blocked I/O operations (usually disk activity), and some measures of how much physical memory your program occupied when it ran.† I will describe each of them in turn.

Percent utilization

Percent utilization corresponds to the ratio of elapsed time to CPU time. As I mentioned above, there can be a number of reasons why the CPU utilization wouldn't be 100%, or mighty close. You can often get a hint from the other fields as to whether it is a problem with your program, or whether you were sharing the machine when you ran it.

---

*The *uptime* command will tell you how many other jobs are running on your machine. The last three fields tell the average number of processes ready to run during the last 1, 5, and 15 minutes, respectively.

†A System V utility called *timex* provides an even more comprehensive set of statistics. We won't discuss *timex*; check the manual entry for information.

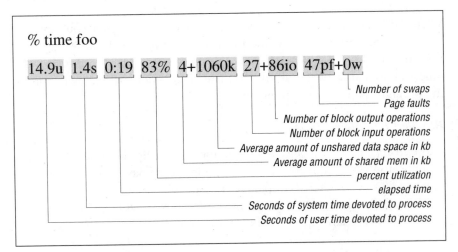

Figure 7-1: The built-in csh time function

Average real memory utilization

The two *average memory utilization* measurements shown in Figure 7-1 characterize the program's resource requirements as it ran.

The first measurement, *shared memory space*, accounts for the average amount of *real* memory taken by your program's text segment—the portion that holds the machine instructions. It is called "shared" because several concurrently running copies of a program can share the same text segment (to save memory). Years ago, it was possible for the text segment to consume a significant portion of the memory system, but these days, with memory sizes starting around 32 megabytes, you would have to compile a pretty huge source program and use every bit of it to create a shared memory usage figure big enough to cause concern. The shared memory space requirement will usually be quite low relative to the amount of memory available on your machine.

The second average memory utilization measurement, *unshared memory space*, describes the average *real* storage dedicated to your program's data structures as it ran. This would include saved local variables and COMMON for FORTRAN, and static and external variables for C. I stress the word "real" here and above because these numbers talk about physical memory usage, taken over time. It may be that you have allocated arrays with 1 trillion elements (virtual space), but if your program only crawls into a corner of that space, your run time memory requirements will be pretty low.

What the unshared memory space measurement doesn't tell you, unfortunately, is your program's demand for memory at its greediest. An application that requires 100 MB 1/10th of the time and 1 KB all the rest of the time will appear to need only 10 MB on average—not a revealing picture of the program's memory requirements.

Blocked I/O operations

The two figures for *blocked I/O* operations primarily describe disk usage, though tape devices and some other peripherals may also be used with blocked I/O. Character I/O operations, such as terminal input and output, do not appear here. A large number of blocked I/O operations could explain a lower than expected CPU utilization.

Page faults and swaps

An unusually high number of *page faults* or any *swaps* probably indicates a system that is choked for memory, which would also explain a longer than expected elapsed time. It may be that other programs are competing for the same space. And don't forget that even under optimal conditions every program will suffer some number of page faults, as explained in Chapter 3. Techniques for minimizing paging are described in Chapter 11.

Timing a Portion of the Program

Suppose that you are interested in knowing the average lap time for a race car competition. I can suggest two methods—one that will cost you nothing and another that will cost you the price of admission to the raceway. The second method will give you a better quality number, but you will have to pay for it.

To benefit from my "cheap" method, we will have to assume that the race starts soon after the gates open and continues until closing time. This is how you go about it: make yourself inconspicuous at the far end of the parking lot and watch as the crowd arrives for the event. Record the time. Stay there a few more hours until the crowd starts to shuffle back out, and record the time again. Provided that you know how many laps were involved, you can derive a rough estimate for the average lap time as follows:

```
(time the crowd left - time the crowd arrived) / number of laps
```

Of course, the average includes the overhead associated with people finding their seats, concessioneering before the start of the race, etc., but the numbers will be correct within perhaps 10% or so.

My second method, paying admission and witnessing the actual start and finish times first hand, will give you a more accurate figure, but you will have to go "inside" and be a part of the event.

Similarly, for most benchmarking or tuning efforts, measurements taken on the "outside" of the program will tell you everything you need to know. But if you are trying to isolate performance figures for individual loops or portions of the code, you may want to include timing routines on the inside too. The basic technique is simple enough:

1. Record the time before you start doing X.
2. Do X.
3. Record the time at completion of X.
4. Subtract the start time from the completion time.

If, for instance, *X*'s primary job is to calculate geometric friggs, you can divide by the total time to obtain a number for geometric friggs/second. You have to be careful though; a few too many calls to the timing routines and you become part of the experiment. The timing routines take time too, and their very presence can increase instruction cache miss or paging. Furthermore, you want *X* to take a significant amount of time so that the measurements are meaningful. This is really important because the clock used by the timing functions has a limited resolution, usually in 60ths or 100ths of seconds. An event that occurs within a fraction of a second will be hard to measure with any accuracy.

For FORTRAN programs, a library timing function found on many machines is called *etime*, which takes a two element REAL*4 array as an argument and fills the slots with the user time and system time, respectively. The value returned by the function is the sum of the two. Here's how *etime* is often used:

Example 7-1: FORTRAN program using etime

```
      real*4 tarray(2), etime
      real*4 start, finish

      start  = etime(tarray)
      .... compute something
      finish = etime(tarray)

      write (*,*) 'CPU time: ', finish - start
```

Not every vendor supplies an etime function; in fact, one doesn't provide a timing routine for FORTRAN at all. Try it first. If it shows up as an undefined symbol when the program is linked, you can use the C routine below. It provides the same functionality as *etime*.*

Example 7-2: etime implemented in C

```
#include <sys/times.h>
#define TICKS    100.

float etime (parts)
struct {
        float user;
        float system;
} *parts;
{
        struct tms local;
        times (&local);
        parts->user   = (float) local.tms_utime/TICKS;
        parts->system = (float) local.tms_stime/TICKS;
        return (parts->user + parts->system);
}
```

C programmers could call the *times* routine directly, though a routine called *getrusage* provides more information. It is supported on some machines, particularly Berkeley UNIX variants. *getrusage* returns the kind of information about page faults, swaps, blocked I/O operations, etc., that came from the *csh* time command, as described above. Look for a complete description in your vendor's documentation.

Using Timing Information

You can get a lot information from the timing facilities on a UNIX machine. Not only can you tell how long it takes to perform a given job, but you can also get hints about whether the machine is operating efficiently, or whether there is some other problem that needs to be factored in, such as inadequate memory.

---

*There are a couple of things you might have to tweak to make it work. First of all, linking C routines with FORTRAN routines on your computer may require that you add an underscore (_) after the function name. This would change the entry to float etime_ (parts). Furthermore, you might have to adjust the TICKS parameter. I assumed that the system clock had a resolution of 1/100 of a second (true for the Hewlett-Packard machines which this version of *etime* was written for). 1/60 is very common. On an RS6000 the number would be 1000. You may find the value in a file named */usr/include/sys/param.h* on your machine, or you can determine it empirically.

Once the program is running with all anomalies explained away, you can record the time as a baseline. If you are tuning, the baseline will be a reference with which you can tell how much (or little) tuning has improved things. If you are benchmarking, you can use the baseline to judge how much overall incremental performance a new machine will give you. But remember to watch the other figures—paging, CPU utilization, etc. These may differ from machine to machine for reasons unrelated to raw CPU performance. You want to be sure that you are getting the full picture. In Chapter 14 I talk about benchmarking in more detail.

Subroutine Profiling

Say you have been hired as an efficiency expert for a large municipality. Your job is to make recommendations for how the city can get a better return on the salaries it pays its employees. The first day of work they hand you a stack of job descriptions and a key to the washroom, and show you to your office. You have a list of employees and the jobs they do, but you really can't tell anything about their day-to-day schedules. A person may profess to be a ditch digger or a police officer, but until you study how they spend their time, you don't really know what ditch diggers and police officers do.

Your first duty would be to *profile* the work day of a typical employee in a given position. What you find will have a great bearing on your ability to help them become more efficient. For instance, if you discover that the city librarian spends most of the week carrying books from the return desk to the stacks, one at a time, a cart might triple her efficiency. A city hall clerk, on the other hand, does a little of this and a little of that, so doubling his efficiency on any single job might benefit his weekly throughput by only 1% or so. Changes in city hall would have to affect every job the clerk does by a significant amount if you wanted the total benefit to be significant as well.

These two cases represent different types of profiles. They are analogous to the extremes you see when profiling programs to determine where the time is being spent. Some concentrate activity in one or two routines; others are more spread out. Likewise, depending on what you discover, you will have to adjust your tuning approach to match the profile, if you decide to tune at all; different profile shapes suggest different tuning methods and different probabilities of success.

Let's investigate this notion of profile shape a little more. Assume for the moment that you have a way to break down the total time an application takes into time-per-routine. That is, you can see that 10% of the time is spent in subroutine A, 5% in subroutine B, etc. Naturally, if you add all of the routines together they should account for 100% of the overall time spent. From these percentages you can construct a picture—a *profile*—of how execution is distributed when the program runs. Though not representative of any particular profiling tool, the histograms in Figure 7-2 and Figure 7-3 depict these percentages, sorted from left to right, with each vertical column representing a different routine. They will help illustrate different profile shapes.

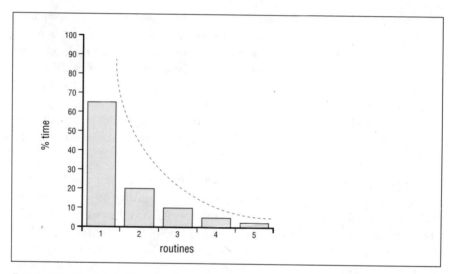

Figure 7-2: Sharp profile—dominated by routine 1

As with the hypothetical librarian, a *sharp profile* says that most of the time is spent doing one or two things, and if you want to improve the program's performance you should focus your efforts on tuning those things. A minor optimization in a heavily traveled line of code can sometimes have a great effect on the overall run time—20% or more, given the right opportunity. A relatively *flat profile*,* on the other hand, tells you that the run time is spread across many routines, and effort spent optimizing any one or two

---

*The term "flat profile" is a little overloaded. I am using it to describe a profile that shows an even distribution of time throughout the program. You will also see the label flat profile used to draw distinction from a call graph profile, as described below.

will have little benefit in speeding up the program. Of course, there are also programs whose execution profile falls somewhere in the middle.

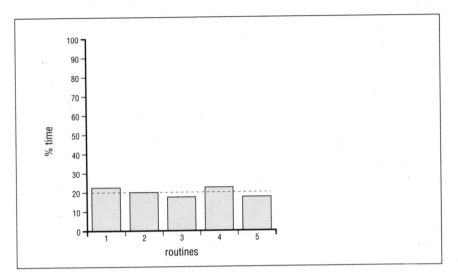

Figure 7-3: Flat profile—no routine predominates

I couldn't predict with absolute certainty what you are likely to find when you profile your programs, but there are some general trends. For instance, engineering and scientific codes built around matrix solutions often exhibit very sharp profiles. The run time will be dominated by the work performed in a handful of solver routines. To tune the code, you need to focus your efforts on those routines to make them more efficient. It may involve res-tructuring loops to expose parallelism, providing hints to the compiler, or re-arranging memory references. In any case, the challenge is tangible—you can see the problems you have to fix.

There are limits to how much tuning one or two routines will improve your run time, of course. An often quoted rule of thumb is *Amdahl's Law*, derived from remarks made in 1967 by one of the designers of the IBM 360 series, and founder of Amdahl Computer, Gene Amdahl. Strictly speaking, his remarks were about the performance potential of parallel computers, but people have adapted Amdahl's Law to describe other things too. For our purposes, it goes like this: Say you have a program with two parts, one that can be optimized so that it goes infinitely fast, and another that can't be optimized at all. Even if the optimizable portion makes up 50% of the initial run time, you will at best be able to cut the total run time in half. That is, your run time will eventually be dominated by the portion that can't be optimized. This puts an upper limit on your expectations when tuning.

Even given the finite return on effort suggested by Amdahl's Law, tuning a program with a sharp profile can be rewarding. Programs with flat profiles are much more difficult to tune. These are often system codes, non-numeric applications, and varieties of numerical codes without matrix solutions. It takes a global tuning approach to reduce, to any justifiable degree, the run time of a program with a flat profile. For instance, you can sometimes optimize instruction cache usage, which is complicated because of the program's equal distribution of activity among a large number of routines. It can also help to reduce subroutine call overhead by folding callees into callers. Occasionally, you can find a memory reference problem that is endemic to the whole program—and one that can be fixed all at once.

In any case, to get a profile you need a profiler. One or two subroutine profilers come standard with the software development environments on all UNIX machines. I'll discuss two of them: *prof* and *gprof*. In addition, I'll mention a few line-by-line profilers. Subroutine profilers can give you a general overall of where time is being spent. You will probably want to start with *gprof*, if you have it (most machines do). Otherwise, use *prof*. After that, you can move to a line-by-line profiler if you need to know which statements take the most time.

prof

prof is the most common of the UNIX profiling tools. In a sense, it is an extension of the compiler, linker, object libraries, plus a few extra utilities, so it is hard to look at any one thing and say "this profiles your code." *prof* works by periodically sampling the program counter as your application runs. To enable profiling, you must recompile and relink using the -p flag.* For example, if your program has two modules, *stuff.c* and *junk.c*, you will need to compile and link according to the following code.

```
% cc stuff.c -p -O -c
% cc junk.c -p -O -c
% cc stuff.o junk.o -p -o stuff
```

This will create a *stuff* binary which is ready for profiling. You don't need to do anything special to run it. Just treat it normally by entering stuff.

---

*You don't *have* to recompile (you can just relink). However, information regarding the number of times routines are called will be missing from the profile.

Because run time statistics are being gathered, it will take a little longer than usual to execute.* At completion there will be a new file called *mon.out* in the directory where you ran it. This will contain the history of *stuff* in binary form, but you can't look at it directly. You use the *prof* utility to read *mon.out* and create a profile of *stuff*. By default, the information is written to your screen on standard output, though you can easily redirect it to a file:

```
% prof stuff > stuff.prof
```

For illustration, I have created a ridiculous little application, *loops.c*, below. It contains a main routine and three subroutines for which you can predict the time distribution just by looking at the code.

Example 7-3: loops.c—a program for testing profilers

```
main () {
    int l;
    for (l=0;l<1000;l++) {
        if (l == 2*(1/2)) foo ();
        bar();
        baz();
    }
}
foo (){
    int j;
    for (j=0;j<200;j++)
}
bar () {
    int i;
    for (i=0;i<200;i++);
}
baz () {
    int k;
    for (k=0;k<300;k++);
}
```

Again, you need to compile and link *loops* with the **-p** flag, run the program, and then run the *prof* utility to extract a profile, as follows.

```
% cc loops.c -p -o loops
% ./loops
% prof loops > loops.prof
```

---

*Remember: code with profiling enabled takes longer to run. You will want to recompile and relink the whole thing *without* the *-p* flag when you have finished profiling.

Example 7-4 shows what a *loops.prof* should look like. There are six columns.

Example 7-4: Profile of loops.c

%Time	Seconds	Cumsecs	#Calls	msec/call	Name
56.8	0.50	0.50	1000	0.500	_baz
27.3	0.24	0.74	1000	0.240	_bar
15.9	0.14	0.88	500	0.28	_foo
0.0	0.00	0.88	1	0.	_creat
0.0	0.00	0.88	2	0.	_profil
0.0	0.00	0.88	1	0.	_main
0.0	0.00	0.88	3	0.	_getenv
0.0	0.00	0.88	1	0.	_strcpy
0.0	0.00	0.88	1	0.	_write

The columns mean:

%Time	Percentage of CPU time consumed by this routine
Seconds	CPU time consumed by this routine
Cumsecs	A running total of time consumed by this and all preceding routines in the list
Calls	The number of times this particular routine was called
msec/call	Seconds divided by number of calls. This gives the average length of time taken by each invocation of the routine.
Name	The name of this routine

The top three routines listed are from *loops.c* itself. You can see an entry for the "main" routine more than halfway down the list. Depending on the vendor, the names of the routines may contain leading or trailing underscores, and there will always be some routines listed that you don't recognize. These are contributions from the C library and possibly the FORTRAN libraries, if you are using FORTRAN. Profiling also introduces some overhead into the run, and will often show up as one or two subroutines in the *prof* output. In this case, the entry for _profil represents code inserted by the linker for collecting run time profiling data.

If it was my intention to tune *loops*, I would consider a profile like the one in the figure above to be a fairly good sign. The lead routine takes 50% of the run time, so at least there is a chance that I could do something with it that would have a significant impact on the overall run time. (Of course with a program as trivial as *loops*, there is plenty I can do, since *loops* does nothing.)

gprof

Just as it is important to know how time is distributed when your program runs, it is also valuable to be able to tell who called who in the list of routines. Imagine, for instance, if something labeled _exp showed up high in the list in the *prof* output. You might say: "Hmmm, I don't remember calling anything named exp(). I wonder where that came from." A profiler could help you find it.

Subroutines and functions can be thought of as members of a family tree. The top of the tree, or root, is actually a routine that precedes the main routine you coded for the application. It calls your main routine, which in turn calls others, and so on, all the way down to the leaf nodes of the tree. This tree is properly known as a *call graph.** The relationship between routines and nodes in the graph is one of parents and children. Nodes separated by more than one hop are referred to as ancestors and descendants.

Figure 7-3 graphically depicts the kind of call graph you might see in a small application. main is the parent or ancestor of most of the rest of the routines. G has two parents, E and C. Another routine, A, doesn't appear to have any ancestors or descendants at all. This can happen when routines are not compiled with profiling enabled, or when they aren't invoked with a subroutine call—such as would be the case if A was an exception handler.

The UNIX profiler that can extract this kind of information is called *gprof.* It replicates the abilities of *prof*, plus it gives a call graph profile so you can see who calls who, and how often. The call graph profile is handy if you are trying to figure out how a piece of code works, where an unknown routine came from, or if you are looking for candidates for subroutine inlining.

To use call graph profiling you need go through all of the same steps as with *prof*, except that a **-pg** flag is substituted for the -p flag.† Additionally, when it comes time to produce the actual profile, you use the *gprof* utility

---

*It doesn't have to be a tree. Any subroutine can have more than one parent. Furthermore, recursive subroutine calls introduce cycles into the graph, in which a child calls one of its parents.

†On HP machines the flag is **-G**.

instead of *prof.* One other difference is that the name of the statistics file will be *gmon.out* instead of *mon.out*:

```
% cc -pg stuff.c -c
% cc stuff.o -pg -o stuff
% stuff
% gprof stuff > stuff.gprof
```

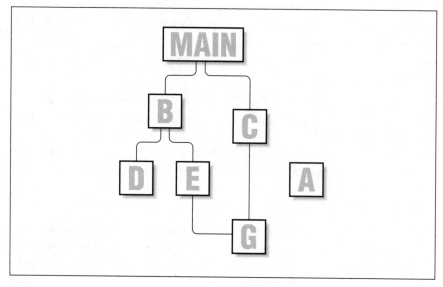

Figure 7-4: Simple call graph

The output from *gprof* is divided into three sections:

* Call Graph Profile
* Timing Profile
* Index

The first section textually maps out the call graph. The second section lists routines, the percentage of time devoted to each, the number of calls, etc. (similar to *prof*). The third section is a cross reference so that you can locate routines by number, rather than by name. This is especially useful for large applications because routines are sorted based on the amount of time they use, and it can be difficult to locate a particular routine by scanning for its name.

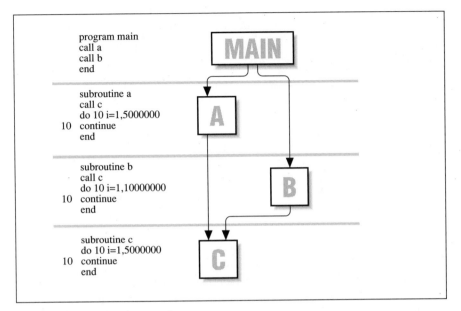

Figure 7-5: FORTRAN example

Let's invent another trivial application to illustrate how *gprof* works. Figure 7-5 shows a short piece of FORTRAN code, along with a diagram of how the routines are connected together. Subroutines A and B are both called by MAIN, and in turn each calls C. Example 7-5 shows a section of the output from *gprof*'s call graph profile.*

Example 7-5: A portion of gprof output

index	%time	self	descendents	called/total called+self called/total	parents name index children
....			....		....
		0.00	8.08	1/1	_main [2]
[3]	99.9	0.00	8.08	1	_MAIN_ [3]
		3.23	1.62	1/1	_b_ [4]
		1.62	1.62	1/1	_a_ [5]
-----	-----	----	-----------	--------------------------------------	----------------------------
		3.23	1.62	1/1	_MAIN_ [3]

---

*In the interest of conserving space, I clipped out the section most relevant to our discussion and included it in Example 7-5. There was a lot more to it, including calls of setup and system routines, the likes of which you will see when you run *gprof*.

Example 7-5: A portion of gprof output (continued)

```
[4]     59.9     3.23         1.62          1         _b_ [4]
                 1.62         0.00          1/2          _c_ [6]

        ---------------------------------------------

                 1.62         1.62          1/1          _MAIN_ [3]
[5]     40.0     1.62         1.62          1         _a_ [5]
                 1.62         0.00          1/2          _c_ [6]

        ---------------------------------------------

                 1.62         0.00          1/2          _a_ [5]
                 1.62         0.00          1/2          _b_ [4]
[6]     39.9     3.23         0.00          2         _c_ [6]

  ....                      ....                            ....
```

Sandwiched between each set of dashed lines is information describing a given routine and its relationship to parents and children. It is easy to tell which routine the block represents because the name is shifted farther to the left than the others. Parents are listed above, children below. As with *prof,* underscores are tacked onto the labels.* A description of each of the columns follows.

Index

You will notice that each routine name is associated with a number in brackets ([n]). This is a cross reference for locating the routine elsewhere in the profile. If, for example, you were looking at the block describing _MAIN_ and wanted to know more about one of its children, say _a_, you could find it by scanning down the left hand side of the page for its index, [5].

%Time

The meaning of the %time field is a little different than it was for *prof.* In this case it describes the percentage of time spent in this routine *plus* the time spent in all of its children. It gives you a quick way to determine where the busiest sections of the call graph can be found.

Self

Listed in seconds, the self column has different meanings for parents, the routine in question, and its children. Starting with the middle entry—the

---

*You may have noticed that there are two main routines: _MAIN_ and _main. In a FORTRAN program; _MAIN_ is the actual FORTRAN main routine. It is called as a subroutine by _main, provided from a system library at link time. When you're profiling C code, you won't see _MAIN_.

routine itself—the self figure shows how much overall time was dedicated to the routine. In the case _b_, for instance, this amounts to 3.23 seconds.

In Example 7-5, each self column entry shows the amount of time that can be attributed to calls from the parents. If you look at routine _c_, for example, you will see that it consumed a total time of 3.23 seconds. But note that it had two parents. 1.62 seconds of the time was attributable to calls from _a_, and 1.62 to _b_.

For the children, the self figure shows how much time was spent executing each child because of calls from this routine. The children may have used more time overall, but the only time accounted for is time attributable to calls from this routine. For example, _c_ accumulated 3.23 seconds overall, but if you look at the block describing _b_, you will see _c_ listed as a child with only 1.62 seconds. That's the total time spent executing _c_ on behalf of _b_.

Descendants

As with the self column, figures in the descendants column have different meanings for the routine, its parents, and children. For the routine itself, it shows the number of seconds spent in all of its descendants.

For the routine's parents, the descendants figure describes how much time spent in the routine can be traced back to calls by each parent. Looking at routine _c_ again, you can see that of its total time, 3.23 seconds, 1.62 seconds were attributable to each of its two parents, _a_ and _b_.

For the children, the descendants column shows how much of the child's time can be attributed to calls from this routine. The child may have accumulated more time overall, but the only time displayed is time associated with calls from this routine.

Calls

The calls column shows the number of times each routine was invoked, as well as the distribution of those calls associated with both parents and children. Starting with the routine itself, the figure in the calls column shows the total number of entries into the routine. In situations where the routine called itself, you will also see a +n immediately appended, showing that additional n calls were made recursively.

Parent and child figures are expressed as ratios. For the parents, the ratio m/n says "of the n times the routine was called, m of those calls came from this parent."

For the child, it says "of the n times this child was called, m of those calls came from this routine."

gprof's Flat Profile

As I mentioned previously, *gprof* also produces a timing profile (also called a "flat" profile, just to confuse things) similar to the one produced by *prof*. A few of the fields are different from *prof*, and there is some extra information, so it will help if I explain it briefly. Below are the first few lines from a *gprof* flat profile for *stuff*. You will recognize the top three routines from the original program. The others are library functions included at link time.

Example 7-6: gprof flat profile

```
  %   cumulative   self              self     total
 time   seconds   seconds   calls  ms/call  ms/call  name
 39.9      3.23      3.23       2  1615.07  1615.07  _c_ [6]
 39.9      6.46      3.23       1  3230.14  4845.20  _b_ [4]
 20.0      8.08      1.62       1  1620.07  3235.14  _a_ [5]
  0.1      8.09      0.01       3     3.33     3.33  _ioctl [9]
  0.0      8.09      0.00      64     0.00     0.00  .rem [12]
  0.0      8.09      0.00      64     0.00     0.00  _f_clos [177]
  0.0      8.09      0.00      20     0.00     0.00  _sigblock [178]
  ...      ....      ....       .        .        .  ......
```

Here's what each column means:

%Time   Again, we see a field that describes the run time for each routine as a percentage of the overall time taken by the program. As you might expect, all the entries in this column should total to 100% (nearly).

Cumulative
Seconds   For any given routine, the column called "cumulative seconds" tallies a running sum of the time taken by all the preceding routines plus its own time. As you scan down towards the bottom, the numbers asymptotically approach the total run time for the program.

Self
Seconds   Each routine's individual contribution to the run time.

Calls   The number of times this particular routine was called.

Self
ms/call   Seconds spent inside routine, divided by number of calls. This gives the average length of time taken by each invocation of the routine. The figure is presented in milliseconds.

Total
ms/call   Seconds spent inside routine *plus its descendants*, divided by number of calls.

Name   The name of the routine. Notice that the cross reference number appears here too.

Accumulating the Results of Several gprof Runs

It is possible to accumulate statistics from multiple runs so that you can get a picture of how a program is doing with a variety of data sets. For instance, say that you wanted to profile an application, call it *bar*, with three different sets of input data. You could perform the runs separately, saving the *gmon.out* files as you go, and then combine the results into a single profile at the end:

```
% f77 -pg bar.f -o bar
% bar < data1.input
% mv gmon.out gmon.1
% bar < data2.input
% mv gmon.out gmon.2
% bar < data3.input
% gprof bar -s gmon.1 gmon.2 gmon.out > gprof.summary.out
```

In the example profile above, each run along the way creates a new *gmon.out* file, which I quickly renamed to make room for the next one. At the end, *gprof* combines the information from each of the data files to produce a summary profile of *bar* in the file *gprof.summary.out*. Additionally (you don't see it here), *gprof* creates a file named *gmon.sum* that contains the merged data from the original three data files. *gmon.sum* has the same format as *gmon.out*, so you can use it as input for other merged profiles down the road.

In form, the output from a merged profile looks exactly the same as for an individual run. There are a couple of interesting things you will note, however. For one thing, the `main` routine will appear to have been invoked more than once—one time for each run, in fact. Furthermore, depending on the application, multiple runs will tend to either smooth the contour of the profile or exaggerate its features. You can imagine how this might happen. If a single routine is consistently called while others come and go as the input data changes, it will take on increasing importance in your tuning efforts.

A Few Words About Accuracy

For processors running at 50 MHz and more, the time between 60 Hz or 100 Hz samples is a veritable eternity. Furthermore, you can experience quantization errors when the sampling frequency is fixed, as is true of steady 1/100th or 1/60th of a second samples. To take an exaggerated example, assume that the time line in Figure 7-6 shows alternating calls to two subroutines, BAR and FOO. The tick marks represent the sample points for profiling.

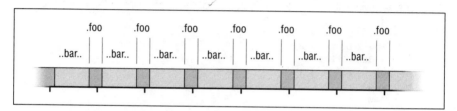

Figure 7-6: Quantization Errors in Profiling

BAR and FOO take turns running. In fact, BAR takes more time than FOO. But because the sampling interval closely matches the frequency at which the two subroutines alternate, we get a quantizing error: most of the samples happen to be taken while FOO is running. Therefore, the profile will tell us that FOO took more CPU time than BAR.

I've described the tried and true (?) UNIX subroutine profilers, which have been available for years. In many cases, vendors have much better tools available for the asking or for a fee. If you are doing some serious tuning, ask your vendor representative to look into other tools for you.

Basic Block Profilers

There are several good reasons to desire a finer level of detail than you can see with a subroutine profiler. For humans trying to understand how a subroutine or function is used, a profiler that tells which lines of source code were actually executed, and how often, is invaluable; a few clues about where to focus your tuning efforts can save you time. Also, such a profiler saves you from discovering that a particularly clever optimization makes no difference because you put it in a section of code that never gets executed.

As part of an overall strategy, a subroutine profile can direct you to a handful of routines that account for most of the run time, but it takes a *basic block profiler** to get you to the associated source code lines.

Basic block profilers can also provide compilers with information they need to perform their own optimizations. Most compilers work in the dark. They can restructure and unroll loops, but they cannot tell when it will pay off. Worse yet, misplaced optimizations often have an adverse effect of slowing down the code! This can be the result of added instruction cache burden, wasted tests introduced by the compiler, or incorrect assumptions about which way a branch would go at run time. If the compiler can automatically interpret the results of a basic block profile, or if you can supply the compiler with hints, it will often mean a reduced run time with little effort on your part.

There are several basic block profilers in the world. The closest thing to a standard, *tcov*, is shipped with Sun workstations; it's standard because the installed base is so big. On UNIX system V machines and some RS6000s you will find a basic block profiler called *lprof*. On MIPS based workstations, such as those from Silicon Graphics and DEC, the profiler (packaged as an extension to *prof*) is called **pixie**. I'll explain briefly how to run each profiler using a reasonable set of switches. You can consult your manual pages for other options.

tcov

tcov, available on Suns and other Sparc machines that run SunOS, gives execution statistics that describe the number of times each source statement was executed. It is very easy to use. Assume for illustration that we have a source program called *foo.c*. The following steps create a basic block profile:

```
% cc -a foo.c -o foo
% foo
% tcov foo.c
```

Several files are created in the process. One called *foo.d* accumulates a history of the execution frequencies within the program *foo*. That is, old data is updated with new data each time *foo* is run, so you can get an overall

---

*A basic block is a section of code with only one entrance and one exit. If you know how many times the block was entered, then you know how many times each of the statements in the block was executed, which gives you a line-by-line profile. The concept of a basic block is explained in detail in Chapter 4.

picture of what happens inside *foo* given a variety of data sets. Just remember to clean out the old data if you want to start over. The profile itself goes into a file called *foo.tcov*.

Let's look at an illustration. Below is a short C program that performs a bubble sort of ten integers:

```
int n[] = {23,12,43,2,98,78,2,51,77,8};
main ()
  {
    int i, j, ktemp;
    for (i=10; i>0; i--) {
      for (j=0; j<i; j++) {
        if (n[j] < n[j+1]) {
          ktemp = n[j+1], n[j+1] = n[j], n[j] = ktemp;
        }
      }
    }
  }
```

tcov produces a basic block profile that contains execution counts for each source line, plus some summary statistics (not shown):

```
          int n[] = {23,12,43,2,98,78,2,51,77,8};
          main ()
  1 ->    {
            int i, j, ktemp;
 10 ->     for (i=10; i>0; i--) {
 10,    55 ->     for (j=0; j<i; j++) {
 55 ->         if (n[j] < n[j+1]) {
 23 ->           ktemp = n[j+1], n[j+1] = n[j], n[j] = ktemp;
               }
             }
           }
  1 ->    }
```

The numbers to the left tell you the number of times each block was entered. For instance, you can see that the routine was entered just once, and that the highest count occurs at the test `n[j] < n[j+1]`. *tcov* shows more than one count on a line in places where the compiler has created more than one block.

lprof

lprof's output looks very much like *tcov*'s. You can find *lprof* on UNIX system V and variants. I have seen it on the RS6000 too, but not all machines have it. You would profile *foo.c* with *lprof*, like so:

```
% cc -ql foo.c -o foo
% foo
% lprof -p -c foo.cnt
```

Run time data is collected in a file called *foo.cnt*. The profile is written to your screen (standard output), though you can easily redirect it to a file:

```
% lprof -p -c foo.cnt > foo.lprof
```

Below, you can see the profile produced for the bubble sort:

```
% lprof -p -c foo.cnt
              int n[] = {23,12,43,2,98,78,2,51,77,8};
              main ()
     1 [3]    {
                  int i, j, ktemp;
     1 [5]        for (i=10; i>0; i--) {
    10 [6]          for (j=0; j<i; j++) {
    55 [7]            if (n[j] < n[j+1]) {
    23 [8]              ktemp  = n[j+1], n[j+1] = n[j], n[j] = ktemp;
                       }
    55 [10]          }
    10 [11]        }
     1 [12]    }
```

As with *tcov*, *lprof* can accumulate statistics from multiple runs. However, it requires that you rename the intermediate *foo.cnt* files between runs and consolidate them at the end. For example, the following line will merge the statistics from three runs into a data file called *final.cnt*:

```
% lprof -m final.cnt run1.cnt run2.cnt run3.cnt
```

pixie

pixie is a little different from *tcov* and *lprof*. Rather than reporting the number of times each source line was executed, *pixie* reports the number of machine clock cycles devoted to executing each line. In theory, you could use this to calculate the amount of time spent per statement, although anomalies like cache misses are not represented.

pixie works by "pixifying" an executable file that has been compiled and linked in the normal way. Below I ran *pixie* on *foo* to create a new executable called *foo.pixie*:

```
% cc foo.c -o foo
% pixie foo
% foo.pixie
% prof -pixie foo
```

Also created was a file named *foo.Addrs*, which contains addresses for the basic blocks within *foo*. When the new program, *foo.pixie*, is run, it creates a file called *foo.Counts*, containing execution counts for the basic blocks whose addresses are stored in *foo.Addrs*. *pixie* data will accumulate from run to run. The statistics are retrieved using *prof* and a special *-pixie* flag.

pixie's default output comes in three sections, and shows:

- Cycles per routine
- Procedure invocation counts
- Cycles per basic line

Below, I have listed the output of the third section for the bubble sort:

procedure (file)	line	bytes	cycles	%	cum %
main (foo.c)	7	44	605	12.11	12.11
_cleanup (flsbuf.c)	59	20	500	10.01	22.13
fclose (flsbuf.c)	81	20	500	10.01	32.14
fclose (flsbuf.c)	94	20	500	10.01	42.15
_cleanup (flsbuf.c)	54	20	500	10.01	52.16
fclose (flsbuf.c)	76	16	400	8.01	60.17
main (foo.c)	10	24	298	5.97	66.14
main (foo.c)	8	36	207	4.14	70.28
....	..	..	..	...	...

Here you can see three entries for the `main` routine from *foo.c*, plus a number of system library routines. The entries show the associated line number and the number of machine cycles dedicated to executing that line as the program ran. For instance, line 7 of *foo.c* took 605 cycles (12% of the run time). Given a clock speed of 33 MHz (30 nanoseconds), this would suggest that a total of `605*30e-9=18.3` microseconds was spent in line seven.

Closing Notes

We have seen some of the tools for timing and profiling. Even though it seems like we covered a lot, there are other kinds of profiles we would like to be able to cover—cache miss measurements, run time dependency analysis, flop measurements, and so on. These profiles are good when you are looking for particular anomalies, such as cache miss or floating point pipeline utilization. Profilers for these quantities exist for some machines, but they aren't widely distributed.

One thing to keep in mind: when you profile code you sometimes get a very limited view of the way a program is used. This is especially true if it can perform many types of analyses for many different sets of input data. Working with just one or two profiles can give you a distorted picture of how the code operates overall. Imagine the following scenario: Someone invites you to take your very first ride in an automobile. You get in the passenger's seat with a sketch pad and a pen, and record everything that happens. Your observations include some of the following:

- The radio is always on.
- The windshield wipers are never used.
- The car only moves in a forward direction.

The danger is that given this limited view of the way a car is operated, you might want to disconnect the radio's on/off knob, remove the windshield wipers, and eliminate the reverse gear. This would come as a real surprise to the next person who tries to back the car out on a rainy day! The point is that unless you are careful to gather data for *all kinds* of uses, you may not really have a picture of how the program operates. A single profile is fine for tuning a benchmark, but you may miss some important details on a multi-purpose application. Worse yet, if you optimize it for one case and cripple it for another, you may do far more harm than good.

Speaking of tuning, all last summer I had to listen to a teenager up the street optimize the engine in his mom's old Impala. It was hot, the windows were open, and I wanted to kill him. But I have to admit that he understands the tuning process. He tweaks some component (carburetor, distributor, steam valve, whatever) and then guns the engine to to see if it helped; he iterates. Chances are good that he didn't start by sticking his hand into whirring machinery and pulling out the first piece that came loose. Rather, he made some kind of judgement about what needed adjustment and then tried a few things.

Profiling, as we saw in this chapter, is pretty mechanical. Tuning requires insight. It's only fair to warn you that it isn't always rewarding. Sometimes you pour your soul into a clever modification that actually *increases* the run time. Argh! What went wrong? You'll need to depend on your profiling tools to answer that.

Exercises

1. Profile the following program using gprof. Is there any way to tell how much of the time spent in routine c was due to recursive calls?

```
main()
{
    int i, n=10;
    for (i=0; i<1000; i++) {
        c(n);
        a(n);
    }
}
c(n)
int n;
{
    if (n > 0) {
        a(n-1);
        c(n-1);
    }
}
a(n)
int n;
{
    c(n);
}
```

2. Profile an engineering code (floating point intensive) with full optimization on and off. How does the profile change? Can you explain the change?

8

Understanding Parallelism

Now that we have discussed different ways to measure the performance of programs, it is time to talk about how to improve it. Really, the subject is quite big—and not independent of architecture. However, the list of things you would want to try first is going to be the right approach on most of the machines out there. That being true, it is possible to treat application tuning generically.

The best way to understand what constitutes good code—at least as far as performance is concerned—is to learn to appreciate it from the compiler's point of view. Choices you make when coding or tuning an application directly affect the compiler's ability to generate a fast and efficient machine language representation. This is especially true for newer RISC workstations, with their ability to issue more than one instruction at a time, though it applies to other types of machines as well. Accordingly, this chapter is devoted to understanding what is needed to extract the most (fine-grained) *parallelism* from a piece of code.* But the answer is elimination of *dependencies*—interrelationships between instructions and data that bind the order in which they can occur. When parts of the program become less dependent on other parts, there is an increase in the pool of things that can be done simultaneously; that is, the parallelism increases.

This chapter supplements Chapter 4 in many ways. We looked at the mechanics of compiling code, all of which apply here, but we didn't answer all of the "why's." Basic block analysis techniques form the basis for the work the compiler does when looking for more parallelism. Looking at two

---

*Parallel computations have a notion of granularity associated with them. On one hand we have *fine-grained* or *instruction level* parallelism (which is what I'm really talking about here). On the other we have *coarse-grained* parallelism, found between large chunks of computations (see Chapters 15 and 16).

pieces of data, instructions or data and instructions, a modern compiler asks the question, "Do these things depend on each other?" The three possible answers are: yes, no, and I don't know. The third answer is effectively the same as a yes, because a compiler has to be conservative whenever it is unsure whether it is safe to tweak the ordering of instructions.

Helping the compiler to recognize parallelism is one of the basic approaches specialists take to tuning code. A slight rewording of a loop or some supplementary information supplied to the compiler can change an "I don't know" answer into an opportunity for overlapped instruction execution. To be certain, there are other facets to tuning as well, such as optimizing memory access patterns so that they best suit the hardware, or recasting an algorithm. And there is no single best approach to every problem; any tuning effort will have to be a combination of techniques.

I have intentionally avoided creating a cookbook tuning guide—so you won't have to sort through 100 cases to pick the one that best matches yours. This chapter, and the ones that follow, are written to give you an appreciation for the "why's" of performance. Of course, you will see a number of "how's" too. It is interesting material, and my hope is that arming you with knowledge will be more useful than arming you with a prescription pad.

A Few Important Concepts

Let's begin by formalizing a few terms that I've been using throughout the book. These are terms you have heard before, but a few of them are overloaded with definitions, so it is a good idea to describe them as we have been and will be using them.

Constants

Earlier I said that it is usually better to name constants than to sprinkle numbers through your code. This was in the interest of making the code clear and understandable. In fact, I claimed that the compiler will even treat local variables as constants—if they are used as constants—so you shouldn't be afraid to create them too, if they help make your code more understandable. (A constant is a single expression, of any type, the value of which is known at compile time and fixed for the life of the program.) Anyway, the point is that a constant isn't simply a numerical value typed into the program. From the compiler's point of view, it is an expression whose value is unchanging and can be determined at compile time. The code below shows a short subroutine, FOO, that modifies N.

```
SUBROUTINE FOO (N)
PARAMETER (J = 4, K = 3)
PARAMETER (L = J * K)
INTEGER M
DATA M /K/
IF (L .NE. M*2) N = M
END
```

The values for variables J, K, and L are defined in PARAMETER statements—obvious constants. But there are a lot of other candidates too. We have not specified M in a parameter statement, but its value is derived from constants, so M is also a constant. What about expressions such as K*2, M*2, and L.EQ.M*2? These, too, are made up solely from other constants. Well, as it turns out, the only thing that a sophisticated compiler won't consider as a constant is the variable being passed in, N.

It may not be obvious that M is a constant. Even though we have declared storage for it, a smart compiler will note that the value is never changed after initialization in the data statement. Expressions that are made up solely of constants evaluate to constants also, as with K*2, M*2, and L.EQ.M*2. A good compiler will replace them with their equivalent values. For example, K*2 evaluates to 6, and L.NE.M*2 evaluates to .TRUE.. After all of the constants have been *folded*, the following subroutine will be an exact replacement for the one above:

```
SUBROUTINE FOO (N)
N = 6
END
```

Constants can be any type—character, logical, etc.—though we are most interested in numerical types. You do not see the notion of a constant in arrays; that is, there is no commonly accepted concept of a "constant array." It's not that such a thing couldn't exist, it just doesn't. Even if you initialize a local array with data statements and never redefine it, the compiler will allocate storage for it and treat it like a variable that can be changed.

Scalars

Scalars are individual pieces of data. Constants, variables, and individual array elements are all scalars. When we talk about scalars, we are usually interested in some kind of numerical data. However, you should realize that logical variables and data structures are scalars as well. (A scalar is a single quantity of any data type.)

The terms scalar and scalar processor often travel together. Frankly, a scalar processor is nothing more than a general purpose computer— this is another one of those labels that was created to make room for something else—in this case, a "vector processor." It is called a scalar processor because it operates on scalars. That is, it performs computations on individual pieces of data— not whole collections of data. Consider the following vector addition.

Example 8-1: Vector Addition

```
for (i+0; i<n; i++)
    a[i] = a[i] + b[i];
```

On a scalar processor, executing this loop means taking a pair of elements, adding them together, and storing the result, incrementing an index variable, taking another pair, adding them, storing the next result, and so on. A vector processor would take all of a and all of b (or at least chunks of each) and sum them (conceptually) all at once.

Vectors and Vector Processing

A vector is a collection of scalars. Admittedly, this is a weak definition. In practice, a vector is more exclusive than just a collection of scalars. Members of the list are "peers"—all expressed in the same units and part of the same problem. This gives a vector a higher social standing than, say, any old array, where the elements could be totally unrelated. Vectors are built from elements of a single array; no one would ever call a handful of scalar variables a vector.

What people do with vectors depends on the problem they are trying to solve. Often, vectors make up the columns or rows of matrices representing a system of linear equations. Correspondingly, we generally assume that the elements of a vector are stored in a regular pattern within an array. Vectors stored this way are the easiest to handle. But a vector can also be composed of array elements that appear to be randomly organized or scattered about, where in reality their arrangement reflects some physical or computational ordering. For instance, the elements of the array A (A(1), A(2), A(3), etc.) can be considered a vector. But so can the same elements in a different sequence, such as A(3), A(1), A(2). Whether or not a collection of data is a vector depends on how the data are used, rather than how they are stored.

Numerical manipulation of vectors is called *vector arithmetic.* Primitive arithmetic vector operations take one or two vectors, or possibly a scalar, and produce either another vector or a scalar. For example, a simple vector sum takes two vectors and forms a third. It's the way elements of a vector are treated that makes them most interesting—at least from the computer's point of view. A vector sum is inherently regular: in each iteration, the same operations are repeated on different data. However, because there is a loop body, there is also an explicit order to the way the elements are added together: a[i]+b[i], followed by a[i+1]+b[i+1], etc. If we relax that restriction, so that there is no implied order, then we can express the whole loop as a single *vector operation*:

```
a <- a + b
```

When there is no implied order, you can perform iterations two at a time, three at a time, *n* at a time or even all at once, given suitable hardware. Looked at another way, it means that vector operations contain a lot of unbridled parallelism. Consider the following code:

```
      DO 10 I=1,N
         A(I) = A(I) + B(I) * C
   10 CONTINUE
```

This loop performs two vector operations: multiplication by a scalar and vector addition. Note that C is not a vector, but a scalar. Here is the same loop, expressed using our vector shorthand:

```
A <- A + B * C
```

The regularity of vector operations makes it relatively easy to build hardware that can execute them very quickly. This hardware is usually called a *vector unit* or *vector processor.* The underlying architecture may differ between vendors, but on the outside, a vector unit is a box that can perform idempotent operations on whole vectors.

As you'd expect, vector hardware provides very high throughput. However, there is always some minimum startup time associated with using one. In practice, this places a lower limit on the length, or number of elements, of vectors you would want to process with the vector unit. This lower limit is usually between 16 and 64 elements. Below that limit, a scalar unit will give you better performance. At the other extreme, very long vectors do quite well. The longer the vector, the less significant the startup cost and the higher the average throughput.

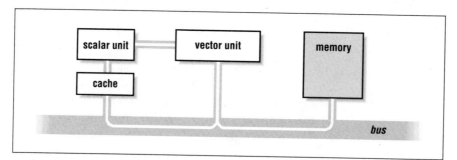

Figure 8-1: Vector Computer

If you strap a vector and scalar unit together as in Figure 8-1, you will then have a machine that can execute either kind of instruction, and is extremely good at running vector code. Short vector operations will be steered to run on the scalar unit; longer operations will be steered towards the vector unit; and operations that don't involve vectors at all will run exclusively on the scalar unit. This is essentially the description of a *vector supercomputer*, like the Cray C90. Each of its 16 CPUs is divided into separate portions devoted to vector and scalar processing. There are also a number of *minisupercomputer* class machines with the same general architecture, such as the Convex C3.* The extent to which a program can be run on the vector processor is the extent to which it is vectorizable. Of course, not all code is made up of vector operations. And not all vector arithmetic is vectorizable; some constructs don't allow vectorization. However, most scientific codes contain some vectorizable portions. Naturally, you expect good performance when the whole program (or most of it) runs on the vector processor. However, any time spent running on the scalar processor can loom large in the foreground. Contrasted with vector processing, scalar processing is considerably slower, which makes trying to vectorize a particular loop or code fragment an all or nothing experience.

---

*Parallel machines (you have probably heard the term "massively parallel") can also exploit the regularity of vector operations. They get their speed by passing portions of vector operations out to many processors to be run in parallel. For instance, processor 1 may run the first 10 iterations, processor 2 will run the second 10, etc. We will look at these machines in detail near the end of the book.

Vector processing has a rich past. For the last 30 years, supercomputing has been essentially synonymous with vector computing.* Accordingly, we owe something to the users and vendors of vector computers for what we know about parallel processing. In some respects, performance RISC workstations represent a new start because they are not direct descendents of vector computers. They don't (generally) have hardware specifically dedicated to vector processing, and they don't have the memory systems of real vector machines. But the parallelism found in vector operations can be exploited by newer RISC processors. Vector operations are compiled into long sequences of independent scalar operations that can be pipelined. However, there are some things you would want to change for the sake of a RISC workstation. As we go along I'll be pointing out the differences.

Dependencies

Imagine a symphony orchestra where each musician plays without regard to the conductor or the other musicians. At the first tap of the conductor's baton, each musician goes through all of his or her sheet music. Some finish far ahead of others, leave the stage, and go home. The cacophony wouldn't resemble music (come to think of it, it would resemble experimental jazz) because it would be totally uncoordinated. Of course this isn't how music is played. A computer program, like a musical piece, is woven on a fabric that unfolds in time (though perhaps woven more loosely). Certain things must happen before or along with others, and there is a rate to the whole process.

With computer programs, whenever event **A** must occur before event **B** can, we say that **B** is *dependent* on **A**. We call the relationship between them a *dependency*. Sometimes dependencies exist because of calculations or memory operations; we call these *data dependencies*. Other times, we are waiting for a branch or do-loop exit to take place; this is called a *control dependency*. Each is present in every program to varying degrees. The goal is to eliminate as many as possible. Rearranging a program so that two chunks of the computation are less dependent exposes *parallelism*, or opportunities to do several things at once.

---

*Though in recent years, "supercomputing" has come to include parallel computers too. In fact, all major vector computer manufacturers have announced plans to build parallel machines.

Data Dependencies

A calculation that is in some way bound to a previous calculation is said to be *data dependent* upon that calculation. In the code below, the value of B is data dependent on the value of A. That's because you can't calculate B until the value of A is available.

```
A = X + Y + COS(Z)
B = A * C
```

This dependency is easy to recognize and easy to eliminate, but others are not so simple. There may be unknown relationships between variables, such as can occur with array references located at the center of a loop nest. Even determining whether a dependency exists can be a challenge. At other times, you must be careful not to rewrite a variable with a new value before every other computation has finished using the old value. We can group all data dependencies into three separate categories:

- Flow Dependencies
- Anti-Dependencies
- Output Dependencies

There wouldn't be any reason to talk about these categories at all if computers still performed operations one after another, the way programs are coded. But parallel architectures exploit opportunities to overlap execution, and with that comes the danger of doing things in the wrong order. You have to be sure that a given calculation isn't performed out of turn. That is, you have to be sure that a data dependency is honored, otherwise the results will be incorrect. The notion of data dependence is particularly important when we look at loops, the hub of activity inside numerical applications. Loops often contain vector operations, and often those operations contain dependencies that span from one iteration to another, so eliminating a dependency within a loop often has a big pay-back.

The first step toward eliminating dependencies in loops is recognizing whether they exist. Some constructs are completely independent, right out of the box. The question we want to ask is "can two different iterations execute at the same time, or is there a data dependency between them?" Consider the following vector addition:

```
      DO 10 I=1,N
         A(I) = A(I) + B(I)
   10    CONTINUE
```

For any two values of I and K, can I calculate the value of A(I) and A(K) at the same time? Below, I have rewritten several iterations of the previous loop, so they can be executed together:

```
A(I)   = A(I)   + B(I)
A(I+1) = A(I+1) + B(I+1)
A(I+2) = A(I+2) + B(I+2)
```

You can see that none of the results are used as an operand for another calculation. For instance, the calculation for A(I+1) can occur at the same time as the calculation for A(I) because the calculations are independent; you don't need the results of the first to determine the second. In fact, mixing up the order of the calculations will not change the results in the least. Relaxing the serial order imposed on these calculations makes it possible to execute this loop very quickly on parallel hardware, such as a vector unit.

Flow dependencies

For comparison, look at the next code fragment:

```
      DO 10 I=2,N
         A(I) = A(I-1) + B(I)
10    CONTINUE
```

This loop has the regularity of the previous example, but one of the subscripts is changed. Again, it is useful to pull the loop apart and look at several iterations together:

```
A(I)   = A(I-1) + B(I)
A(I+1) = A(I)   + B(I+1)
A(I+2) = A(I+1) + B(I+2)
```

In this case, there is a dependency problem. The value of A(I+1) depends on the value of A(I), the value of A(I+2) depends on A(I+1), and so on; every iteration depends on the result of a previous one. Dependencies that extend back to a previous calculation and perhaps a previous iteration (like this one), are called *flow dependencies* or *backward dependencies*. You often see such dependencies in applications that perform Gaussian elimination on certain type of matrices, or numerical solutions to systems of differential equations. However, it is impossible to run such a loop in parallel (as written); the processor must wait for intermediate results before it can proceed.

In some cases, flow dependencies are impossible to fix; calculations are so dependent upon one another that we have no choice but to wait for previous ones to complete. Other times, dependencies are a function of the way the calculations are expressed. For instance, the loop above can be changed to reduce the dependency. By replicating some of the arithmetic, we can make it so that the second and third iterations depend on the first, but not on one another. The operation count goes up—we have an extra addition that we didn't have before—but we have reduced the dependency between iterations:

```
DO 10 I=2,N,2
   A(I)   = A(I-1) + B(I)
   A(I+1) = A(I-1) + B(I) + B(I+1)
10 CONTINUE
```

The speedup on a workstation won't be great (and some machines will run the recast loop more slowly). However, some parallel computers can trade-off additional calculations for reduced dependency and chalk up a big win.

Anti-dependencies

A fundamentally different kind of dependency exists when all calculations using a particular variable must be finished before the variable gets redefined. For instance, if you calculated a value for a variable X, used it to define another variable Y, and then redefined X, you would want to be sure to use the first definition of X to define Y (got that?).

It's easier to see with an example. In the following code fragment, the problem isn't much of a challenge as long as you perform all the calculations in the right order:

```
X = A/B
Y = X + 2.0
X = D - E
```

But you don't want to be restricted to sequential calculations if you can avoid it, because this limits parallelism. You would rather be free to overlap execution of the statements, if possible, but re-use of the variable X stands in your way. This is another form of data dependency known as an *anti-dependency*. Unlike the flow dependency above, we are not waiting for the output of a previous calculation, rather we are waiting for a previous calculation to finish so we can reuse the variable. A simple fix, and one that your compiler should be capable of, is to create a new, temporary variable to be used instead of X in the first two statements, as in the following code, which eliminates the anti-dependency completely:

```
Xtemp = A/B
Y = Xtemp + 2.0
X = D - E
```

It's a different story when the anti-dependency involves vectors, as in the code below:

```
      DO 10 I=1,N
         A(I)    = B(I) * E
         B(I)    = A(I+2) * C
 10   CONTINUE
```

The kind of regularity you want for a vector processor is present, except that there is an anti-dependency between the variable A(I) and the variable A(I+2). That is, you must be sure that the instruction that uses A(I+2) does so before the previous one redefines it. Clearly, this is not a problem if the loop is executed serially, but remember, we are looking for opportunities to overlap instructions. Again, it helps to pull the loop apart and look at several iterations together. First, I will illustrate how a vector processor views this code. I've recast the loop by making many copies of the first statement, followed by copies of the second.

```
A(I)   = B(I)   * E
A(I+1) = B(I+1) * E
A(I+2) = B(I+2) * E
 . . .
B(I)   = A(I+2) * C   ← assignment makes use of the new
B(I+1) = A(I+3) * C        value of A(I+2)  incorrect.
B(I+2) = A(I+4) * C
```

Vector processors work by taking a whole vector operation and logically executing it as one instruction. That is, the vector processor wants to execute one instruction to compute all of the As, followed by another instruction to compute the Bs. This poses a problem. The reference to A(I+2) needs to access an "old" value, rather than one of the new ones being calculated. If you perform all of the first statement, followed by all of the second statement, the answer will be wrong. This is not to say that there aren't ways to recast the loop for use with a vector processor. Vectorizing compilers have several options. New values for A could go to a temporary vector, to be stored back later. Or the statements in the loop could be reversed, and B could go to temporary storage. A clever compiler should be able to come up with a workable solution. Now, let's look at this loop as a RISC processor would see it:

```
A(I)   = B(I)   * E
B(I)   = A(I+2) * C
A(I+1) = B(I+1) * E
B(I+1) = A(I+3) * C
A(I+2) = B(I+2) * E
B(I+2) = A(I+4) * C
 . . .
```

The statements are interleaved, as if the loop were unrolled. Arranging calculations this way is not an option that is open to a vector processor. By carefully selecting when to perform each operation, a RISC compiler can generate efficient code without violating the dependency.

Output dependencies

The third class of data dependencies, *output dependencies*, is of particular interest to users of parallel computers, particularly multiprocessors. Output dependencies involve getting the right values to the right variables when all calculations have been completed. For instance, if there are assignments to the variable K in several places, for several purposes, a sophisticated compiler may determine that it is more efficient to make several copies of K, rather than work with just one. Additionally, the calculations may be overlapped or executed in a different order than they are written. Several different values for K may be generated along the way. When the dust settles, the value that should get stored away is the last one calculated, according to the original source program. Otherwise, an output dependency will be violated. The loop below assigns new values to two elements of the vector A with each iteration:

```
      DO 10 I=1,N
         A(I)   = C(I) * 2.
         A(I+2) = D(I) + E
 10   CONTINUE
```

As always, we won't have any problems if we execute the code sequentially. But if several iterations are performed together, and statements are reordered, then incorrect values can be assigned to the last elements of A. For example, in the naive vectorized equivalent below, A(I+2) takes the wrong value because the assignments occur out of order:

```
      ...
      A(I)   = C(I)   * 2.
      A(I+1) = C(I+1) * 2.
      A(I+2) = C(I+2) * 2.
      ...
      A(I+2) = D(I)   + E      ← output dependency violated
      A(I+3) = D(I+1) + E
      A(I+4) = D(I+2) + E
      ...
```

Whether or not you have to worry about output dependencies depends on whether you are actually parallelizing the code. Your compiler will be conscious of the danger, and will be able to generate legal code—and possibly even fast code, if it's clever enough. But output dependencies occasionally become a problem for programmers. These situations usually arise when you are dividing a program for parallel execution on a multiprocessor, a topic I discuss later in the book.

Control Dependencies

Just as variable assignments can depend on other assignments, a variable's value can also depend on the *flow of control* within the program. For instance, an assignment within an if-statement can only occur if the conditional evaluates to *true*. The same can be said of an assignment within a loop. If the loop is never entered, then no statements inside the loop will be executed.

When calculations occur as a consequence of the flow of control, we say there exists a *control dependency*, as in the code below. The assignment located inside the block-if may or may not be executed, depending on the outcome of the test I .EQ. 10. In other words, the value of A depends on the flow of control in the code around it.

```
IF (I .EQ. 10) THEN
  A = B * C
ENDIF
```

Again, this may sound to you like a concern for compiler designers, not programmers, and that's mostly true. But there are times when you might want to move control-dependent instructions around to get expensive calculations out of the way (provided your compiler isn't smart enough to do it for you). For example, say that Figure 8-2 represents a little section of your program.

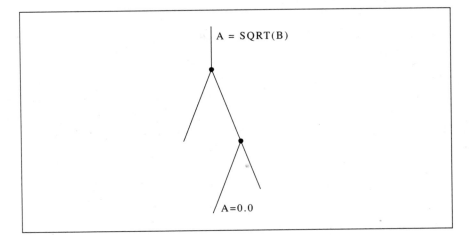

A = SQRT(B)

A=0.0

Figure 8-2: A little section of your program

Flow of control enters at the top and goes through two branch decisions. Furthermore, say that there is a square root operation at the entry point, and that the flow of control almost always goes from the top, down to the leg containing the statement A=0.0. This means that the results of the calculation A=SQRT(B) are almost always discarded because A gets a new value of 0.0 each time through. A square root operation is always "expensive" because it takes a lot of time to execute. The trouble is that you can't just get rid of it; occasionally it is needed. However, you could move it out of the way, and continue to observe the control dependencies by making two copies of the square root operation along the less traveled branches, as shown in Figure 8-3.

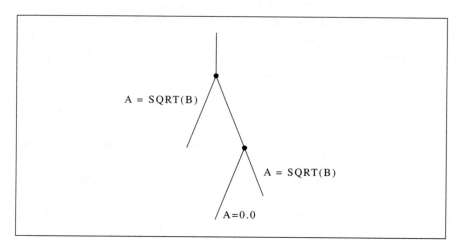

Figure 8-3: Expensive operation moved so that it's rarely executed

This way the SQRT would only execute along those paths where it was actually needed.

This kind of instruction scheduling will be appearing in compilers (and even hardware) more and more as time goes on. A variation on this technique is to calculate results that might be needed at times when there is a gap in the instruction stream (because of dependencies), thus using some spare cycles that might otherwise go wasted.

Ambiguous References

Every dependency we have looked at so far has been clear cut—you could see exactly what you were dealing with by looking at the source. But other times, describing a dependency isn't so easy. Recall this loop from the "Anti-Dependencies" section, earlier in this chapter:

```
      DO 10 I=1,N
        A(I)   = B(I) * E
        B(I)   = A(I+2) * C
  10    CONTINUE
```

Because each variable reference is solely a function of the index, I, it is clear what kind of dependency we are dealing with. Furthermore, we can describe how far apart (in iterations) a variable reference is from its definition. This is called the *dependency distance*. A negative value represents a flow dependency; a positive value means there is an anti-dependency. A value of zero says that no dependency exists between the reference and the definition. In this loop, the dependency distance for A is +2 iterations.

However, array subscripts may be functions of other variables besides the loop index. It may be difficult to tell the distance between the use and definition of a particular element. It may even be impossible to tell whether the dependency is a flow dependency or an anti-dependency, or whether a dependency exists at all. Consequently, it may be impossible to determine if it is safe to overlap execution of different statements, as in the following loop:

```
      DO 10 I=1,N
        A(I)   = B(I) * E
        B(I)   = A(I+K) * C    ← K unknown
  10    CONTINUE
```

If the loop made use of A(I+K), where the value of K was unknown, then we wouldn't be able to tell (at least by looking at the code) anything about the kind of dependency we might be facing.

Consider the effect that *ambiguous references*, like A(I+K), have on vector operations. Each statement in the previous loop is vectorizable by itself, but because of the ambiguous memory references, we can't be sure whether they are vectorizable together—at least not without more information. It may be that they are actually two independent calculations that the author whimsically decided to throw into a single loop. But when they appear together, the compiler has to treat them conservatively—as if they were inter-related. This has a big effect on performance. If the compiler has to assume that consecutive memory references may ultimately access the same location, the instructions involved *cannot* be overlapped.*

A similar situation occurs when we use indirectly addressed vectors. The loop below only contains a single statement, but you cannot be sure that any iteration is independent of the last because you can't tell what the pattern of subscripts will be:

```
      DO 10 I=1,N
         A(K(I)) = A(K(I)) + B(J(I)) * C
   10    CONTINUE
```

For instance, what if all of the values for K(I) were the same? This would cause the same element of the array A to be re-referenced with each iteration! That may seem ridiculous to you, but the compiler can't tell.

With code like this, it's common for every value of K(I) to be unique. This is called a *permutation*. If you can tell a compiler that it is dealing with a permutation, the penalty is lessened in some cases. Even so, there is insult being added to injury. Indirect references require more memory activity than direct references, and this will slow you down. We will visit this subject again when we look at memory reference tuning, a couple of chapters ahead.

Closing Notes

You already knew that there was a limit to the amount of parallelism in any given program. Now you know why. Clearly, if a program had no dependencies, you could execute the whole thing at once, given suitable hardware. But programs aren't infinitely parallel; they are often hardly parallel at all. This is because they contain dependencies of the types we saw above. In the coming chapters we'll call on this information repeatedly. We will see ways to restructure loops and branches so that dependencies are decreased and parallelism is increased.

Exercises

1. Identify the dependencies (if there are any) in following loops. Can you think of ways to organize each loop for more parallelism?

---

*In Chapter 2, I described a piece of hardware called a stunt box. It can lower the performance penalty of ambiguous references for those machines that have one.

(a)
```
        DO 10 I=1,N-2
          A(I+2) = A(I) + 1.
     10 CONTINUE
```

(b)
```
        DO 10 I=1,N-1,2
          A(I+1) = A(I) + 1.
     10 CONTINUE
```

(c)
```
        DO 10 I=2,N
          A(I) = A(I-1) * 2.
          B = A(I-1)
     10 CONTINUE
```

(d)
```
        DO 10 I=1,N
          IF(N .GT. M)
            A(I) = 1.
     10 CONTINUE
```

(e)
```
        DO 10 I=1,N
          A(I,J) = A(I,K) + B
     10 CONTINUE
```

(f)
```
        DO 10 I=1,N-1
          A(I+1,J) = A(I,K) + B
     10 CONTINUE
```

(g)
```
        for (i=0; i<n; i++)
          a[i] = b[i];
```

2. Imagine that you are a vectorizing compiler, trying to generate code for the loop below. Why are references to A a challenge? Why would it help to know that K is equal to zero? Explain how you could partially vectorize the statements involving A if you knew that K had an absolute value of at least 8?

```
        DO 10 I=1,N
          E(I,M) = E(I-1,M+1) - 1.0
          B(I) = A(I+K) * C
          A(I) = D(I) * 2.0
     10 CONTINUE
```

3. The following three statements contain a flow dependency, an anti-dependency and an output dependency. Can you identify each? Given that you are allowed to reorder the statements, can you find a permutation that produces the same values for the variables C and B? Show how

you can reduce the dependencies by combining or rearranging calculations, and using temporary variables.

```
B = A + C
B = C + D
C = B + D
```

9

Eliminating Clutter

...at code from the compiler's point of view, and before that, ...ne to find the trouble spots. It's good information, but if you ...satisfied with a code's performance, you might still be wondering what to do about it. Ultimately, you want to make changes that expose parallelism, provided of course that your program has some parallelism in it. But before that, you want to remove the clutter that slows a program down. Clutter is anything that contributes to the run time, without contributing to the answer. It comes in two forms:

Things that contribute to overhead
> Subroutine calls, indirect memory references, tests within loops, wordy tests, type conversions, variables preserved unnecessarily

Things that restrict parallelism
> Subroutine calls, indirect memory references, tests within loops, ambiguous pointers

It's not a mistake that some of the same items appear in both lists. Subroutine calls or if-statements within loops can both bite and scratch you by taking too much time and by creating "fences" to parallelism—places in the program where instructions that appear before can't be safely intermixed with instructions that appear after, at least not without a great degree of care. The goal of this chapter is to show you how to eliminate clutter, so we can restructure what's left over for the most parallelism. I'll save a few specific topics that might fit here, especially those regarding memory references, for later chapters where they are treated as subjects by themselves.

Before we start, let me remind you: as you look for ways to improve what you have, keep your eyes and mind open to the possibility that there might be a fundamentally better way to do something—a more efficient sorting technique, random number generator, or solver. A different algorithm may buy you far more speed than tuning. Algorithms are beyond the scope of this book, but what we are discussing here should help you recognize "good" code, or help you to code a new algorithm to get the best performance.

Subroutine Calls

A typical big company is full of frightening examples of overhead. Say that your department has prepared a stack of paperwork to be completed by another department. What do you have to do to transfer that work? First, you have to be sure that your portion is completed; you can't ask them to take over if the materials they need aren't ready. Next, you need to package the materials—data, forms, charge numbers, and the like. And finally comes the official transfer. Upon receiving what you sent, the other department has to unpack it, do their job, repackage it, and send it back.

A lot of time gets wasted moving work between departments. Of course, if the overhead is minimal compared to the amount of useful work being done, it won't be that big a deal. But it might be more efficient for small jobs to stay within one department. The same is true of subroutine and function calls. If you only enter and exit modules once in a relative while, then the overhead of saving registers and preparing argument lists won't be significant. However, if you are repeatedly calling a few small subroutines, the overhead can buoy them to the top of the profile. It might be better if the work stayed where it was, in the calling routine.

Additionally, subroutine calls inhibit parallelism. Given the right opportunity, you'd like your compiler to have the freedom to intermix instructions that are not dependent upon each other. These could be found on either side of a subroutine call, in the caller and callee. But the opportunity is lost because the compiler can't peer into subroutine and function calls. Instructions that might overlap very nicely have to stay on their respective sides of the fence.

It will help if I illustrate the challenge that subroutine boundaries present with an exaggerated example. The following loop is very vectorizable, which means it will run very well on a parallel RISC processor:

```
      DO 10 I=1,N
        A(I) = A(I) + B(I) * C
 10    CONTINUE
```

tion per clock cycle. If there are few floating point operations to perform between subroutine calls, then the time spent winding-up and winding-down pipelines will figure prominently.

Last, subroutine and function calls complicate the compiler's ability to efficiently manage COMMON and external variables. The compiler uses registers to hold the "live" values of many variables. When you make a call, the compiler cannot tell whether the subroutine will be changing variables that are declared as external or COMMON. Therefore, it's forced to store any modified external or COMMON variables back into memory so that the callee can find them. Likewise, after the call has returned, the same variables have to be reloaded into registers because the compiler can no longer trust the old, register-resident copies. The penalty for saving and restoring variables can be substantial, especially if you are using lots of them. It can also be unwarranted if variables that probably ought to be local are specified as external or COMMON, as in the following code:

```
      COMMON /USELESS/ K
      DO 10 K=1,1000
        IF (K .EQ. 1) CALL AUX
10    CONTINUE
```

In this example, K has been declared as a COMMON variable. It is only used as a do-loop counter, so there really is no reason for it to be anything but local. However, because it is in a COMMON block, the call to AUX forces the compiler to store and reload K each iteration. This is because the side effects of the call are unknown.

Macros are little procedures that are substituted inline at compile time. Unlike subroutines or functions, which are included once during the link, macros are replicated every place they are used. When the compiler makes its first pass through your program, it looks for patterns that match previous macro definitions and expands them inline. No arguments are passed. In fact, in later stages the compiler sees an expanded macro as source code.

Macros are part of both C and FORTRAN (although the FORTRAN notion of a macro, the *statement function*, is reviled by the FORTRAN community, and won't survive much longer).* For C programs, macros are created with a #define construct.

Example 9-1: Macro definition and use

```
#define average(x,y) ((x+y)/2)
main ()
{
    float q = 100, p = 50;
    float a;
    a = average(p,q);
    printf ("%f\n",a);
}
```

The first compilation step for a C program is a pass through the C preprocessor, *cpp*. This happens automatically when you invoke the compiler.

---

*The statement function has been eliminated in Fortran 90.

```
        a = ((p+q)/2);
```

You have to be careful how you use the macro because it literally replaces
the pattern located by *cpp*. For instance, if the macro definition said:

```
#define multiply(a,b) (a*b)
```

and you invoked it as

```
c = multiply(x+t,y+v);
```

the resulting expansion would be x+t*y+v—probably not what you
intended.

If you are a C programmer you may be using macros without being conscious of it. Many C header files (.*h*) contain macro definitions. In fact,
some "standard" C library functions are really defined as macros in the
header files. For instance, the function *getchar* can be linked in when you
build your program. However, if you have a statement:

```
#include <stdio.h>
```

in your file, *getchar* will be replaced with a macro definition at compile
time, replacing the C library function.

You can make *cpp* macros work for FORTRAN programs too.* For example,
a FORTRAN version of the C program above might look like this:

```
#define AVERAG(X,Y) ((X+Y)/2)
C
      PROGRAM MAIN
      REAL A,P,Q
      DATA P,Q /50.,100./
      A = AVERAG(P,Q)
      WRITE (*,*) A
      END
```

Without a little preparation, the #define statement will be rejected by the
FORTRAN compiler. The program first has to be preprocessed through *cpp*
to replace the use of AVERAG with its macro definition. It makes compilation a two-step procedure, but that shouldn't be too much of a burden,
especially if you are building your programs under the control of the *make*

---

*Some programmers use the *m4* preprocessor for FORTRAN.

utility. I would also suggest that you store FORTRAN programs containing *cpp* directives under *filename.F* to distinguish them from unadorned FORTRAN. Just be sure that you make your changes only to the *.F* files, and not to the output from *cpp*. This is how you would preprocess FORTRAN *.F* files by hand:

```
% /lib/cpp -P < average.F > average.f
% f77 average.f -c
```

The FORTRAN compiler never sees the original code. Instead, the macro definition is substituted inline as if you had typed it yourself:

```
C
        PROGRAM MAIN
        REAL A,P,Q
        DATA P,Q /50.,100./
        A = ((P+Q)/2)
        WRITE (*,*) A
        END
```

By the way, some FORTRAN compilers recognize the *.F* extension already, making the two step process unnecessary. If the compiler sees the *.F* extension it will invoke *cpp* automatically, compile the output and throw away the intermediate *.f* file. Try compiling a *.F* on your computer to see if it works.

Also, be aware that macro expansions may make source lines extend past column 72, which will probably make your FORTRAN compiler complain (or worse: it might pass unnoticed). Many FORTRAN compilers support *tab extended* source lines (taken from VAX FORTRAN): if a tab character appears in column 1, then the source line can extend out to column 256. Although it may be inviting to extend source lines with a tab character, I suggest that you avoid it. Tab extended source lines are not portable to all FORTRAN compilers.

Procedure Inlining

Macro definitions tend to be pretty short, usually just a single statement. Sometimes you have slightly longer (but not too long) bits of code that might also benefit from being copied inline, rather than called as a subroutine or function. Again, the reason for doing this is to eliminate procedure call overhead and expose parallelism. If your compiler is capable of *inlining* subroutine and function definitions into the modules that call them, then you have a very natural, very portable way to write modular code without suffering the cost of subroutine calls.

line

- Putting inlining directives into the source program
- Letting the compiler inline automatically (if it can)

The directives and compile line options are not standard, so you will have to check with your compiler documentation. Unfortunately, you may learn that there is no such feature ("yet", always yet), or that it's an expensive extra. The third form of inlining in the list, automatic, is available from just a few vendors. Automatic inlining depends on a sophisticated compiler that can view the definitions of several modules at once.

There are some words of caution with regard to procedure inlining. You can easily do too much of it. If everything and anything is ingested into the body of its parents, the resulting executable may be so obese that it will repeatedly spill out of the instruction cache and become a net performance loss. My advice is that you use the caller/callee information that profilers give you and make some intelligent decisions about inlining, rather than trying to inline every subroutine available. Again, small routines that are called often are generally the best candidates for inlining.

Branches

It takes me about a week to make a decision, so I can't fault a computer if it takes a few tens of nanoseconds. However, if an if-statement appears in some heavily traveled section of the code, you might get tired of the delay. There are two basic approaches to reducing the impact of branches:

- Streamline them.
- Move them out to the computational suburbs. Particularly, get them out of loops.

In this section I'll show you some easy ways to reorganize conditionals so that they execute more quickly.

Wordy Conditionals

A wordy conditional is a compound logical expression that has so many terms that deciding whether the outcome will be true or false is a fair piece of work by itself. Depending on the frequency with which it gets executed, it may be worth reorganizing such a conditional for speed.

Conditionals are evaluated according to precedence rules (&& is higher than
| |, for instance), and from left to right. With most FORTRAN compilers, and
all C compilers, evaluation stops as soon as the machine has determined
that the conditional is true (or false). That makes sense. There is no reason
to evaluate the rest of statement if you already know the outcome. For illustration, here's a very wordy conditional:

```
    . . .
    if (((~i & j) && a <= 0. && m == -1) || k == 0) {
    . . .
```

If all that stuff within the lefthand expression is true *or* k==0, the outcome
will be true. If it turns out that k is usually equal to zero, it will be more
efficient to rearrange the test so that k==0 is evaluated first. When k==0,
you will save the time spent evaluating the remaining tests. Here's the
same statement, rearranged for better performance:

```
    . . .
    if (k == 0 || ((~i & j) && a <= 0. && m == -1)) {
    . . .
```

For logical *and*-clauses, you will want to arrange it so that the condition
that is most likely to fail is farthest to the left. Again, this will get you out of
the if-statement as early as possible. Your compiler may be smart enough
to rearrange the conditional by itself, but if you order it manually you can
be sure that the code will perform well on any machine, even ones that
don't have smart compilers.

Redundant Tests

Another technique for streamlining branches is to avoid checking for conditions you know can't be true. For instance, the following conditionals
appear back-to-back, checking for different cases that necessarily exclude
one another:

```
        if (c == 'A')
          FoundA = TRUE;
        if (c == 'F')
          FoundF = TRUE;
        if (c == 'Q')
          FoundQ = TRUE;
        . . .
```

Obviously, if c=='A' is true then c=='F' can't be true. You know that,
but still the compiler will test for the possibility that c equals 'f' and 'Q',
even after finding that c equals 'A'. You can avoid redundant tests by
using a logical construct that discriminates among a number of choices, like

```
      case 'A':
         FoundA = TRUE;
         break;
      case 'F':
         FoundF = TRUE;
         break;
      case 'Q':
         FoundQ = TRUE;
         break;
      . . .
```

Branches Within Loops

Numerical codes usually spend most of their time in loops, so you don't want anything inside a loop that doesn't have to be there, especially an if-statement. Not only do if-statements gum up the works with extra instructions, they add control dependencies and, as you'll recall, dependencies reduce parallelism. Of course, you can't always avoid conditionals. Sometimes, though, people place them in loops to process events that could have been handled outside, or even ignored.

To take you back a few years, the following code shows a loop with a test for a value close to zero:

```
         PARAMETER (SMALL = 1.E-20)
         DO 10 I=1,N
            IF (ABS(A(I)) .GE. SMALL) THEN
               B(I) = B(I) + A(I) * C
            ENDIF
10       CONTINUE
```

The idea was that if the multiplier, A(I), were reasonably small there would be no reason to perform the math in the center of the loop. Because floating point operations weren't pipelined on many machines, a comparison and a branch was cheaper—the test would save time. On a home computer a comparison and branch is probably still a savings.* But on other architectures it will cost a lot less to just perform the math and skip the test. Eliminating the branch eliminates a control dependency and allows the compiler to pipeline more arithmetic operations. Of course, the

---

*An RS/6000 runs four times faster without the test. A 386 without a 387 (math coprocessor) runs slower without the test.

answer could change slightly if the test is eliminated. It then becomes a question of whether the difference is significant. Here's another example where a branch isn't necessary. The loop finds the absolute value of each element in a vector:

```
      DO 10 I=1,N
         IF (A(I) .LT. 0.) A(I) = -A(I)
   10    CONTINUE
```

But why perform the test at all? On most machines, it will be quicker to perform the `abs()` operation on every element of the vector:

```
#define ABS(Q) (Q < 0. ? -Q : Q)
  ...
  for (i=0; i<n; i++)
    a[i] = ABS(a[i]);
```

I do have to give you a warning though: If you are coding in C, the absolute value, `fabs()`, is a subroutine call. In this particular case you are better off leaving the conditional in the loop.*

When you can't always throw out the conditional, there are often things you can do for damage control. First, we have to learn to recognize which conditionals within loops can be restructured and which cannot. Conditionals in loops fall into four categories:

- Loop Invariant
- Loop Index Dependent
- Independent Loop Conditionals
- Dependent Loop Conditionals

The last two types look hopeless when you see them on paper. I am forcing the distinction because you can do more with conditionals in the third category than in the fourth. Let's look at all four types in turn.

Loop Invariant Conditionals

The following loop contains an *invariant* test:

```
      DO 10 I=1,K
         IF (N .EQ. 0) THEN
            A(I) = A(I) + B(I) * C
```

---

*The machine representation of a floating point number starts with a *sign bit*. If the bit is "0" then the number is positive. If it is "1" then the number is negative. The fastest absolute value function is one that merely "ands" out the sign bit. See macros in */usr/include/macros.h* and */usr/include/math.h*.

Invariant means that the outcome will always be the same. Regardless of what happens to the variables **A**, **B**, **C** and **I**, the value of N will not change, so neither will the outcome of the test.

You can recast the loop by making the test outside and replicating the loop body twice—once for when the test is true, and once for when it is false, as in the following example:

```
      IF (N .EQ. 0) THEN
         DO 10 I=1,K
            A(I) = A(I) + B(I) * C
10       CONTINUE
      ELSE
         DO 11 I=1,K
            A(I) = 0
11       CONTINUE
      ENDIF
```

The effect on the run time will be dramatic. Not only have we eliminated N-1 copies of the test, we have also assured that the computations in the middle of the loop are not control dependent on the if-statement, and are therefore much easier for the compiler to pipeline.

I remember helping someone optimize a program with loops containing similar conditionals. They were checking to see whether debug output should be printed each iteration inside an otherwise vectorizable loop. I can't fault the person for not realizing how much this slowed his program down. Performance wasn't important at the time. He was just trying to get the code to produce good answers. But later on, when performance mattered, we were able to speed up the program by a factor of 100 by cleaning up invariant conditionals.

Loop Index Dependent Conditionals

For *loop index dependent* conditionals, the test is true for certain ranges of the loop index variables. It isn't always true or always false, like the conditionals we just looked at, but it does change with a predictable pattern, and one that we can use to our advantage. The following loop has two index variables, I and J.

```
        DO 10 I=1,N
          DO 20 J=1,N
            IF (J .LT. I)
              A(J,I) = A(J,I) + B(J,I) * C
            ELSE
              A(J,I) = 0.0
            ENDIF
  20      CONTINUE
  10    CONTINUE
```

Notice how the if-statement partitions the iterations into distinct sets: those for which it is true and those for which it is false. You can take advantage of the predictability of the test to restructure the loop into several loops—each custom made for a different partition:

```
        DO 10 I=1,N
          DO 20 J=1,I-1
            A(J,I) = A(J,I) + B(J,I) * C
  20      CONTINUE
          DO 30 J=I,N
            A(J,I) = 0.0
  30      CONTINUE
  10    CONTINUE
```

The new version will almost always be faster. A possible exception is when N is a small value, like 3, in which case we will have created more clutter. But then, the loop probably has such a small impact on the total run time that it won't matter which way it is coded.

Independent Loop Conditionals

It would be nice if you could optimize every loop by partitioning it. But more often than not, the conditional doesn't directly depend on the value of the index variables. Although an index variable may be involved in addressing a vector, it doesn't create a recognizable pattern in advance—at least not one you can see when you are writing the program. Here's such a loop:

```
        DO 10 I=1,N
          DO 10 J=1,N
            IF (B(J,I) .GT. 1.0)
     +        A(J,I) = A(J,I) + B(J,I) * C
  10    CONTINUE
```

So, what can you do about loops like these? Well, the first thing to look for is independence *between* iterations. Even though the if-statement is a rock

```
      DO 10 I=1,N
        DO 10 J=1,N,2
          IF (B(J,I) .GT. 1.0)
     +       A(J,I)   =    A(J,I)    + B(J,I)    * C
          IF (B(J+1,I) .GT. 1.0)
     +       A(J+1,I) = A(J+1,I) + B(J+1,I) * C
   10    CONTINUE
```

When unrolled, some of the math can be pipelined while the conditionals are evaluated. Unrolling also reduces the loop overhead, so you can expect an added speedup. Am I recommending that you unroll the loops by hand? Perhaps, although I'll leave that for the next chapter.

On some architectures it is even possible to calculate values for several iterations speculatively, just in case the tests are true. More floating point operations are actually performed, but because they are pipelined, and because a good portion of them will be needed, it can be a performance win. This is particularly true of vector machines. Based on a vector of "trues" and "falses" calculated by vectorizing the test for **B .GT. 1.0**, new values of **A** can be calculated and conditionally assigned.

Dependent Loop Conditionals

As with any loop, loops with if-statements can have dependencies between iterations, making them difficult to optimize. For instance, the following loop has an if-statement with built-in scalar recursion:

```
      DO 10 I=1,N
        IF (X .LT. A(I)) X = X + B(I)*2.
   10    CONTINUE
```

You can't know which way the branch will go for the next iteration until you are done with the current one. To recognize the recursion, try to unroll the loop slightly. If you can't start the second test until the first has finished, you have a dependent loop conditional. What can you do about loops like this? As with all recursive loops, you could manipulate the body

---

*Of course, if *n* is an odd number, the above loop is going to get me into trouble. I'll talk about how to precondition loops in the next chapter.

algebraically to increase the pool of operations that can be overlapped. But let me show you the resulting disaster:

```
     DO 10 I=1,N,2
        IF (X .LT. A(I)) THEN
           IF (X + B(I)*2 .LT. A(I+1)) THEN
              X = X+(B(I) + B(I+1))*2
           ELSE
              X = X + B(I)*2
           ENDIF
        ELSE
           IF (X .LT. A(I+1)) THEN
              X = X + B(I+1)*2
           ENDIF
        ENDIF
  10    CONTINUE
```

It's a good thing that this chapter is about eliminating clutter, not creating it. (That's the next chapter.) Although there is opportunity for increased instruction overlap, this new loop is so busy with new calculations it's almost guaranteed to run more slowly. When you encounter a loop with a branch and dependencies between iterations my advice is to suffer and be happy about it.

Reductions

Keep an eye out for loops in which the if-statement is performing a *max* or *min* function on a vector. This is a *vector reduction*, so called because it reduces a vector to a scalar result (the previous example was a reduction too, by the way). Again, I'm getting a little bit ahead of myself, but since we are talking about if-statements in loops, I want to introduce a trick for restructuring reductions `max` and `min` to expose more parallelism. The following loop searches for the maximum value, z, in the vector a by going through the elements one at a time:

```
     for (i=0; i<n; i++)
        z = a[i] > z ? a[i] : z;
```

As written, it is recursive like the loop from the previous section. You need the result of a given iteration before you can proceed to the next. However, since we are looking for the greatest element in the whole vector, and since that will be the same element (essentially) no matter how we go about looking for it, we can restructure the loop to check several elements at a time:

players competing at a time while the rest sat around, the new loop runs several matches side by side.

Conditionals That Transfer Control

Let's step back a second. Have you noticed a similarity among all the loops so far? We have looked only at a particular type of conditional: *conditional assignments*—based on the outcome of the test, a variable gets reassigned. Of course, not every conditional ends up in an assignment. You can have statements that transfer flow of control, such as subroutine calls or goto statements. There's not much you can do about the subroutine calls, but it will help if you restructure the gotos back into conditional assignments. You might say "Who uses gotos!?" Here's an example of a loop containing an arithmetic if-statement, fairly common in old FORTRAN programs:

```
      DO 10 I=1,N
        DO 10 J=1,N
          IF (B(J,I) - 1.0) 20, 30, 30
20          A(J,I) = A(J,I) + B(J,I) * C
            GO TO 10
30          A(J,I) = 0.
10      CONTINUE
```

On many machines, this will execute much better if cast as a block if-statement. After restructuring it looks like one of the independent loops we saw above:

```
      DO 10 I=1,N
        DO 10 J=1,N
          IF (B(J,I) .GT. 1.0) THEN
            A(J,I) = 0.
          ELSE
            A(J,I) = A(J,I) + B(J,I) * C
          ENDIF
10      CONTINUE
```

A Few Words About Branch Probability

In Chapter 2 I told you about delayed branches and the penalty for guessing incorrectly which way a branch will go at run time. Usually the penalty is no more than a cycle or two, so it isn't going to make a great deal of difference if your compiler gets it wrong. However, it will make some difference, so I thought you might be interested in it anyway. Let's stage a little mental exercise. Pick any conditional and try to predict the probability that it will be true:

```
if (something) then something_else
```

You will most likely code for the odd condition—things that happen once in a while. You might be checking for an error condition or an exceptional element in a list. The probability of branching will be low because the condition is true less often than it is false. As far as compiler is concerned, a branch with a less than 50% probability is unlikely to occur, so it will probably optimize the branch for the fall-through case.

Similarly with do-loops, while-loops, and until-loops, the compiler will assume that the probability of exiting the loop is low. Again, it makes sense. How many times do you code a loop that goes around less than twice? If the loop only performs three iterations then the probability of exiting is 33%—another low figure.

So now you know the heuristics compilers use to guess branch probability. You could try to code a critical conditional backwards, so that the fall-through is less likely than the branch, especially one in a loop, and see if it makes a difference in the run time. It might not. The compiler may be able to find something useful to fill the "delay slot," whether or not the branch is taken.

The most exceptional case I ever saw was a piece of scalar code that was translated by a preprocessor into FORTRAN from a language called Flecs. The preprocessor was unlike any human: every branch was coded to check for conditions that were probably *true*. The machine it was running on, a Multiflow Trace, had an architecture and compiler that depended on branch prediction to get the best performance. Having all the branches coded backwards accounted for a 20% difference in the run time—probably the most you could ever expect to see.

Statements that contain run time type conversions suffer a little performance penalty each time the statement is executed. If the statement is located in a portion of the program where there is a lot of activity, the total penalty can be significant.

People have their reasons for writing applications with mixed typing. Often it is a matter of saving memory space, memory bandwidth, or time. In the past, for instance, double precision calculations took twice as long as their single precision counterparts, so if some of the calculations could be arranged to take place in single precision, there could be a performance win.* But any time saved by performing part of the calculations in single precision, and part in double precision, has to be measured against the additional overhead caused by the run time type conversions. In the following code, the addition of A(I) to B(I) is *mixed type:*

```
      ...
      INTEGER NUMEL, I
      PARAMETER (NUMEL = 1000)
      REAL*8 A(NUMEL)
      REAL*4 B(NUMEL)
      ...
      DO 10 I=1,NUMEL
        A(I) = A(I) + B(I)
10    CONTINUE
      ...
```

Each iteration, B(I) has to be promoted to double precision before the addition can occur. You don't see the promotion in the source code, but it's there, and it takes time.

_____

*Nowadays, single precision calculations often take *longer* than double precision calculations. The RS/6000 is an example of an architecture for which this is true.

C programmers beware: In Kernighan and Ritchie C, all floating point calculations in C programs take place in double precision—even if all the variables involved are declared as float. It is possible for you to write a whole K+R application in one precision, yet suffer the penalty of many type conversions. *ANSI C* compilers, on the other hand, may treat float declarations as doubles, avoiding the mismatch altogether.

Doing Your Own Common Subexpression Elimination

So far I have given your compiler the benefit of the doubt. *Common subexpression elimination*—the ability of the compiler to recognize repeated patterns in the code and replace all but one with a temporary variable—probably works on your machine for simple expressions. In the following lines of code, most compilers would recognize a+b as a common subexpression:

```
c = a + b + d
e = q + a + b
```

becomes

```
temp = a + b
c = temp + d
e = q + temp
```

Substituting for a+b eliminates some of the arithmetic. If the expression is reused many times, the savings can be significant. However, a compiler's ability to recognize common subexpressions is limited, especially when there are multiple components or their order is permuted. A compiler might not recognize that a+b+c and c+b+a are equivalent.* For important parts of the program, you might consider doing common subexpression elimination of complicated expressions by hand. This will guarantee that it gets done. It compromises beauty somewhat, but there are some situations where it is worth it.

Here's another example in which the function *sin* is called twice with the same argument:

```
x = r*sin(a)*cos(b);
y = r*sin(a)*sin(b);
z = r*cos(a);
```

becomes

---

*And because of overflow and roundoff errors, in some situations they might not be equivalent.

The only time a compiler might eliminate common subexpressions containing function calls is when they are intrinsics, as in FORTRAN. This is because the compiler can assume some things about their side-effects. You, on the other hand, can see into subroutines, which means you are better qualified than the compiler to group together common subexpressions involving subroutines or functions.

Doing Your Own Code Motion

All of these optimizations have their biggest payback within loops because that's where all of a program's activity is concentrated. One of the best ways to cut down on run time is to move unnecessary or repeated (invariant) instructions out of the main flow of the code and into the suburbs. For loops, it's called *hoisting* instructions when they are pulled out from the top, and *sinking* when they are pushed down below. Here's an example:

```
      DO 10 I=1,N
         A(I) = A(I) / SQRT(X*X + Y*Y)
10    CONTINUE
```

becomes

```
      TEMP = 1 / SQRT(X*X + Y*Y)
      DO 10 I=1,N
         A(I) = A(I) * TEMP
10    CONTINUE
```

Above, I hoisted an expensive, invariant operation out of the loop and assigned the result to a temporary variable. Notice, too, that I made an algebraic simplification when I exchanged a division for multiplication by an inverse. This will execute much more quickly. Your compiler might be smart enough to make these transformations itself; but without crawling through the assembly language, you can't be positive. Of course, if you rearrange code by hand and the run time for the loop suddenly goes down, you will know that the compiler has been sandbagging all along.

Sometimes you want to sink an operation below the loop. Usually, it's some calculation performed each iteration but whose result is only needed for the last. To illustrate, here's a sort of loop that is different from the ones we have been looking at. It searches for the final character in a character string.

```
while (*p != ' ')
    c = *p++;
```

becomes

```
while (*p++ != ' ');
c = *(--p);
```

The new version of the loop moves the assignment of c beyond the last iteration. Admittedly, this transformation would be a reach for a compiler and the savings wouldn't even be that great. But it illustrates the notion of sinking an operation very well.

Again, hoisting or sinking instructions to get them out of loops is something your compiler should be capable of doing. But often, as in these two examples, you can slightly restructure the calculations yourself at the same time you move them to get an even greater benefit.

Handling Array Elements in Loops

Here's another area where you would like to trust the compiler to do the right thing. When making repeated use of an array element within a loop, you want to be charged just once for loading it from memory. Take the following loop as an example. It reuses X(I) twice:

```
      DO 10 I=1,N
        XOLD(I) = X(I)
        X(I)    = X(I) + XINC(I)
 10   CONTINUE
```

In reality, the steps that go into retrieving X(I) are just additional common subexpressions: an address calculation (possibly) and a memory load operation. You can see that the operation is repeated by rewriting the loop slightly:

```
      DO 10 I=1,N
        TEMP    = X(I)
        XOLD(I) = TEMP
        X(I)    = TEMP + XINC(I)
 10   CONTINUE
```

FORTRAN compilers *should* recognize that the same X(I) is being used twice and that it only needs to be loaded once, but compilers aren't always

Unless the compiler can see the definitions of **x**, **xinc**, and **xold**, it has to assume that they are pointers leading back to the same storage, and repeat the loads and stores. In this case, introducing temporary variables to hold the values **x**, `xinc`, and `xold`, will be an optimization the compiler wasn't free to make.

Interestingly, while putting scalar temporaries in the loop is useful for RISC and superscalar machines, it doesn't help code that will run on vector hardware. A vector compiler will be looking for opportunities to eliminate the scalars or, at the very least, to replace them with temporary vectors. If you run your code on a vector machine from time to time, you might want to be careful about introducing scalar temporary variables into a loop. A dubious performance gain in one instance could be a real performance loss in another.

Closing Notes

In this chapter, I introduced tuning techniques for eliminating program clutter—anything that contributes to the run time without contributing to the answer. We saw many examples of tuning techniques—enough that you may be asking yourself, "What's left?" Well, as we will see in the next two chapters, there are a few ways we can help the compiler:

- Find more parallelism.
- Use memory as effectively as possible.

Often this means changes that are not beautiful. However, they will often be quick.

Exercises

1. Explain why inlining procedure *cat* into *dog* would probably be of dubious value. How could a profiler help you decide?

```
dog (bark, scratch, pant, sleep)
    int bark;
{
    if (bark < 10)
        return (cat (bark-1, scratch, pant, sleep));
    else if (bark > 100)
        return (cat (bark-1, scratch-1, pant, sleep));
    else
        return (cat (bark, scratch, pant, sleep));
}
cat (meow, preen, sneeze, sleep)
    int meow;
{
    int get_mouse;
    if (meow == 10)
        return (1);
    getmouse = sleep + (preen * meow) - sneeze * 2;
    if ((getmouse % 4) == 3) {
        preen += sleep;
        get_mouse = getmouse + preen;
    }
    return (getmouse);
}
```

2. How would you simplify the following loop conditional?

```
      DO 10 I=1,N
        A(I) = A(I) * B
        IF (I .EQ. N/2)
   +      A(I) = 0.
   10 CONTINUE
```

3. The following loop is taken from this chapter. Time it on your computer, both with and without the test. Run it with three sets of data; one with all A(I)s less than SMALL, one with all A(I)s greater than SMALL, and one with an even split. When is it better to leave the test in the loop, if ever?

```
        PARAMETER (SMALL = 1.E-20)
        DO 10 I=1,N
          IF (ABS(A(I)) .GE. SMALL) THEN
            B(I) = B(I) + A(I) * C
          ENDIF
   10     CONTINUE
```

Suppose that a particular program has no loops in it, which is essentially the same as supposing that a program never re-executes the same code twice. How long will it take to run? Well, say for argument that the text section (the part of the program that houses the instructions) is one megabyte in size. Also, assume that you have a 10 MIPS processor, and that all instructions are four bytes long. In this case, the program would run for .025 seconds:

```
1,000,000 bytes / (4 bytes/instr) / (10,000,000 instrs/sec) = .025 seconds
```

Unless it's a real-time application, .025 seconds hardly seems like something to get upset about. For a program's run time to be substantial, you have to execute some of the same code more than once—there are going to be loops in it somewhere.

For tuning purposes, the scope of the loops is important. Your approach will vary if, for instance, the perimeter of the program is surrounded by one huge loop, as opposed to containing many small loops inside. The first situation may offer an opportunity for some large-grained parallelism (provided you have a parallel processor of some sort), whereas the second may suggest that you tune fine-grained parallel or vectorizable loops. Of course, there are situations in between too. In this chapter (and to some extent the next) I'll talk about tuning the small, primarily vectorizable loops. Later in the book I'll discuss larger-grained parallelism when I cover parallel processors.

With loop optimizations we hope to accomplish three things:

- Reduce loop overhead
- Increase parallelism
- Improve memory reference patterns

We talked about the first item in the last chapter, *Eliminating Clutter*, and I'll discuss the third item in the next chapter. Here I will discuss ways to increase parallelism, primarily in loops that contain floating point operations, and mostly by unrolling loops and loop nests.

Basic Loop Unrolling

Say, for illustration, that you have a job as a baloney tester. Part of your day-to-day labor is to consume one full blister-pack of baloney each morning before you go to lunch. You are further required to eat all the baloney in sandwiches; you are not allowed to lower shrouds of baloney into your mouth without bread and mayonnaise.

On your first day of work you arrive at 7 AM. They give you two loaves of white bread, a plastic squeeze-jar of mayonnaise, and a blister-pack of baloney. You eagerly begin making and eating sandwiches so that you will be finished by the time the doughnut truck comes at 10:00. At 9:39, the veal loaf tester, assigned to the station next to yours, finally arrives for work. She pulls out two pieces of bread, squirts on some mayonnaise, and heaps the whole contents of her blister-pack into a sandwich. She wolfs it down with a glass of milk, smiles at you with breaded teeth and walks outside to meet the doughnut truck. When the truck arrives she is able to consume more than twice as many doughnuts as you. What happened?

Basically, your co-worker ate less bread and more meat. This is the idea behind *loop unrolling*. If you can get more meat into your loops, you'll be chewing several pieces in parallel and swallowing less bread. For illustration, consider the loop below. It has a single statement wrapped in a do-loop:

```
      DO 10 I=1,N
        A(I) = A(I) + B(I) * C
10    CONTINUE
```

You can unroll the loop, as I have below, giving you the same operations in less iterations with less loop overhead. You can imagine how this would

```
        A(I+1)  = A(I+1) + B(I+1) * C
        A(I+2)  = A(I+2) + B(I+2) * C
        A(I+3)  = A(I+3) + B(I+3) * C
10    CONTINUE
```

However, there is also potential for big trouble. The loop is unrolled four times, but what if N is not divisible by four? If not, there will be one, two, or three spare iterations that don't get executed. To handle these extra iterations, we add another little loop to soak them up. This extra loop is called a *preconditioning loop*:

```
      II = IMOD (N,4)
      DO 9 I=1,II
        A(I) = A(I) + B(I) * C
9     CONTINUE

      DO 10 I=1+II,N,4
        A(I)    = A(I)   + B(I)    * C
        A(I+1) = A(I+1) + B(I+1) * C
        A(I+2) = A(I+2) + B(I+2) * C
        A(I+3) = A(I+3) + B(I+3) * C
10    CONTINUE
```

You calculate the number of preconditioning iterations by taking the total iteration count modulo the unrolling amount. If, at run time, N turns out to be divisible by four, there will be no spare iterations, and the preconditioning loop will not be executed.

Qualifying Candidates for Loop Unrolling

The previous loop was an ideal candidate for loop unrolling. The iterations were independent and the loop innards were small. But as you might suspect, this isn't always the case; some kinds of loops can't be unrolled so easily. Additionally, the way a loop is actually used when the program runs can disqualify it for loop unrolling, even if it looks promising.

In this section I am going to discuss a few categories of loops that are generally not prime candidates for unrolling, and give you some ideas of what you can do about them. I talked about several of these in the last chapter as well, but they are also relevant here. They are:

- Loops with low trip counts
- Fat loops
- Loops containing procedure calls
- Loops containing branches
- Recursive loops

A few of other topics, such as *vector reductions*, need special attention, too. I'll talk about them separately, later in this chapter.

Loops with Low Trip Counts

To be effective, loop unrolling requires that there be a fairly large number of iterations in the original loop. To understand why, picture what happens if the total iteration count is low, perhaps less than ten, or even less than four. With a trip count this low, the preconditioning loop is doing a proportionately large amount of the work. It's not supposed to be that way. The preconditioning loop is supposed to catch the few leftover iterations missed by the unrolled, main loop. However, when the trip count is low, you will make one or two passes through the unrolled loop, plus one or two passes through the preconditioning loop. In other words, you have more clutter; the loop shouldn't have been unrolled in the first place.

Probably the only time it makes sense to unroll a loop with a low trip count is when the number of iterations is fixed at compile time. For instance, suppose that you had the loop below:

```
      PARAMETER (NITER = 3)
      ....
      DO 10 I=1,NITER
        A(I) = B(I) * C
10    CONTINUE
```

Because NITER is hard-wired to 3, you can safely unroll to a *depth* of 3 without worrying about a preconditioning loop. In fact, you can throw out the loop structure altogether and just leave the unrolled loop innards:

```
      PARAMETER (NITER = 3)
      ....
      A(1) = B(1) * C
      A(2) = B(2) * C
      A(3) = A(3) * C
```

Of course, if a loop's trip count is low it probably won't contribute significantly to the overall run time, unless you find such a loop at the center of a loop nest. Then you will either want to unroll it completely or leave it alone.

Fat Loops

Loop unrolling helps performance because it fattens up a loop with calculations that can be done in parallel. By the same token, if a particular loop is already fat, then unrolling isn't going to help much; you already have a pool of operations that can be overlapped (possibly), and the loop overhead is already spread over a fair number of instructions. In fact, unrolling a fat loop may even slow your program down because it increases the size of the text segment, placing an added burden on the memory system (I'll explain this in greater detail, shortly). A good rule of thumb is to look elsewhere for performance when the loop innards exceed three or four statements.

Loops Containing Procedure Calls

As with fat loops, loops containing subroutine or function calls generally aren't good candidates for unrolling. There are several reasons. First, they often contain a fair number of instructions already. And if the subroutine being called is fat, it makes the loop which calls it fat as well. This may not be apparent when you look at the loop; the function call can conceal many more instructions.

Second, when the calling routine and the subroutine are compiled separately it is impossible for the compiler to intermix instructions. A loop that is unrolled into a series of function calls behaves much like the original loop, before unrolling.

Last, function call overhead is expensive. Registers have to be saved, argument lists have to be prepared. The time spent calling and returning from a subroutine can be much greater than that of the loop overhead. Unrolling to amortize the cost of the loop structure over several calls doesn't buy you enough to be worth the effort.

There are, however, a few rare cases where unrolling a loop with a procedure call will help, if you can answer yes to all of the following questions:

- Does your compiler support procedure inlining?
- Is the procedure very short?
- Is the loop trip count high?

Example 10-1 shows the inlining example from the last chapter. The code is a little ridiculous, I admit, but it illustrates when you can unroll a loop containing a procedure call.

Example 10-1: Loop containing a procedure call

```
        DO 10 I=1,N
          CALL SHORT (A(I), B(I), C)
   10   CONTINUE
        ....
        SUBROUTINE SHORT (A,B,C)
        A = A + B * C
        RETURN
        END
```

If a look at the source code indicates that inlining is feasible—i.e., that the function you call is short and won't have any side-effects, go ahead and unroll the DO 10 . . . loop. Then compile with procedure inlining enabled. The body of the subroutine SHORT will be incorporated directly into the loop as if it was written that way in the first place. If your compiler doesn't support inlining, you will have to incorporate the subroutine into its caller by hand. Here's the previous loop, with procedure inlining and unrolling, including a preconditioning loop:

```
        II = IMOD (N,4)
        DO 9 I=1,II
          CALL SHORT (A(I), B(I), C)
    9   CONTINUE

        DO 10 I=1+II,N,4
          CALL SHORT (A(I), B(I), C)
          CALL SHORT (A(I+1), B(I+1), C)
          CALL SHORT (A(I+2), B(I+2), C)
          CALL SHORT (A(I+3), B(I+3), C)
   10   CONTINUE
```

Unfortunately, there are times when you don't have source code for whatever you want to inline, so you are sort of stuck. This would be the case if you were using a third party application library or system routines.

There are a couple of special cases that will benefit from unrolling, even without source code. A few of the FORTRAN intrinsics and some C functions (which are actually header file macros) are replaced by a handful of instructions at compile time. These intrinsics and macros don't generate procedure calls anyway, so the loop can be unrolled. FORTRAN examples are INT, FLOAT, ABS, and MOD. The SQRT function may or may not cause a procedure call, depending on whether or not your processor supports square roots in hardware. Transcendental functions such as SIN, LOG and

TAN are not implemented in hardware, but they take a relatively long time to compute anyway, so the ability to unroll them within a loop wouldn't help much.

In C, some functions appear to be procedure calls, but are actually macros which can be found in header files. Examples include the character macros isalpha, isupper, isdigit, etc., found in */usr/include/ctype.h*, and numerical functions max, min and abs, found in */usr/include/macros.h* and */usr/include/math.h*. There are others as well.

Loops with Branches in Them

Like subroutines, branches in loops can break up the flow of control: they erect fences between patches of parallelism. In the last chapter I showed you how to eliminate certain types of branches, but of course, we couldn't get rid of them all. In cases of iteration independent branches I suggested that you might want to try a little unrolling. The pay-back won't be as great for unrolled loops that don't contain branches, but you should see some improvement. Below is a doubly-nested loop. The inner loop tests the value of B(J,I):

```
         DO 10 I=1,N
           DO 10 J=1,N
             IF (B(J,I) .GT. 1.0)
     +         A(J,I) = A(J,I) + B(J,I) * C
    10     CONTINUE
```

Each iteration is independent of every other, so unrolling it won't be a problem. We'll just leave the outer loop undisturbed:

```
         II = IMOD (N,4)
         DO 10 I=1,N
           DO 9   J=1,II
             IF (B(J,I) .GT. 1.0)
     +         A(J,I) = A(J,I) + B(J,I) * C
     9     CONTINUE
           DO 10 J=II+1,N,4
             IF (B(J,I)   .GT. 1.0)
     +         A(J,I)   = A(J,I)   + B(J,I)   * C
             IF (B(J+1,I) .GT. 1.0)
     +         A(J+1,I) = A(J+1,I) + B(J+1,I) * C
             IF (B(J+2,I) .GT. 1.0)
     +         A(J+2,I) = A(J+2,I) + B(J+2,I) * C
             IF (B(J+3,I) .GT. 1.0)
     +         A(J+3,I) = A(J+3,I) + B(J+3,I) * C
    10     CONTINUE
```

Modern RISC and CISC processors can execute multiple instructions per clock cycle, so the branch tests and the arithmetic can often be overlapped. In many cases, the compiler can push the tests up early in this instruction stream so that they won't cause branch delays. A particularly clever compiler, paired with the right hardware, can even schedule the arithmetic and conditionally store the results, depending on the outcomes of the tests. This allows the floating point pipelines to become filled without gaps, and increases the speed of the loop. Some machines (DEC Alpha/AXP is one) even have conditional assignment instructions, which replace the test and branch combination altogether.

Recursive Loops

Whether you are dealing with conditionals or not, you need iteration independence to get the best benefit from loop unrolling. When I first introduced the topic of dependencies in Chapter 8, I talked particularly about *flow dependencies*—situations in which you need the results of a previous calculation before you can start another. For a reminder, here's a simple flow dependence on the variable **x**:

```
x = a+b;
y = x*2;
```

The second equation depends on the results of the first equation, **x**, before it can proceed.

Chances are that your compiler can optimize this automatically. More challenging would be a flow dependency that appears in a loop *and* spans iterations. In this case, equations would be dependent on the results of at least one previous iteration. Here's one such case, a first order linear recursion:

```
      DO 10 I=2,N
         A(I) = A(I) + A(I-1) * B
   10    CONTINUE
```

In the loop above, the value of A(I) depends on A(I-1), which depends on A(I-2), etc. You can unroll such a loop, but that's not going to increase the pool of operations that can be performed in parallel. The dependencies still exist; the calculation in the second statement depends on the first, the third depends on the second, and so on:

```
   A(I)   = A(I)   + A(I-1) * B
   A(I+1) = A(I+1) + A(I)   * B
   A(I+2) = A(I+2) + A(I+1) * B
   A(I+3) = A(I+3) + A(I+2) * B
```

It's almost completely academic for our purposes, but notice below that it is possible to calculate two iterations at a time independently by increasing the total number of calculations performed. That is, if you algebraically substitute every other statement into the one following it, you can decrease dependency at the expense of creating more work:

```
A(I+1) = A(I+1) + A(I)   * B + A(I-1) * B * B
A(I)   = A(I)   + A(I-1) * B

A(I+3) = A(I+3) + A(I+2) * B + A(I+1) * B * B
A(I+2) = A(I+2) + A(I+1) * B
```

Expressed in a loop, the recast calculations look like this:

```
      DO 10 I=2,N,2
         A(I+1) = A(I+1) + A(I)   * B + A(I-1) * B * B
         A(I)   = A(I)   + A(I-1) * B
   10 CONTINUE
```

Will this execute more quickly? Perhaps marginally, though it might even go slower (and it's pretty ugly too).* To go faster, the restructured loop will need a machine with the ability to execute more than one operation per clock tick, and a smart compiler to trade the increased number of operations for a reduction in dependency. It is interesting because it hints at an approach that is becoming more common with algorithms for highly parallel computers: trading-off dependencies at the expense of more computations.

The loop above is an example of a simple vector recursion—though very difficult to improve. Scalar recursions are often easier to handle. We'll see more of this when we look at associative transformations and vector reductions, below. You might also look at the last chapter where I talked briefly about restructuring the *min* and *max* functions.

Negatives of Loop Unrolling

You never get something for nothing. Loop unrolling always adds some run time to the program. It's just that often the good outweighs the bad. If you unroll a loop and see the performance dip a little, you can assume that either:

- The loop wasn't a good candidate for unrolling in the first place, or
- A secondary effect absorbed your performance increase.

---

*A good compiler can make the rolled up version go faster by recognizing the dependency as an opportunity to save memory traffic. Since A(I+1) is going to be needed next iteration anyway, the compiler can forward the value to another register and skip the store and subsequent load.

We just finished looking at what makes good and bad candidates for loop unrolling. Remember to use your profilers to tell you whether a loop that looks like it will optimize nicely actually gets executed often enough to warrant restructuring. Anyway, let's say that you did your homework. There are other possible reasons why you can come up short after making a perfectly good optimization:

- Unrolling by the Wrong Factor
- Register Spilling
- . Instruction Cache Miss
- Other Hardware Delays

I'll describe each in turn.

Unrolling by the Wrong Factor

For loops with a relatively small number of iterations (say tens of iterations), it is particularly important to avoid executing the preconditioning loop. The time spent cleaning up can eat away at the performance benefits of unrolling. Picking an unrolling amount that evenly divides the expected number of iterations (provided you know what that is), will help. Of course, if the loop goes around many thousands of times, a handful of preconditioning iterations won't matter quite as much.

Register Thrashing

When offered too many things that can be done in parallel, compilers sometimes struggle with register allocation. Too much to do—too few registers. Visualize a child with her mouth so full of candy she can't chew. She will probably become more concerned with keeping the candy in her mouth than enjoying the taste. Eventually, she may have to spit some out.

A compiler copes with a shortage of registers by spilling off their contents to temporary storage, to free them up for other operations. It is a short-sighted thing to do in many cases, since the spilled values will probably have to be reloaded soon. In pathological cases, the compiler stops all useful work while it shuffles the spilled register variables around.

You won't see the problem on every compiler and every machine. However, register thrashing is one of the reasons that infinite unrolling doesn't work very well. Workstation's CPUs become saturated with about four copies of the inner loop, depending on the memory usage and the processor. Therefore, you want to be conservative with loop unrolling. Too much is a bad thing.

Instruction Cache Miss

Unwanted activity in the instruction cache is another incentive to be conservative. When you unroll loops, you expand the size of the compiled program. This, in turn, increases contention over space in the instruction cache. Granted, it would take an incredibly large loop to cover the whole cache, but it only takes a handful of instructions to eat up a cache line. Because it's part of a loop, you can bet that the line will be needed often (remember, all the activity is in loops). The larger the loop when it sits in the cache, the more likely pieces of it will get bumped out for other parts of the same program, other programs, or the kernel.

Other Hardware Delays

For some architectures, particularly multiprocessors, there are other hardware delays that you encounter when you unroll excessively. These don't have so much to do with allocation of particular CPU resources, like cache entries or registers, but instead involve the particulars of a shared memory system.

First of all, shared memory multiprocessors (Chapter 16) have to ensure that all the processors see the same data in their caches and memory. The updates usually proceed quietly in the background. If these updates occur too often, however, they can affect activity in the foreground, and take a piece out of your run time. This may be true even if you are running alone or on a single CPU machine. Processors designed for multiprocessing often run with shared memory policies enabled.

Another consequence of running in a shared memory environment is that there is generally less total memory bandwidth available than all of the processors could absorb all at one time. That is, a processor running alone may have as much bandwidth as it needs, but all processors running together may not. You would see this as a frustrating lack of performance past a certain point, no matter how hard you tried to optimize.

Outer Loop Unrolling

When you embed loops within other loops you create a *loop nest*. The loop or loops in the center are called the *inner* loops. The surrounding loops are called *outer* loops. Unrolling the innermost loop in a nest isn't any different from what we saw above. You just pretend the rest of the loop nest doesn't exist and approach it in the normal way. However, there are times when you want to apply loop unrolling not just to the inner loop, but to outer loops as well—or perhaps only to the outer loops. First I'll tell you how and then I'll tell you why. Here's a typical loop nest:

```
for (i=0; i<n; i++)
    for (j=0; j<n; j++)
        for (k=0; k<n; k++)
            a[i][j][k] = a[i][j][k] + b[i][j][k] * c;
```

To unroll an outer loop, you pick one of the outer loop index variables and replicate the innermost loop body so that several iterations are performed at the same time, just like we saw when we looked at unrolling a single loop, above. The difference is in the index variable for which you unroll. In the code below, we have unrolled the middle (j) loop twice:

```
for (i=0; i<n; i++)
    for (j=0; j<n; j+=2)
        for (k=0; k<n; k++) {
            a[i][j][k]   = a[i][j][k]   + b[i][k][j]   * c;
            a[i][j+1][k] = a[i][j+1][k] + b[i][k][j+1] * c;
        }
```

I left the k loop untouched; however, I could unroll that one, too. That would give me outer *and* inner loop unrollings at the same time:

```
for (i=0; i<n; i++)
    for (j=0; j<n; j+=2)
        for (k=0; k<n; k+=2) {
            a[i][j][k]     = a[i][j][k]     + b[i][k][j]     * c;
            a[i][j+1][k]   = a[i][j+1][k]   + b[i][k][j+1]   * c;
            a[i][j][k+1]   = a[i][j][k+1]   + b[i][k+1][j]   * c;
            a[i][j+1][k+1] = a[i][j+1][k+1] + b[i][k+1][j+1] * c;
        }
```

I could even unroll the i loop too, giving me eight copies of the loop innards. (Notice that I completely ignored preconditioning; in a real application, of course, you couldn't.) Why would you want to go to all this trouble? The reasons for applying outer loop unrolling are (as ever):

- To expose more computations
- To improve memory reference patterns

The most important reason is the second one, which I will discuss in the next chapter; therefore, I will limit my discussion here to how outer loop unrolling exposes computations. Note that loop nests that are candidates for outer loop unrolling are also candidates for loop reversal.

Outer Loop Unrolling to Expose Computations

Say that you have a doubly nested loop, and that the inner loop trip count is low—perhaps four or five on average. Inner loop unrolling doesn't make sense in this case because there won't be enough iterations to justify the cost of the preconditioning loop. However, you may be able to unroll an outer loop. Consider this loop, assuming that M is small and N is large:

```
      DO 10 I=1,N
        DO 20 J=1,M
          A(J,I) = B(J,I) + C(J,I) * D
20        CONTINUE
10      CONTINUE
```

We are looking for a way to increase the parallelism without adding to the clutter, which rules out inner loop unrolling. However, unrolling the I loop will give you lots of floating point operations that can be overlapped:

```
      II = IMOD (N,4)
      DO 9 I=1,II
        DO 19 J=1,M
          A(J,I)   = B(J,I)   + C(J,I) * D
19        CONTINUE
9       CONTINUE

      DO 10 I=II,N,4
        DO 20 J=1,M
          A(J,I)   = B(J,I)   + C(J,I)   * D
          A(J,I+1) = B(J,I+1) + C(J,I+1) * D
          A(J,I+2) = B(J,I+2) + C(J,I+2) * D
          A(J,I+3) = B(J,I+3) + C(J,I+3) * D
20        CONTINUE
10      CONTINUE
```

In this particular case there is bad news to go with the good news: unrolling the outer loop causes strided memory references on A, B, and C.* However, it probably won't be too much of a problem because the inner loop trip count is small, so it naturally groups references to conserve cache entries.

Outer loop unrolling can also be helpful when you have a nest with recursion in the inner loop, but not in the outer loops. For illustration, I have borrowed the first order linear recursion from above and placed it into a loop nest.

---

*Stride is something I'll discuss in more detail in the next chapter. For now, though, we can say that the stride of a memory reference is the distance (in memory) between successive memory accesses.

```
        DO 10 J=1,M
          DO 10 I=2,N
            A(I,J) = A(I,J) + A(I-1,J) * B
 10     CONTINUE
```

I still can't unroll the inner loop, but I can work on several copies of the outer loop at the same time. When unrolled it looks like this:

```
        JJ = IMOD (M,4)
        DO 9 J=1,JJ
          DO 19 I=2,N
            A(I,J) = A(I,J) + A(I-1,J) * B
 19       CONTINUE
  9     CONTINUE

        DO 10 J=1+JJ,M,4
          DO 10 I=2,N
            A(I,J)   = A(I,J)   + A(I-1,J)   * B
            A(I,J+1) = A(I,J+1) + A(I-1,J+1) * B
            A(I,J+2) = A(I,J+2) + A(I-1,J+2) * B
            A(I,J+3) = A(I,J+3) + A(I-1,J+3) * B
 10     CONTINUE
```

You can see the recursion still exists in the I loop, but we have succeeded in finding lots of parallelism anyway.

Sometimes the reason for unrolling the outer loop is to get a hold of much larger chunks of things that can be done in parallel. If the outer loop iterations are independent, and the inner loop trip count is high, then each outer loop iteration represents a significant, parallel chunk of work. On a single CPU that doesn't matter very much, but on a tightly-coupled multiprocessor it can translate into a tremendous speedup.

Associative Transformations

Imagine that you are about to bake a cake requiring over 100 ingredients. The recipe reads as follows:

- Measure 1 cup of corn syrup into a large mixing bowl.
- Add 1/2 teaspoons of vanilla extract.
- Blend in 2 cups of flour.
- Add 1/4 cup distilled water.
- Mix in 8 1/2 cups of salt.
- Add 1 tablespoon clam broth.
- and so on . . .

As written, the recipe is very serial—one ingredient follows another. It could take you a long time. Perhaps you could ask a friend to mix all the even numbered ingredients in a separate bowl, while you handle the odd ones. Maybe that would cut the mixing time in half. Watch out! There is some danger that the cake won't come out the way you expect. Say, for instance, that with the exception of the first ingredient, corn syrup, all the rest of the odd ingredients are powders of various sorts. Likewise, say that all of the even numbered ingredients are liquids. Corn syrup+ flour+salt+whatever might make a formidable cement. After several minutes of stirring you could have a bowl of stones, and your friend could be discovering a recipe for motor oil. When you get together to combine ingredients it could be like throwing your rocks into his pond, not at all like food.

Similarly, some source code optimizations aren't strictly one-to-one replacements for the original code. Algebraically, they are equivalent to the originals, but because of limits to the precision of a computer, rearranging the calculations can change the answers—like the modified cake recipe.

There is *some* freedom, of course. For instance, the answer you obtain from X+Y will be the same as Y+X, as per the commutative law for addition. Whichever operand you pick first, the operation yields the same result; they are mathematically equivalent. It also means that you can choose either of the following two forms and get the same answer:

```
(X + Y) + Z
(Y + X) + Z
```

However, this is not equivalent:

```
(Y + Z) + X
```

The third version isn't equivalent to the first two because the order of the calculations has changed. Again, the rearrangement is equivalent algebraically, but not computationally. By changing the order of the calculations, we have taken advantage of the associativity of the operations—we have made an *associative transformation* of the original code.

To understand why the order of the calculations matters, imagine that your computer can perform arithmetic significant to only five decimal places.

Also assume that the values of X, Y, and Z are .00005, .00005, and 1.0000, respectively. This means that:

```
X + Y + Z =   .00005 +   .00005 + 1.0000
          =   .0001            + 1.0000     = 1.0001
```

but

```
Y + Z + X =   .00005 + 1.0000  +   .00005
          = 1.0000            +   .00005   = 1.0000
```

The two versions give slightly different answers. When adding Y+Z+X, the sum of the smaller numbers was insignificant when added to the larger number. But when computing X+Y+Z, we add the two small numbers first, and their combined sum is large enough to influence the final answer. For this reason, compilers that rearrange operations for the sake of performance generally only do so after the user has requested optimizations beyond the defaults.

C precedence rules are different.* Although the precedences between operators are honored (i.e., * comes before +, and evaluation generally occurs left to right for operators of equal precedence) the compiler is allowed to treat a few commutative operations (+, *, &, ^ and |) as if they were fully associative, even if they are parenthesized. For instance, you might tell the compiler:

```
a = x + (y + z);
```

However, the compiler is free to ignore you, and combine X, Y, and Z in any order it pleases.

Reductions

Let's look at a case where you can put associative transformations to work in hand-code optimizations. Suppose that you had a loop with a dot product in it:

```
        SUM = 0.0
        DO 10 I=1,N
          SUM = SUM + A(I) * B(I)
10      CONTINUE
```

The dot product is a running sum of the pairwise product of two vectors, one example of a *reduction*—so-called because it reduces a vector to a scalar. The calculation is simple enough. The problem is the same as before: we would like to unroll the loop to get more meat into the center.

---

*Kernighan and Ritchie C.

However, there are two new challenges:

- The loop is recursive on that single variable (a scalar); every iteration needs the result of the previous iteration.

- Because the assignment is being made to a scalar, unrolling isn't as straightforward as before.

As with the cake recipe, there are ways to divide up the work for a loop like this. The most obvious is to try to calculate several iterations at a time. Here's what a loop looks like with four iterations exposed:*

```
      SUM = 0.0
      DO 10 I=1,N,4
         SUM = SUM + A(I)   * B(I)
       .           + A(I+1) * B(I+1)
       .           + A(I+2) * B(I+2)
       .           + A(I+3) * B(I+3)
   10 CONTINUE
```

It looks like we have made greater gains than we actually have. Unrolling the loop this way spreads out the loop overhead somewhat, but the calculations are still going to take place serially, as they did in the original loop. We would like to overlap the calculations so that the components of different iterations are calculated together. This will mean transforming the loop into one that is algebraically equivalent, but not computationally equivalent:

```
      SUM0 = 0.0
      SUM1 = 0.0
      SUM2 = 0.0
      SUM3 = 0.0
      DO 10 I=1,N,4
         SUM0 = SUM0 + A(I)   * B(I)
         SUM1 = SUM1 + A(I+1) * B(I+1)
         SUM2 = SUM2 + A(I+2) * B(I+2)
         SUM3 = SUM3 + A(I+3) * B(I+3)
   10 CONTINUE
      SUM = SUM0 + SUM1 + SUM2 + SUM3
```

The restructured loop incorporates associative transformations. Again, as with the cake, there is a chance that the results won't be exactly the same as if we had stuck with the original recipe. However, we have overcome the serial, recursive nature of the loop by collecting four partial sums instead of one. Dot products are just one form of vector reduction. Loops that look for the maximum or minimum elements in an array, multiply all the elements of an array or sum all the elements of an array are also

---

*Again, I have disregarded any iterations that might be left over.

reductions. Likewise, some of these can be reorganized into partial products or sums, as with the dot product, to expose more computations.

Dot Products and daxpys

The best known floating point benchmark is proably the Linpack benchmark, often quoted as a standard for floating point performance. (See Chapter 13). The inner loop of Linpack is a piece of code called *daxpy* and, at one time, it was the optimal construct for the fastest computers on the market. However, it isn't optimal for your workstation.

The name *daxpy* stands for "*d*ouble precision *A* times *X p*lus *Y*": a vector plus a vector times a constant (*saxpy* is the single precision form). It is a common inner loop for Gaussian Elimination, like the Linpack benchmark. Coded in FORTRAN it looks like this:

```
      DO 10 I=1,N
         DY(I) = DY(I) + DA*DX(I)
10    CONTINUE
```

If you count the number of memory and floating point operations inside the loop you come up with a ratio of three memory operations to two floating point operations. We have already identified that memory operations aren't the strong suit of workstations on the market today. However, this is a perfect ratio for modern supercomputers, such as the Cray Y/MP. These machines can perform three memory operations and two (or more) vector flops per clock cycle. Therefore, they can run daxpy very fast—much faster by proportion than a workstation that can do only one memory operation (at most) per flop.

However, vector computers don't do so well on dot products, another very common construct:

```
      DO 10 I=1,N
         S = S + DX(I) * DY(I)
10    CONTINUE
```

As we've just seen, dot products aren't vectorizable. If you interpret the dot product code literally, each iteration requires the results from the previous iteration before computation can proceed. In other words, a scalar dependency between loop iterations prevents vectorization.

A dot product can be partially vectorized, if you take the kind of liberties with associative transformations I discussed above. The loop can be broken into partial sums. The sums can be created using the vector processor and assembled later, using the scalar processor. Most vectorizing compilers will do this for you automatically, but for illustration I have hand-coded a coarse approach. The TEMP array is folded over on itself a couple of times until the end, where the last part is done in scalar mode:

```
      DO 10 I=1,N
        TEMP(I) = A(I) * B(I)
 10   CONTINUE
      DO 20 I=1,N/2
        TEMP(I) = TEMP(I) + TEMP(I+N/2)
 20   CONTINUE
      DO 30 I=1,N/4
        TEMP(I) = TEMP(I) + TEMP(I+N/4)
 30   CONTINUE
      DO 40 I=1,N/8
        TEMP(I) = TEMP(I) + TEMP(I+N/8)
 40   CONTINUE
C
C Assemble the results in scalar mode
C
      X = 0
      DO 50 I=1,N/8
        X = X + TEMP(I)
 50   CONTINUE
```

Unlike vector supercomputers, parallel RISC workstations are better with dot products than they are with daxpys. Many new architectures, such as RS/6000, the Intel i860, H-P's PA RISC, and the DEC Alpha AXP, feature pipelined floating point multiply-add instructions that can take the contents of two registers, multiply them, add in a third, and store the result to a fourth—all from one opcode.

```
r1 * r2 + r3 -> r4
```

While this hardly sounds like RISC, it is the perfect primitive from which to construct a dot product.

Looking at the loop above again, you will notice that there are only two memory operations per iteration; the variable S can be kept in a register. This means that a loop constructed with a dot product will have a lower demand for memory than one made from a daxpy. Theoretically, if the demand could be further reduced to roughly one memory operation per clock, then the workstation CPU could produce results at its highest rate—two floating point operations (a multiply and an add) and one memory operation every one or two clock cycles, depending on the brand.

Matrix Multiplication

With full matrix multiplication you get to choose whether you would prefer to construct the inner loop from a dot product or a daxpy. Example 10-2 shows how matrix multiplication looks, using daxpy as the inner loop.

Example 10-2: Matrix multiply with daxpy inner loop

```
        DO 10 I=1,N
         DO 20 J=1,N
          C(J,I) = 0.0
  20     CONTINUE
  10    CONTINUE

        DO 50 K=1,N
         DO 60 J=1,N
          DO 70 I=1,N
           C(I,J) = C(I,J) + A(I,K) * B(K,J)
  70      CONTINUE
  60     CONTINUE
  50    CONTINUE
```

There are three memory operations per iteration—two loads and a store. A mature compiler will recognize that B(K,J) needs to be loaded only once inside the inner loop, so references to **B** won't contribute to memory traffic.

You can easily turn a matrix multiply with a daxpy at its center into one with a dot product at the center by interchanging (explained below) the inner and outer loops.

Example 10-3: Matrix multiply with dot product inner loop

```
        DO 10 I=1,N
         DO 20 J=1,N
          C(J,I) = 0.0
  20     CONTINUE
  10    CONTINUE

        DO 60 J=1,N
         DO 70 I=1,N
          DO 50 K=1,N
           C(I,J) = C(I,J) + A(I,K) * B(K,J)
  50      CONTINUE
  70     CONTINUE
  60    CONTINUE
```

Now, with a dot product at the center, you can perform the reduction optimization to expose more parallelism.

The following code will execute very quickly:

```
        DO 10 I=1,N
         DO 20 J=1,N
          C(J,I) = 0.0
  20     CONTINUE
  10    CONTINUE

        DO 60 J=1,N
         DO 70 I=1,N

           KK = IMOD (N,4)
           DO 80 K=1,KK
             C(I,J) = C(I,J) + A(I,K) * B(K,J)
  80       CONTINUE

           TEMP0 = 0.0
           TEMP1 = 0.0
           TEMP2 = 0.0
           TEMP3 = 0.0
           DO 50 K=1+KK,N,4
              TEMP0 = TEMP0 + A(I,K)   * B(K,J)
              TEMP1 = TEMP1 + A(I,K+1) * B(K+1,J)
              TEMP2 = TEMP2 + A(I,K+2) * B(K+2,J)
              TEMP3 = TEMP3 + A(I,K+3) * B(K+3,J)
  50       CONTINUE
           C(I,J) = C(I,J) + TEMP0 + TEMP1 + TEMP2 + TEMP3
  70     CONTINUE
  60    CONTINUE
```

To further reduce the amount of memory traffic, you can perform some additional optimizations on the loop nest. The same B(K,J) is going to be needed for many different values of the index I in the middle loop. Provided the compiler cooperates, outer loop unrolling or blocking could preserve copies of B(K,J) in registers. This is also how you would approach it if you were hand coding the multiplication in assembly language. By blocking iterations (next chapter) and keeping copies of B(K,J), B(K+1,J), B(K+1,J), etc., in registers, you can reduce the demand for memory in the inner loop to nearly one load operation per iteration, giving you performance close to peak. A hand coded matrix multiply has slightly more than one memory operation and a multiply-add instruction in the inner loop, which corresponds to the best you can hope for from many of the superscalar RISC architectures on the market today.

Loop Interchange

Loop interchange is a technique for rearranging a loop nest so that the right stuff is at the center. What the right stuff is depends upon what you are trying to accomplish. I just showed you how to invert loops in matrix multiplication to turn a daxpy into a dot product. In many situations, loop interchange also lets you swap high trip count loops for low trip count loops, so that activity gets pulled into the center of the loop nest. It's also good for improving memory access patterns; iterating on the wrong subscript can cause a large stride and hurt your performance.* If you invert the loops, so that the iterating variables causing the lesser strides are in the center, you can get a performance win.

Again, memory access patterns are something I'll be covering in detail in the next chapter, so here I will just describe how loop interchange can increase parallelism.

Loop Interchange to Move Computations to the Center

When someone writes a program that represents some kind of real world model, they often structure the code in terms of the model. This makes perfect sense. The computer is an analysis tool. You are not writing the code on the computer's behalf. However, a model expressed naturally often works on one point in space at a time, which tends to give you insignificant inner loops—at least in terms of the trip count. For performance, you might want to reverse inner and outer loops to pull the activity into the center, where you can then do some unrolling. Let me illustrate with an example. Here's a loop where KDIM time dependent quantities for points in a two-dimensional mesh are being updated:

```
      PARAMETER (IDIM = 1000, JDIM = 1000, KDIM = 4)
        ...
      DO 10 I=1,IDIM
        DO 20 J=1,JDIM
          DO 30 K=1,KDIM
            D(K,J,I) = D(K,J,I) + V(K,J,I) * DT
30        CONTINUE
20      CONTINUE
10    CONTINUE
```

---

*Remember, I'm talking about machines with caches. Machines with the ability to bypass cache don't (necessarily) have problems with large strides.

In practice, KDIM is probably equal to two or three, where J or I, representing the number of points, may be in the thousands. The way it is written, the inner loop has a very low trip count, making it a poor candidate for unrolling.

By interchanging the loops, you update one quantity at a time, across all of the points. For tuning purposes, this moves larger trip counts into the inner loop and allow you to do some strategic unrolling:

```
          DO 10 K=1,IDIM
            DO 20 I=1,KDIM
              DO 30 J=1,JDIM
                D(K,J,I) = D(K,J,I) + V(K,J,I) * DT
30            CONTINUE
20          CONTINUE
10        CONTINUE
```

This example is straightforward; it is easy to see that are no inter-iteration dependencies. But how can you tell, in general, when two loops can be interchanged? Interchanging loops might violate some dependency, or worse, only violate it occasionally, meaning you might not catch it when optimizing. Can we merge the loops below?

```
          DO 10 I=1,N-1
            DO 20 J=2,N
              A(I,J) = A(I+1,J-1) * B(I,J)
              C(I,J) = B(J,I)
20          CONTINUE
10        CONTINUE
```

In Appendix B I'll show you a graphical technique for determining when loop interchange is OK, for relatively simple loop nests. I'll also talk about the possibility of running loops backwards—starting from the loop upper limit and working towards the lower limit—as a technique for overcoming dependencies.

Operation Counting

Operation counting is simply the process of surveying a loop to understand the operation mix. We counted operations in the discussions about daxpys, dot products, and matrix multiplication, above. From that, we could see how well the operation mix of a given loop matched the capabilities of the processor. Of course, operation counting doesn't guarantee that the compiler will generate an efficient representation of a loop.* But it generally provides enough insight to the loop to direct tuning efforts.

Bear in mind that an instruction mix that is balanced for one machine may be imbalanced for another. We saw this when we compared a superscalar RISC workstation to a Cray supercomputer, above. Workstations on the market today can generally issue one (dual) floating point operation and one memory operation (or integer operation), per clock cycle, as a minimum (see Appendix A). Address arithmetic is often embedded in the instructions that reference memory. Because the compiler can replace complicated loop address calculations with simple expressions (provided the pattern of addresses is predictable), you can often ignore address arithmetic when counting operations.†

Let's look at a few loops and see what we can learn about the instruction mix:

```
      DO 10 I=1,N
        A(I,J,K) = A(I,J,K) + B(J,I,K)
   10 CONTINUE
```

The loop above contains one floating point addition and three memory references (two loads and a store). There are some complicated array index expressions, but these will probably be simplified by the compiler, and executed in the same cycle as the memory and floating point operations.

A 3:1 ratio of memory references to floating point operations suggests that we can hope for no more than 1/3 peak floating point performance from the loop, even after unrolling it many times. That's bad news, but good information. The ratio tells us that we ought to consider memory reference optimizations first.

The loop below contains one floating point addition and two memory operations—a load and a store. Operand B(J) is loop-invariant, so its value only needs to be loaded once, upon entry to the loop.

```
      DO 10 I=1,N
        A(I) = A(I) + B(J)
   10 CONTINUE
```

---

*We would have to look at the assembly language output to be sure, which may be going a bit overboard. To get an assembly language listing on most machines, compile with the **-S** flag. On an RS/6000, use the **-qlist** flag.

†The compiler reduces the complexity of loop index expressions with a technique called *induction variable simplification*. See Chapter 4.

Again, our floating point throughput is limited, though not as severely as in the previous loop. The ratio of memory references to floating point operations is 2:1.

Below we have a loop with better prospects. It performs element-wise multiplication of two vectors of imaginary numbers, and assigns the results back to the first. There are six memory operations (four loads and two stores) and six floating point operations (two additions and four multiplications).

```
for (i=0; i<n; i++) {
    xr[i] = xr[i] * yr[i] + xi[i] * yi[i];
    xi[i] = xr[i] * yi[i] + xi[i] * yr[i];
}
```

It appears that this loop is balanced for a workstation that can perform one memory operation and one floating point operation per cycle. However, it might not be. Recall that newer RISC processors can issue dual-operation multiply-add instructions. If the compiler is good enough to recognize that the multiply-add is appropriate, this loop may also be limited by memory references; each iteration would be compiled into two multiplications and two multiply-adds.

Again, operation counting is a simple way to estimate how well the requirements of a loop will map onto the capabilities of the machine. For floating point applications, you will often find the performance of the loops dominated by memory references, as we have seen in the last three examples. This suggests that memory reference tuning will be very important.

Closing Notes

Many chapters back, I promised to show you some optimizations that would mar the beauty of your programs. I feel that I have kept my promise.

We've actually looked at two different kinds of activities:

1. Rearranging loops to make them vectorizable (eliminating if-statements, inlining short routines, loop interchange, etc.)

2. Exposing parallelism, particularly for a (super)scalar processor (unrolling, restructuring reductions)

For some purposes we've gone too far. If you are writing code for a vector machine, or are planning to feed it to an optimizing preprocessor (not much different from a vectorizing compiler), you may want to go as far as rearranging loops so that they are more vectorizable. But stop short of unrolling them; let the compiler take it from there. Vector hardware or hand-coded vector libraries will almost always execute more quickly than the code the compiler creates from unrolled loops. I'll have more to say about this later on.

Chapter 11 is about memory optimizations. Some (not all) are loop optimizations, and many look an awful lot like the ones we saw in this chapter.* Accordingly, the techniques aren't independent of one another—tuning for parallelism affects memory patterns and vice versa. Is it possible to tune for one and satisfy the other? Sort of. We'll look at that next.

Exercises

1. Why is an unrolling amount of three or four iterations generally sufficient for simple vector loops on a RISC processor? What relationship does the unrolling amount have to floating point pipeline depths?

2. On a processor that can execute one floating point multiply, one floating point addition/subtraction, and one memory reference per cycle, what's the best performance you could expect from the following loop?

```
      DO 10 I = 1,10000
  10    A(I) = B(I) * C(I) - D(I) * E(I)
```

3. Show how you could unroll the following reduction:

```
   for (i=0; i<n; i++)
      a[i] = a[i] < b[i] ? b[i] : c[i];
```

4. Can you interchange the loops in the following loop nest?

```
      DO 10 I=1,N-1
        DO 20 J=2,M
          A(I+1,J) = A(I,J-1) + B(J)
  20      CONTINUE
  10    CONTINUE
```

---

*It's the same way that a wrench can double as a hammer and a crowbar.

11

Memory Reference Optimizations

We continue to benefit from tremendous increases in the raw speed of microprocessors without proportional increases in the speed of memory. This means that "good" performance is becoming more closely tied to good memory access patterns, and careful re-use of operands.

No one could afford a memory system fast enough to satisfy every reference immediately, so vendors depend on caches, interleaving, and other devices to deliver reasonable memory performance. The efficiency of these depends on the behavior of your program—bad memory access patterns give you bad performance. In pathological cases, you would simply be better off without them. A single problem, structured two different ways, could run at very different speeds because of the way it plays to the memory system.

Clarity is another key element. Although not directly related to the speed of the memory system, it is important for parallelism and good memory throughput. When the compiler can see how memory references interplay, it can safely schedule them alongside other operations for improved performance. This is especially important for multiprocessors and vector computers.

Memory Access Patterns

The best pattern is the most straightforward: increasing and unit sequential. For an array with a single dimension, stepping through one element at a time will give you this.* For multiply dimensioned arrays, access will be fastest if you iterate on the array subscript offering the smallest *stride* or step size. In FORTRAN programs this is the leftmost subscript; in C it is the rightmost. The FORTRAN loop below has unit stride, and therefore will run quickly:

```
      DO 10 J=1,N
        DO 10 I=1,N
          A(I,J) = B(I,J) + C(I,J) * D
   10 CONTINUE
```

In contrast, the next loop will be slower because its stride is N (which, we assume, is greater than 1). The larger the value of N, the more significant the performance difference will be:

```
      DO 10 J=1,N
        DO 10 I=1,N
          A(J,I) = B(J,I) + C(J,I) * D
   10 CONTINUE
```

In C programs, the subscripts appear in reverse order. Here's a unit stride loop like the one above, but written in C:

```
  for (i=0; i<n; i++)
    for (j=0; j<n; j++)
      a[i][j] = a[i][j] + c[i][j] * d;
```

Unit stride gives you the best performance because it conserves cache entries. Recall how a data cache works.† Your program makes a memory reference; if the data is in the cache, it gets returned immediately. If not, your program suffers a cache miss while a new cache line is fetched from main memory, replacing an old one. The line holds the values taken from a handful of neighboring memory locations, including the one that caused the cache miss. If you loaded a cache line, took one piece of data from it and threw the rest away, you would be wasting a lot of time and memory bandwidth. However, if you brought a line into the cache and consumed everything in it, you would benefit from a large number of memory refer-

---

*I'm talking about machines with caches. Strided references are not necessarily bad for machines that access a multibanked memory system directly, though some strides can cause bank stalls. See Chapter 3 for a discussion of multi-banked memory systems.
†See Chapter 3.

ences for a small number of cache misses. This is exactly what you get when your program makes unit stride memory references.

The worst case patterns are those that jump through memory, especially a large amount of memory, and particularly those that do so without apparent rhyme or reason (viewed from the outside). On large jobs, you not only pay a penalty for cache misses, but for TLB misses too.* It would be nice to be able to rein these jobs in so that they make better use of memory. Of course, you can't eliminate memory references; programs have to get to their data one way or another. The question is, then: how can we restructure memory access patterns for the best performance?

In the next few sections we are going to look at some tricks for restructuring loops with strided, albeit predictable, access patterns. The tricks will be familiar; they are mostly loop optimizations from the last chapter, used here for different reasons. The underlying goal is to minimize cache and TLB misses as much as possible. You will see that we can do quite a lot, although, here again, some of this is going to be ugly.

Loop Interchange to Ease Memory Access Patterns

Loop interchange is a good technique for lessening the impact of strided memory references. Let's revisit our FORTRAN loop with non-unit stride. The good news is that we can easily interchange the loops; each iteration is independent of every other:†

```
        DO 10 J=1,N
          DO 10 I=1,N
            A(J,I) = B(J,I) + C(J,I) * D
   10     CONTINUE
```

After interchange, **A**, **B**, and **C** are referenced with the leftmost subscript varying most quickly. This can make an important difference in performance. We traded three N-strided memory references for unit strides:

```
        DO 10 I=1,N
          DO 10 J=1,N
            A(J,I) = B(J,I) + C(J,I) * D
   10     CONTINUE
```

---

*The Translation Lookaside Buffer (TLB) is a cache of translations from virtual memory addresses to physical memory addresses. For more information, see Chapter 3.

†See Appendix B for a method to recognize when loops can be interchanged.

Life is rarely this simple, of course. Often you find some mix of variables with small and large strides, in which case interchanging the loops moves the damage around, but doesn't make it go away.

These loops represent a dilemma:

```
      DO 10 I=1,N              DO 20 J=1,M
        DO 20 J=1,M              DO 10 I=1,N
          A(J,I) = B(I,J)          A(J,I) = B(I,J)
   20     CONTINUE          10     CONTINUE
   10   CONTINUE            20   CONTINUE
```

Whichever way you interchange them, you will break the memory access pattern for either **A** or **B**. Even more interesting, you have to make a choice between strided loads vs. strided stores—which will it be?* We really need a general method for improving the memory access patterns for *both* **A** and **B**, not one or the other. I'll show you such a method in the next section.

Blocking to Ease Memory Access Patterns

Blocking is another kind of memory reference optimization. As with loop interchange, the challenge is to retrieve as much data as possible with as few cache misses as possible. We'd like to rearrange the loop nest so that it works on data in little neighborhoods, rather than striding through memory like a man on stilts. Given the sample vector sum in Example 11-1, how can we rearrange the loop?

Example 11-1: Two-dimensional vector sum

```
      DO 10 I=1,N
        DO 20 J=1,N
          A(J,I) = A(J,I) + B(I,J)
   20     CONTINUE
   10   CONTINUE
```

This loop involves two vectors. One is referenced with unit stride, the other with a stride of N. We can interchange the loops, but one way or another we will still have N-strided array references on either **A** or **B**, either of which is undesirable. The trick is to *block* references so that you grab a

---

*I can't tell you which is the better way to cast it—it depends on the brand of computer. Some perform better with the loops left as they are, sometimes by more than a factor of two. Others perform better with them interchanged. The difference is in the way the processor handles updates of main memory from cache.

few elements of **A**, and then a few of **B**, and then a few of **A**, and so on—in neighborhoods. You make this happen by combining inner and outer loop unrolling.

Example 11-2: Outer and inner loop unrolled

```
      DO 10 I=1,N,2
        DO 20 J=1,N,2
          A(J,I)     = A(J,I)      + B(I,J)
          A(J+1,I)   = A(J+1,I)    + B(I,J+1)
          A(J,I+1)   = A(J,I+1)    + B(I+1,J)
          A(J+1,I+1) = A(J+1,I+1)  + B(I+1,J+1)
   20   CONTINUE
   10   CONTINUE
```

Lend me your imagination so I can show you why this helps. Usually, when you think of a two dimensional array, you think of a rectangle or a square.

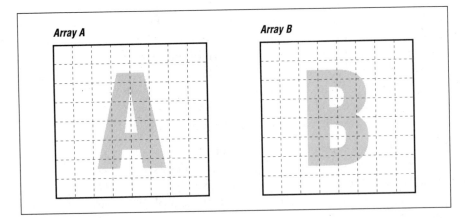

Figure 11-1: Arrays A and B

Remember, to make programming easier, the compiler provides the illusion that two dimensional arrays **A** and **B** are rectangular plots of memory. Actually, memory is sequential storage. In FORTRAN, a two dimensional array is constructed from memory by logically lining memory "strips" up against each other, like the pickets of a cedar fence. (It's the other way around in C—rows are stacked on top of one another). Array storage starts at the upper left, proceeds down to the bottom and then starts over at the top of the next column. Stepping through the array with unit stride traces out the shape of a backwards "N", repeated over and over, moving to the right.

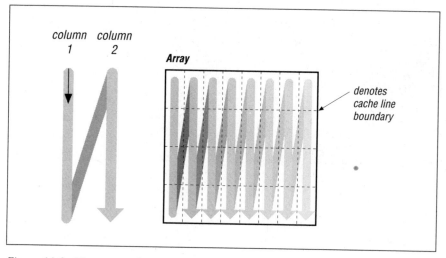

Figure 11-2: How array elements are stored

Imagine that the thin horizontal lines of Figure 11-2 cut memory storage into pieces the size of individual cache entries. Picture how the loop in Example 11-1 will traverse them. Because of their index expressions, references to **A** go from top to bottom (in the backwards "N" shape), consuming every bit of each cache line, but references to **B** dash off to the right, using one piece of each cache entry and discarding the rest (Figure 11-3, top). This will result in a high number of cache misses.

If we could somehow rearrange the loop so that it consumed the arrays in small rectangles, rather than strips, we could conserve some of the cache entries that are being discarded. This is exactly what we accomplished by unrolling both the inner and outer loops of Example 11-2. Array **A** is referenced in several strips side by side, from top to bottom while **B** is referenced in several strips side by side, from left to right (Figure 11-3, bottom). This will improve cache performance and lower the run time.

For really big problems, more than cache entries are at stake. Workstations are virtual memory machines, meaning that memory references have to be translated through a Translation Lookaside Buffer (TLB). A typical workstation's TLB can accommodate entries to cover only several hundred KB of data.* This means that if you are dealing with large arrays, TLB misses are going to add to your run time too, in addition to cache misses.

---

*This is changing. Processors are starting to feature TLBs with variable size page entries. The Intel i860XP and DEC Alpha AXP are examples.

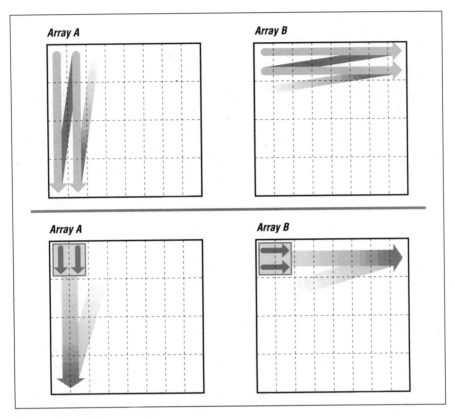

Figure 11-3: 2x2 squares

Here's something that may surprise you. In the code below, I rewrote this loop yet again, this time blocking references at two different levels: in 2×2 squares to save cache entries, and by cutting the original loop in two parts to save TLB entries.

```
        DO 11 I=1,N,2
          DO 21 J=1,N/2,2
            A(J,I) = A(J,I) + B(I,J)
            A(J+1,I) = A(J+1,I) + B(I+1,J)
            A(J,I+1) = A(J,I+1) + B(I+1,J)
            A(J+1,I+1) = A(J+1,I+1) + B(I+1,J+1)
21       CONTINUE
11     CONTINUE
```

```
        DO 10 I=1,N,2
          DO 20 J=N/2+1,N,2
            A(J,I) = A(J,I) + B(I,J)
            A(J+1,I) = A(J+1,I) + B(I+1,J)
            A(J,I+1) = A(J,I+1) + B(I+1,J)
            A(J+1,I+1) = A(J+1,I+1) + B(I+1,J+1)
   20     CONTINUE
   10   CONTINUE
```

You might guess that adding more loops would be the wrong thing to do. But if you work with a reasonably large value of N, say 256, you will see a significant increase in performance. This is because the two arrays **A** and **B** are each 64 KB × 8 bytes = 1/2 MB when N is equal to 256—larger than can be handled by the TLBs and caches of most workstations.

The two boxes in Figure 11-4 illustrate how the first few references to **A** and **B** look superimposed upon one another in the blocked and unblocked cases. Unblocked references to **B** zing off through memory, eating through cache and TLB entries. Blocked references are more sparing with the memory system.

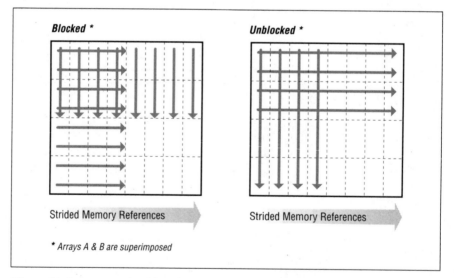

Figure 11-4: Picture of unblocked versus blocked references

You can take blocking even further for larger problems. This code shows another method that limits the size of the inner loop and visits it repeatedly:

```
          II = IMOD (N,16)
          JJ = IMOD (N,4)
          DO 1 J=1,JJ
            DO 2 I=1,II
              A(J,I) = A(J,I) + B(I,J)
  2       CONTINUE
  1     CONTINUE

          DO 10 I=II+1,N,16
            DO 20 J=JJ+1,N,4
              DO 30 K=I,I+16
                A(J,K)   = A(J,K)   + B(K,J)
                A(J+1,K) = A(J+1,K) + B(K,J+1)
                A(J+2,K) = A(J+2,K) + B(K,J+2)
                A(J+3,K) = A(J+3,K) + B(K,J+3)
  30      CONTINUE
  20      CONTINUE
  10      CONTINUE
```

Where the inner I loop used to execute N iterations at a time, the new K loop executes only 16 iterations. This divides and conquers a large memory address space by cutting it into little pieces. Figure 11-5 presents some data that demonstrates how effective these optimizations are. I've selected five variations of the vector sum we've been examining:

- Original unmodified code
- Inner loop unrolling of 4
- Inner loop unrolling of 2, outer loop unrolling of 2
- Inner loop unrolling of 2, outer loop unrolling of 2, 2 inner loops
- Inner loop unrolling of 2, outer loop unrolling of 2, 4 inner loops

Each of the five versions of the loop nest ran on three RISC workstations: the Hewlett-Packard 720B, the IBM RS/6000 530, and the Silicon Graphics 4D/35 with problem sizes varying from 64 KB to 2 MB. For each, I repeated passes through the loop nest hundreds or thousands of times to time each iteration.* I normalized the results to the times for the loop in Figure 11-5 for N equal to 64 on each workstation, and then averaged the numbers for the three brands together. In short, the graph reflects the cumulative results for the tests on all of the workstations combined.

---

*That I repeated passes is significant because it means that cache and TLB misses for the smaller cases will be minimal after the first pass through, as might be the case for small applications that reuse the same memory locations repeatedly. The Linpack benchmark is an example of a program with a small amount of memory that is visited repeatedly.

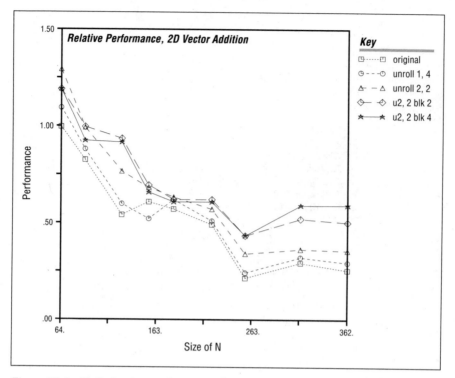

Figure 11-5: Optimization performance for various sized loops

The most striking observation is that performance drops sharply as the problem size increases. This drop-off occurs for all the loops, but it's worst for the original (unmodified) loop—performance drops by a factor of three. This is because of cache and TLB miss. Smaller problems are able to reuse cache and TLB entries left from the previous iterations, but large problems flush them out, so they have to be reloaded.

As we'd hope, the performance of the optimized loops is better than the performance of the original loop, particularly for large values of N. It is also interesting that the loop nest that was split into several loops, although not the best optimization for the small case, is the winner at the far end of the graph, where N is largest.

For fun, the graph in Figure 11-5 shows the workstation data superimposed over the normalized vector performance of a single processor of a Cray Y-MP8E. The Cray isn't operating through a cache, so there are no cache misses to worry about, and it's not a virtual memory machine, so there are no TLB misses, either. The graph illustrates an important difference between memory systems of the two architectural classes. In spite of the cyclic dips caused by oversubscribed memory banks, the performance of the vector machine doesn't fall off as the problem size increases, the way it does with workstations. Moral: Caches don't work well for supercomputing applications that require a lot of memory.

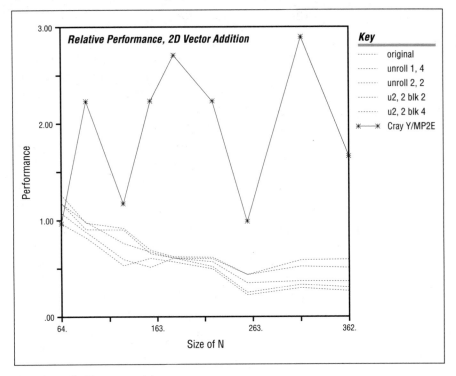

Figure 11-6: Vector machine memory access

Again, the combined unrolling and blocking techniques I just showed you are for loops with *mixed stride* expressions. They work very well for loop nests like the one we have been looking at. However, if all array references are strided the same way, then you will want to try loop unrolling or loop interchange first.

Ambiguity in Memory References

In Chapter 8 we talked about parallelism and what makes good parallel code. We also discussed "Ambiguous Memory References," which I'd like to come back to because it is relative to this chapter as well. Ambiguous memory references are those that are difficult for the compiler to distinguish from other, possibly conflicting references. You *could* call most references ambiguous by themselves; who knows where an expression like A(I) eventually goes? However, this is not what we mean. Memory references are ambiguous when you can't tell how they are related to *other* references located nearby.

Ambiguity in Vector Operations

A RISC processor or vector processor can fly through regular, repeated floating point operations, provided they are not too dependent upon each other. However, there are situations where it is difficult, if not impossible, for the compiler or preprocessor to tell whether two index expressions might point to the same storage location. The compiler has to ask whether these two references can be to the same place? As I said in Chapter 8, an "I don't know" answer is the same as a yes—the compiler has to assume that they could point to the same locations, and be conservative. This will result in reduced performance. For illustration, consider this loop from Chapter 8:

```
      DO 10 I=1,N
         A(I)   = B(I) * E
         B(I)   = A(I+K) * C    ←K unknown
   10    CONTINUE
```

Without information about the value of K, the compiler cannot safely overlap memory references to A(I) and A(I+K). For instance, if K is 0, then the value for A(I) —probably still in a register—is what's needed to calculate B(I). If it's negative, then this loop is recursive—especially if K is -1 or -2. If it's positive, then there really isn't a problem; execution can be safely overlapped.

Sometimes you just don't know what the relationship between the index expressions like I and I+K is going to be. But when you do, you can often supply the compiler or preprocessor with a directive that says: "it's safe to overlap these." This will give the compiler or preprocessor the assurance it needs to cast the loop more efficiently. I'll describe some of these directives in detail in the next chapter.

A similar situation comes up when vector data is stored indirectly, through pointers, as might be the case with a very large, sparse matrix solution or unstructured grid problem. For illustration, here is a *daxpy* from an indirect solution:

```
      DO 10 I=1,N
         A(K(I)) = A(K(I)) + B(I) * C
   10    CONTINUE
```

Again, there is a question of ambiguity. The compiler cannot be sure that each iteration is independent of the others because it can't tell what the pattern of subscripts will be. Successive K(I)s may be recursive, or even repeated, for all the compiler knows. You can improve the performance a little by giving the compiler a directive that says it is OK to overlap memory references and computations.

You can guess that there might be other challenges too. Because elements of **A** may be scattered about, indirect references can exercise the cache more than direct references would. Furthermore, each reference to the array **A** takes two memory references: one for K(I) and one for A(K(I)). The demand for memory bandwidth and the possibility of widely scattered references can make tuning a challenge.

Pointer Ambiguity in Numerical C Applications

FORTRAN compilers depend on programmers to observe aliasing rules. That is, programmers are not supposed to modify locations through pointers that may be aliases of one another. They can become aliases in several ways, such as when two dummy arguments receive pointers to the same storage locations (Chapter 6 describes this in detail):

```
CALL FOO (A,A)
   ...
END
SUBROUTINE FOO (X,Y)   <- X,Y become aliases
```

C compilers don't enjoy the same restrictions on aliasing. In fact, there are cases where aliasing could be desirable. Additionally, C is blessed with pointer types, increasing the opportunities for aliasing to occur. This means that a C compiler has to approach operations through pointers more conservatively than a FORTRAN compiler would. Let's look at some examples to see why.

The following loop nest looks like a FORTRAN loop cast in C. The arrays are declared or allocated all at once at the top of the routine, and the starting address and leading dimensions are visible to the compiler. This is important because it means that the storage relationship between the array elements is well known. Hence, you could expect good performance:

```
#define N ...
double a[N][N], c[N][N], d;
...
for (i=0; i<N; i++)
    for (j=0; j<N; j++)
        a[i][j] = a[i][j] + c[j][i] * d;
```

Now imagine what happens if you allocate the rows dynamically. This makes the address calculations more complicated. The loop nest hasn't changed; however, there is no guaranteed stride that can get you from one row to the next. This is because the storage relationship between the rows is unknown:

```
#define N ...
double *a[N], *c[N], d;
...
for (i=0; i<N; i++) {
    a[i] = (double *) malloc (N*sizeof(double));
    c[i] = (double *) malloc (N*sizeof(double));
}
for (i=0; i<N; i++)
    for (j=0; j<N; j++)
        a[i][j] = a[i][j] + c[j][i] * d;
```

In fact, your compiler knows even less than you might expect about the storage relationship. For instance, how can it be sure that references to a and c aren't aliases? It may be obvious to you that they're not. You might point out that *malloc* never overlaps storage. But the compiler isn't free to assume that. Who knows? You may be substituting your own version of *malloc*!

Let's look at a different example, where storage is allocated all at once, though the declarations are not visible to all routines that are using it. The subroutine foo, below, performs the same computation as our previous example. However, because the compiler can't see the declarations for a and c (they're in the main routine), it doesn't have enough information to be able to overlap memory references from successive iterations; the references could be aliases.

```
#define N ...
main()
{
    double a[N][N], c[N][N], d;
    ...
    foo (a,c,d,N);
}
foo (a,c,d,n)
double *a, *c, d;
int n;
{
    int i,j;
    double *ap, *cp;
    for (i=0;i<n;i++) {
        ap = a + (i*n);
        cp = c + i;
```

```
        for (j=0; j<n; j++)
            *(ap+j) = *(ap+j) + *(cp+(i*n)) * d;
    }
}
```

To get the best performance, make available to the compiler as many details about the size and shape of your data structures as possible. Pointers, whether in the form of formal arguments to a subroutine or whether explicitly declared, can hide important facts about how you are using memory. The more information the compiler has, the more it can overlap memory references. This information can come from compiler directives or from making declarations visible in the routines where performance is most critical.

Programs That Require More Memory Than You Have

People occasionally have programs whose memory size requirements are so great that the data can't fit in memory all at once. At any time, some of the data has to reside outside of main memory on secondary (usually disk) storage. These out-of-core solutions fall into two categories:

- Software-managed, out-of-core solutions
- Virtual memory-managed, out-of-core solutions

With a software-managed approach, the programmer has recognized that the problem is too big, and has written explicit instructions into the source code for heaving sections of the data out to disk for retrieval at a later time. The other method depends of computer's memory system handling the secondary storage requirements on its own, sometimes at a great cost in run time.

Software-Managed, Out-of-Core Solutions

Most codes with software-managed, out-of-core solutions have adjustments—you can tell the program how much memory it has to work with and it will take care of the rest. It is important to make sure that the adjustment is set correctly. Code that was tuned for a machine with limited memory could have been ported to yours without taking into account the storage available. Perhaps the whole problem will fit easily.

If you are writing an out-of-core solution yourself, the trick is to group memory references together so that they are localized. This usually occurs naturally as a side effect of partitioning, say, a matrix factorization into groups of columns. Blocking references the way we did at the start of this chapter will also corral memory references together so you can treat them as memory "pages." Knowing when to ship them off to disk entails being closely involved with what the program is doing.

The reason why anybody would consider writing an out-of-core solution in this day and age is that some of the fastest computers in the world are not virtual memory machines. Cray computers and the nodes of many parallel computers don't support the notion of memory backed up by a swap area. To run larger than core programs, you have to code an out-of-core solution by hand. In the case of the Cray, you would probably use a solid state disk as a "backing store" for the data in your program.

Virtual Memory

There is a common belief that the reason for a virtual memory system is to allow you to run programs of nearly unlimited size. The historical motivation for virtual memory was to allow a handful of users to share 64 KB on a PDP-11 without any of them being thrown out for want of memory. Don't make a mistake: unplanned execution outside the bounds of the memory on your machine can be painfully slow—a factor of 20 or so.

Under most UNIX implementations, the operating system will automatically page pieces of a program that are too large for the available memory out to the *swap area*. The program won't be tossed out completely—that only happens when memory gets extremely tight, or when your program has been inactive for a while. Rather, individual pages are placed in the swap area for retrieval later on. First of all, you need to be aware that this is happening if you don't already know about it. Secondly, if it is happening, then the memory access patterns will be critical. When references are too widely scattered, your run time will be completely dominated by disk I/O.

If you plan in advance, you can make a virtual memory system work with you when your program is too large for the physical memory on the machine. The techniques are exactly the same as those for tuning a software-managed out-of-core solution, or loop nests. "Blocking" memory references so that data is consumed in neighborhoods uses a bigger portion of each virtual memory page before rotating it out to disk to make room for another.

Gauging the Size of Your Program and the Machine's Memory

How can you tell if you are running out-of-core? There are ways to check for paging on the machine, but perhaps the most straightforward check is to compare the size of your program against the amount of available memory. You do this with the *size* command:

```
% size myprogram
```

On a System V UNIX machine, the output will look something like:

```
53872 + 53460 + 10010772 = 10118104
```

On a Berkeley UNIX derivative you will see something like:

```
   text      data       bss        hex      decimal
   53872     53460       10010772   9a63d8   10118104
```

The first three fields describe the amount of memory required for three different portions of your program. The first, text, accounts for the machine instructions that make up your program. The second, data, includes initialized values in your program such as the contents of data statements, common blocks, externals, character strings, etc. The third component, bss, *(block started by symbol)*, is usually the largest. It describes an uninitialized data area in your program. This would be made of common blocks that are not set by a block data. The last field(s) is a total for all three sections added together, in bytes.*

Next, you need to know how much memory you have in your system. Unfortunately, there isn't a standard UNIX command for this. On the RS/6000 */etc/lscfg* will tell you. On an SGI machine, */etc/hinv* will do it. Many System V UNIX implementations have an */etc/memsize* command. On any Berkeley derivative, you can type:

```
% ps aux
```

This will give you a listing of all the processes running on the machine. Find the process with the largest value in the %MEM. Divide the value in the

---

*Warning: The size command will not give you the full picture if your program allocates memory dynamically, or keeps data on the stack. This is especially important for C programs and FORTRAN programs that create large arrays that are not in COMMON.

RSS field by the percentage of memory used to get a rough figure for how much memory your machine has:

```
memory = RSS/(%MEM/100)
```

For instance, if the largest process shows 5% memory usage and a resident set size (RSS) of 840 KB, then your machine has 840000/(5/100) = 16 MB of memory.* If the answer from the size command shows a total that is anywhere near the amount of memory you have, then you stand a good chance of paging when you run—especially if you are doing other things on the machine at the same time.

Checking for Page Faults

Your system's performance monitoring tools will tell you if programs are paging. Some paging is OK; page faults and "page-ins" occur naturally as programs run. Also, be careful if you are competing for system resources along with other users. The picture you get won't be the same as when you have the computer to yourself.

To check for paging activity on a Berkeley UNIX derivative you use the *vmstat* command. Commonly people invoke it with a time increment so that it reports paging at regular intervals:

```
% vmstat 5
```

This produces output every five seconds:

procs			memory		page						disk				faults			cpu		
r	b	w	avm	fre	re	at	pi	po	fr	de	sr	s0	d1	d2	d3	in	sy	cs	us	sy	id
0	0	0	824	21568	0	0	0	0	0	0	0	0	0	0	0	20	37	13	0	1	98
0	0	0	840	21508	0	0	0	0	0	0	0	1	0	0	0	251	186	156	0	10	90
0	0	0	846	21460	0	0	0	0	0	0	0	2	0	0	0	248	149	152	1	9	89
0	0	0	918	21444	0	0	0	0	0	0	0	4	0	0	0	258	143	152	2	10	89

Lots of valuable information is produced. For our purposes, the important fields are avm or *active virtual memory*, the fre or *free real memory* and the pi/po numbers showing paging activity. When the fre figure drops to near zero and the po field shows a lot of activity, it's an indication that the memory system is overworked.

---

*You could also reboot the machine! It will tell you how much memory is available when it comes up.

On a SysV machine, paging activity can be seen with the *sar* command:

```
% sar -r 5 5
```

This will show you the amount of free memory and swap space presently available. If the free memory figure is low, you can assume that your program is paging.

```
Sat Apr 18 20:42:19 1992
[r] freemem freeswap
     4032    82144
```

As I said above, if you must run a job larger than the size of the memory on your machine, then the same sort of advice that applied to conserving cache activity applies to paging activity.* Try to minimize the stride in your code, and where you can't, blocking memory references will help a whole lot.

A note on performance monitoring tools: You should check with your workstation vendor to see what they have available beyond *vmstat* or *sar*. There may be much more sophisticated (and often graphical) tools which can help you understand how your program is using memory.

Instruction Cache Ordering

Up until this point we have been talking exclusively about data access. What about the text—the instructions that make up your program? These too have to be fetched from memory, and these too depend on a cache to make memory references go quickly. And just as with the data cache, there can be contention over certain parts of the *instruction cache* because of high levels of activity. For instance, if *foo* calls *bar* repeatedly, and they both map onto the same instruction cache lines, they will "thrash."

There's no science involved in subroutine arrangement. At link time they are mapped into the executable just as you specify them on the command line. That is, if you say:

```
% cc main.o foo.o bar.o baz.o
```

the routines will be linked in the order *main, foo, bar, baz*—one after the other. This may not be the best mapping as far as the cache is concerned; it may be terrible. The easiest way to tell is by ordering the subroutines

---

*By the way. Are you getting the message "Out of memory?" If you are running the *csh*, try typing unlimit to see if the message goes away. Otherwise, it may mean that you don't have enough swap space available to run the job.

several different ways and noting whether the run time changes. If it does, then you know that you have hit on something. If it doesn't change, the test is inconclusive.

There are ways to link routines to minimize the potential for instruction cache thrashing. For one, when you have a large portion of time spent in several routines which call each other repeatedly, it is a good idea to locate them next to each other in the list of modules being linked together. This way they will be mapped into the cache like peas in a pod. If the total size of these routines is smaller than the cache size, chances are good that your instruction cache miss rate will be pretty reasonable.

Silicon Graphics and MIPS-based DEC workstations come with a utility known as *cord* for ordering routines within the cache. It takes profile data and then modifies the link order so that cache miss will be reduced. Other vendors are aware of the problem of instruction cache miss—they write about it in their manuals—but to my knowledge there are no other tools for instruction cache ordering, so fiddling with the load order is about all you can do. In certain pathological cases, instruction cache reordering can be worth as much as a 25% increase in performance.

Inclusion of new modules, or a change in the size of one module (i.e., from loop unrolling) will change the pattern of activity in the instruction cache, so don't waste too much time reordering routines until you have finished making all of your other optimizations.

Closing Notes

Getting memory references right is the one of the most important challenges of application performance tuning. And you can be sure that as CPUs get faster—and memory systems fail to keep up—that it will become the most important challenge.

In the last two chapters we'll revisit memory references and locality of reference when we talk about parallel computers and multiprocessors. If you believe that it will take some kind of parallel machine to get the performance you are going to need in the future, then your investment in memory reference tuning will payoff down the road too.

Exercises

1. Try unrolling, interchanging or blocking the loop in subroutine BAZFAZ to increase the performance. What method or combination of methods works best? (Notes: compile the main routine and BAZFAZ separately. Adjust NTIMES so that the untuned run takes about one minute. Use the compiler's default optimization level.)

```
      PROGRAM MAIN
      IMPLICIT NONE
      INTEGER M,N,I,J
      PARAMETER (N = 512, M = 640, NTIMES = 500)
      DOUBLE PRECISION Q(N,M), R(N,M)
C
      DO 10 I=1,M
        DO 10 J=1,N
          Q(J,I) = 1.0D0
          R(J,I) = 1.0D0
   10 CONTINUE
C
      DO 20 I=1,NTIMES
   20   CALL BAZFAZ (Q,R,N,M)
      END

      SUBROUTINE BAZFAZ (Q,R,N,M)
      IMPLICIT NONE
      INTEGER M,N,I,J
      DOUBLE PRECISION Q(N,M), R(N,M)
C
      DO 10 I=1,N
        DO 20 J=1,N
          A(I,J) = A(I,J) * B(J,I)
   20   CONTINUE
   10 CONTINUE
C
      END
```

2. Rearrange the subroutine link order for a program with at least 15 subroutines and a run time of at least one minute. Does changing the link order change the run time?

12

Language Support for Performance

OK, I admit it: tuning is like forcing Cinderella's corpulent stepsister's smelly foot into a distressed glass slipper. A reasonable person might ask "Why can't the compiler do this? I'm busy!" True, most of the things I've shown you could be automated. In some cases, the compiler would need a little help to answer questions about how variables are used, whether references overlap, etc. Perhaps this could be solved by providing other ways to express calculations so that it is clear when they are independent. At any rate, it seems like we have to spend an awful lot of time crawling through source code doing a job that ought to be done by a computer.

This chapter is about getting compilers (or precompilers) to do some of the work of tuning loops and memory references. Unfortunately, I may be describing tools you don't own—they aren't always supplied with your workstation. Even so, you can use this chapter as a guide. We'll also be looking at libraries, advanced compiler options, compiler directives, and new dialects of FORTRAN. I'll be jumping around a bit because there is a lot to cover.

Subroutine Libraries

You probably don't write your own transcendental functions, such as sine and cosine, in FORTRAN or C because you expect that the vendor's intrinsics will be faster. This is a safe bet. A hand-coded routine will generally be faster than your best tuning efforts can achieve, particularly since the vendor's numerical analysis staff probably understands (or ought to understand) your system's quirks better than you do.

In addition to the standard math library functions, most vendors have also cobbled together a hand-coded subroutine library, that contains a few of the most important vector subroutines or signal processing kernels. If the library wasn't shipped as part of the standard software distribution then the vendor may make it available on a per-request basis, possibly at extra cost. Passing off particular jobs, such as matrix multiplies or Fourier transforms, to hand-coded subroutine libraries can be an efficient way to tune a program. You look for a routine that matches your problem, supply the correct arguments, and you're done.

Math/vector libraries are also available from third parties. They are often better behaved than the libraries from system vendors, in that they may return more predictable results for fringe values; they also tend to be better documented. But expect them to run slower than the system vendors' libraries. Third party libraries are usually just compiled C or FORTRAN, while the vendors' libraries are often written to take advantage of every optimization; they may even be coded in assembly language. Still, the third-party libraries can probably beat your own untuned, hand-written code. They are often (not always) tuned using some of the techniques we saw in previous chapters.

One thing to keep in mind when using a licensed third party library: because it is licensed, it is going to make it more difficult to pass your code along to somebody else. They too will need to license the same library before using your code. If your application is going to be distributed to other people, you might consider sticking with high quality free or public domain software.

Mathematical libraries operate at all different levels of complexity. For instance, there are libraries of low-level vector operations, like daxpys and dot products.* More complex functions, like matrix-matrix operations or fast Fourier transforms, come in libraries that are either built on these lower level primitives, or designed for efficiency from the ground up. The difference is significant. A matrix solver built from low level functions may not be as efficient as code constructed to be a matrix solver.

Examples of libraries built from BLAS are LINPACK and EISPAK, from Argonne National Laboratory, available free through netlib.† A library that operates at a higher level (using level 2 and level 3 BLAS) is *LAPACK,* or "Linear Algebra Package," available in portions from netlib, but officially

---

*These are called *BLAS* or *BLAS level 1*, for *B*asic *L*inear *A*lgebra *S*ubroutines. Levels 2 and 3 deal with vector-matrix and matrix-matrix functions.

†To learn more about getting a copy of LINPACK and other libraries, send the e-mail message "send index" to *netlib@ornl.gov.*

distributed by Numerical Algorithms Group (NAG), Downers Grover, Illinois. Another source of high quality scientific subroutine libraries, including parallel libraries, is IMSL of Sugar Land, Texas.

Vectorizing Preprocessors

Another way to avoid hand-tuning is to use a special precompiler or *vectorizing preprocessor*. It scans your program in search of BLAS constructs; it then replaces these with subroutine calls or highly optimized source code. The preprocessor doesn't know which loops are important, so it will try to optimize them all. However, it is much faster than you are, so it gets through the job pretty quickly.

Not every vendor supplies a vectorizing preprocessor; if a preprocessor is available, it may come at extra cost. The most commonly distributed preprocessor today comes from Kuck and Associates, available on workstations from IBM and Hewlett-Packard. Silicon Graphics' multiprocessing computers can also be fitted with a Kuck and Associates *parallelizing preprocessor* for taking advantage of multiple CPUs. Other preprocessors are on the market, including a package called Vecpar from the Numerical Algorithms Group (NAG), and VAST-2 from Pacific Sierra Research Corporation.

You may find that a pass through a preprocessor adds all of the additional performance you will need. However, a vectorizing preprocessor sometimes requires your help; the preprocessor may not be able to derive everything you know about the code. To perform some optimizations, it needs insight into what the program will do when it executes. You can give the preprocessor hints with command line switches or *structured comments*. These look like normal comment statements to standard compilers, but the preprocessor recognizes them as directives or assertions. You can also turn off optimizations that aren't needed and may actually add to your run time.

Each vendor uses its own form of compiler directives and assertions, and offers support for some of the others. This is to be expected, because each has some additional capabilities not provided for in the competition's product. Rather than trying to list each vendors' directives and assertions explicitly and risk missing something, I am going to describe the kinds of knobs you get to twiddle when you are working with a vectorizing preprocessor or an advanced optimizing compiler. You will be able to recognize the actual directives and assertions when you see them. I'll also describe a few knobs that aren't part of production compilers, but which you will probably see in the near future.

If you have a preprocessor, the commands you need to invoke it depend on what kind of workstation you own. Therefore, I can't speak concretely (like "do this" or "do that"). But I can describe the situations that you're likely to run into, and the kind of information you need to supply.

Directives and assertions can usually be applied at three levels: Loop, Subroutine, and File. The ability to apply directives and assertions with different scopes makes them more convenient to use. For instance, if you can make a global statement about every loop in the program, you won't have to crawl through the code and add directives by hand to every loop; you can add a single directive that applies to the whole file. On the other hand, many directives and assertions are inappropriate for global application, so you will want to sprinkle them about carefully.

No dependencies

A *no dependencies* or *ignore dependencies* directive tells the preprocessor that references don't overlap. That is, it tells the preprocessor to generate code that may execute incorrectly if there *are* dependencies. You're saying "I know what I'm doing; it's OK to overlap references." A no dependencies directive might help the following loop:

```
for (i=0; i<n; i++)
    a[i] = a[i+k] * b[i];
```

If you know that k is greater than -1, or less than -n, then you can get the preprocessor to match the loop with a vector construct. Of course, blindly telling the compiler that there are no dependencies is a prescription for disaster. If k equals -1, the example above becomes a recursive loop. Vector subroutines for performing element-wise multiplication are not written for recursion, so the answers would be wrong. (But the loop might be really fast . . .)

Relations

You will often see loops that contain some potential dependencies, making them bad candidates for a no dependencies directive. However, you may be able to supply some local facts about certain variables. This would allow partial vectorization without compromising the results. In the code below, there are two potential dependencies because of subscripts involving k and j:

```
for (i=0; i<n; i++) {
    a[i] = a[i+k] * b[i];
    c[i] = c[i+j] * b[i];
}
```

Perhaps we know that there are no conflicts with references to a[i] and a[i+k]. But maybe we aren't so sure about c[i] and c[i+j]. Therefore, we can't say in general that there are no dependencies. However, we may be able to say something explicit about k (like "k is always greater than -1"), leaving j out of it. This information about the relationship of one expression to another is called a *relation assertion*. Applying a relation assertion will allow the compiler to apply vector subroutines to the first statement in the loop, giving us partial vectorization.*

Again, if you supply inaccurate testimony that leads the compiler to make unsafe optimizations, your answer may be wrong.

Permutations

As we have seen elsewhere, when elements of an array are indirectly addressed, you have to worry about whether or not some of the subscripts may be repeated. In the code below, are the values of K(I) all unique? Or are there duplicates?

```
    DO 10 I=1,N
        A(K(I)) = A(K(I)) + B(I) * C
10  CONTINUE
```

If you know that there are no duplicates in K (i.e., that A(K(I)) is a permutation), you can inform the preprocessor so that it can apply a vector construct. You supply the information using a *permutation assertion*.

No equivalences

Equivalenced arrays in FORTRAN programs provide another challenge for the compiler. If any elements of two equivalenced arrays appear in the same loop, most preprocessors and compilers will assume that references could point to the same memory storage location, and optimize very conservatively. This may be true even if it is abundantly apparent to you that there is no overlap whatsoever.

---

*Notice that, if you were tuning by hand, you could split this loop into two: one vectorizable and one not.

You inform the preprocessor or compiler that references to equivalenced arrays are safe with a *no equivalences* assertion. Of course, if you don't use equivalences, this assertion has no effect.

Branch probability

In Chapter 2, I discussed the need for branch prediction and the penalties for guessing wrong. It's up to the compiler to decide whether a branch is more likely to be taken or to fall-through, and to structure the code to be optimal along that path. Of course, the compiler can only guess; it can't know for certain what is going to happen when the program eventually runs. Can you answer the question:

```
C  what is the probability of branching?
       IF (I .EQ. K) THEN
```

If you know, you may be able to tell the compiler with a branch probability assertion. This will help it minimize or eliminate the cost of branching. The difference between choosing all branches correctly, or choosing them incorrectly, probably amounts to 15% or 20% of the total run time, depending on the processor and the number of branches in your program.

Trip count

Each loop can be characterized by an average number of iterations. Some loops are never executed or go around just a few times. Others may go around hundreds of times. Can you answer the question:

```
C what is the average number of times through the loop?
       DO 10 I=L,N
```

Your compiler or preprocessor is going to look at every loop as a candidate for unrolling or vectorization. It's working in the dark, however, because it can't tell which loops are important and will try to optimize them all. This can lead to the surprising experience of seeing your run time *go up* after optimization!

A *trip count assertion* will provide a clue to the compiler that will help it decide how much to unroll a loop or whether to vectorize it.* Loops that aren't important can be identified with low or "zero" trip counts. Important loops will have high trip counts.

---

*The assertion is made either by hand or from a profiler.

Unroll

As its name implies, an *unroll directive* tells the compiler to unroll a loop. It differs from the trip count assertion in that a trip count merely supplies information to help the compiler decide how to optimize the loop. An unroll directive takes away the compiler's choice: it says "unroll this loop!" You usually specify the number of iterations that you want to unroll.

If a loop is too meaty, then the preprocessor or compiler may choose to ignore your unroll directive or pick a halfway point. There are usually some thresholds beyond which unrolling won't occur; the vendor has determined, for most loops, that unrolling past the thresholds creates extra code and flirts with the law of diminishing returns. Even so, the limits may be adjustable. Feel free to change them and see what happens. However, be forewarned: If you bump the thresholds too high, you can create a Frankenstein loop covering three football fields. It will also take a lot of time to compile.

No vectorize

On vector processors, substituting vector subroutines for loop constructs usually yields better performance than source-level loop unrolling. However, you may want to turn off vectorization for some loops and let the preprocessor do loop unrolling in-place. There are several reasons why you might prefer this:

- The associated vector routine has a bug in it.
- You want to tweak the code to improve memory access.
- You may be generating code on one machine for execution on another (without the vector libraries).

Preprocessors provide a *no vectorize* directive that allows you to shut off vectorization for a given loop, subroutine, or file. When you tell the preprocessor "don't vectorize," loops then become candidates for automatic loop unrolling.

Roundoff, no associative transformations

In Chapter 10 I discussed how associative transformations can affect floating point calculations. The effect is slight in most cases. However, for sensitive or ill-conditioned problems, associative transformations can lead to an inaccurate result.

Associative transformations are never enabled at default optimization levels. However, they may be turned on for higher levels. *Roundoff* and *no associative transformation* directives let you tell the compiler that you want them to remain turned off.

Inline substitution

If your compiler or preprocessor supports procedure inlining, you can use directives and command line switches to specify how many nested levels of procedures you would like to inline, thresholds for procedure size, etc. The vendor will have chosen reasonable defaults.

Directives also let you choose subroutines that you think are good candidates for inlining. However, subject to its thresholds, the preprocessor or compiler may reject your choices. Inlining could expand the code so much that increased memory activity would claim back gains made by eliminating the procedure call. At higher optimization levels, the preprocessor or compiler is often capable of making its own choices for inlining candidates, provided it can find the source code for the routine under consideration.

Optimization levels

Every vendor's compiler or preprocessor provides a number of *optimization levels* you can choose from. These are like the various levels of luxury packages offered by car dealers. You may find that going from an LE to an LX package gives you the sunroof you wanted, but also adds something you didn't want, such as simulated air scoops or a rear spoiler (for your front wheel drive car).

Of course, you might just pick an optimization level and trust that the compiler will do the right thing. However, be warned that your code may actually slow down at the highest optimization levels. Increases in program size, number of loop preconditioning iterations, or other baggage might outweigh any optimizations. Generally, it's best to take the recommended optimization level for most of your code, and add your own tweaks where you need them.

Other assertions and directives

I have covered the most important assertions and directives for uniprocessors. There are others, though they can get pretty esoteric. Again, see your compiler manuals for the details.

When you split a single application for execution on several CPUs, some of the more sublime dependencies come into play. The compiler has to be sure that the final states of all variables are the same as they would be on a uniprocessor, even though the intermediate states might be non-vectorizable. There are directives and assertions that can ease the compiler's job. Additionally, compiler assertions and directives can help a parallelizing compiler to place data across multiple CPUs, and to align it with other data within a CPU. I will discuss this more below.

Explicitly Parallel Languages

As we've seen throughout this book, one of biggest tuning challenges is getting the compiler to recognize that a particular code segment can be parallelized. This is particularly true for numerical codes, where the potential payback is greatest. Think about this: If you know that something is parallel, then why should there be any difficulty getting the compiler to recognize it? Why can't you just write it down, and have the compiler say "Oh, I understand this is to be done in parallel."

The problem is that the most commonly used languages don't offer any constructs for expressing parallel computations. You are forced to express yourself in primitive terms, as if you were a cave man with a grand thought, but no vocabulary to voice it. This is particularly true of FORTRAN and C. They do not support a notion of parallel computations, which means that programmers must reduce calculations to sequential steps. That sounds cumbersome, but most programmers do it so naturally that they don't even realize how good they are at it.

For example, let's say that we want to add two vectors, **A** and **B**. How would we do it? We would probably write a little loop without a moment's thought:

```
      DO 10 I=1,N
         C(I) = A(I) + B(I)
10    CONTINUE
```

This seems reasonable, but look what happened. We imposed an order on the calculations! Wouldn't it be enough to say "C gets A plus B, and I don't care how you do it"? That would free the compiler to add the vectors using any hardware at its disposal, using any method it liked. This is what parallel languages are about. They seek to supply primitives suitable for expressing parallel computations.

There are also questions of granularity: at what level do you parallelize? For a vector machine you are clearly looking for vector constructs, but for a multiprocessor, at what level do you want to work? You are usually on the lookout for opportunities to distribute bigger chunks of calculations, like outer loops, before you revert to vectors. This question is important because it affects what you think is valuable in a parallel language. You are going to be most interested in the constructs that map best to your computer.

New parallel languages aren't being proposed as rapidly as they were in the mid 1980s. Developers have realized that you can come up with a wonderful scheme, but if it isn't compatible with FORTRAN or C few people will care about it. The reason is simple: there are billions of lines of C and FORTRAN code, but only a few lines of *Fizgibbet*, or whatever it is you call your new parallel language. Because of the predominance of C and FORTRAN, the most significant parallel language activities today seek to extend those languages, thus protecting the twenty or thirty years of investment in programs already written.

Fortran 90

One of these language extensions is Fortran 90. The last American National Standards Institute (ANSI) FORTRAN standard release, FORTRAN 77 (X3.9-1978), was written to promote portability of FORTRAN programs between different platforms. It didn't invent new language components, but instead incorporated good features that were already available in production compilers. Unlike FORTRAN 77, Fortran 90 (ANSI X3.198-1992) brings *new* extensions and features to the language. Some of these just bring FORTRAN up to date with newer languages like C (dynamic memory allocation, scoping rules) and C++ (generic function interfaces). But some of the new features are unique to FORTRAN (array operations).

The Fortran 90 extensions to FORTRAN 77 include:
- Array Constructs
- Dynamic memory allocation and automatic variables
- Pointers
- New data types, structures
- New Intrinsics functions, including many that operate on vectors or matrices
- New control structures, such as DO WHILE and CASE statements
- Enhanced procedure interfaces

Fortran 90 array constructs

With Fortran 90 array constructs you can specify whole arrays or array sections as the participants in unary and binary operations. These constructs are a key feature for "unserializing" applications so that they are better suited to vector computers and parallel processors. For example, say you wish to add two vectors, **A** and **B**. In Fortran 90 you can express this as a simple addition operation, rather than a traditional loop. That is, you can write:

```
A = A + B
```

instead of the traditional FORTRAN 77 loop:

```
       DO 10 I=1,N
   10     A(I) = A(I) + B(I)
```

The code generated by the compiler on your workstation may not look any different, but for some of the parallel machines available now, and workstations just around the corner, the difference will be significant. The Fortran 90 version states explicitly that the computations can be performed in parallel.

You are not limited to one dimensional arrays. For instance, the element-wise addition of two 2-D arrays could be stated like this:*

```
       A = A + B
```

in lieu of:

```
       DO 20 J=1,M
         DO 10 I=1,N
            A(I,J) = A(I,J) + B(I,J)
   10     CONTINUE
   20     CONTINUE
```

Naturally, when you want to combine two arrays in an operation, their shapes have to be compatible. Adding a seven element vector to an eight element vector doesn't make sense. Neither would multiplying a 2×4 array by a 3×4 array. When the two arrays have compatible shapes, relative to

---

*Just in case you are wondering, A * B will give you an element-wise multiplication of array members—not matrix multiplication. That is covered by a Fortran 90 intrinsic function.

the operation being performed upon them, we say they are in *shape confor-mance*, as in the following code:

```
DOUBLE PRECISION A(8), B(8)
   ...
A = A + B
```

Scalars are always considered to be in shape conformance with arrays (and other scalars). In a binary operation with an array, a scalar will be treated as an array of the same size with a single element duplicated throughout.

Still, we are limited. When you reference a particular array, **A**, for example, you reference the whole thing, from the first element to the last. You can imagine cases where you might be interested in specifying a subset of an array. This could either be a group of consecutive elements or something like "every eighth element" (i.e., a non-unit stride through the array). Parts of arrays (possibly non-contiguous) are called *array sections*.

Fortran 90 array sections can be specified by replacing traditional subscripts with triplets of the form a:b:c, meaning "elements a through b, taken with an increment of c." You can omit parts of the triplet, provided the meaning remains clear. For example, a:b means "elements a through b"; a: means "elements from a to the upper bound." Remember that a triplet replaces a single subscript—so an *n*-dimension array can have *n* triplets.

You can use triplets in expressions, again making sure that the parts of the expression are in conformance. Consider these statements:

```
REAL X(10,10), Y(100), Z(5,5,5)
   ...
X(10,1:10)   = Y(91:100)
X(10,:)      = Y(91:100)
Z(10:1:-2,5) = Y(1:5)
```

The first statement above assigns the last ten elements of **Y** to the 10th row of **X**. The second statement expresses the same thing slightly differently. The lone ":" tells the compiler that the whole range (one through ten) is implied. The third statement assigns the first five elements of **Y** to elements 10, 8, 6, 4, and 2 of column 5 of **Z**.

Fortran 90 intrinsics

Fortran 90 extends the functionality of FORTRAN 77 intrinsics, and adds many new ones as well, including some intrinsic subroutines. Most can be *array-valued*: they can return arrays sections or scalars, depending on how they are invoked. For example, here's a new, array-valued use of the SIN intrinsic:

```
REAL A(100,10,2)
  ...
A = SIN(A)
```

Each element of array **A** is replaced with its sine. Fortran 90 intrinsics work with array sections too, as long as the variable receiving the result is in shape conformance with the one passed:

```
REAL A(100,10,2)
REAL B(10,10,100)
  ...
B(:,:,1) = COS(A(1:100:10,:,1))
```

Other intrinsics, such as SQRT, LOG, etc., have been extended as well. Among the new intrinsics are:

Reductions

> Fortran 90 has vector reductions such as MAXVAL, MINVAL, and SUM. For higher order arrays (anything more than a vector) these functions can perform a reduction along a particular dimension. Additionally, there is a DOT_PRODUCT function for the vectors.

Matrix Manipulation

> Intrinsics MATMUL and TRANSPOSE can manipulate whole matrices.

Constructing or Reshaping Arrays

> RESHAPE allows you to create a new array from elements of an old one with a different shape. SPREAD replicates an array along a new dimension. MERGE copies portions of one array into another under control of a mask.

Inquiry Functions

> SHAPE, SIZE, LBOUND, and UBOUND let you ask questions about how an array is constructed.

Parallel Tests

> Two other new reduction intrinsics, ANY and ALL, are for testing many array elements in parallel.

New control features

Fortran 90 includes some new control features, including a conditional *assignment primitive* called WHERE, which puts shape conforming array assignments under control of a mask as in the following example. Here's an example of the WHERE primitive:

```
REAL A(2,2), B(2,2), C(2,2)
DATA B/1,2,3,4/, C/1,1,5,5/

  ...
WHERE (B .EQ. C)
```

```
       A =  1.0
       C =  B + 1.0
    ELSEWHERE
       A = -1.0
    ENDWHERE
    ...
```

In places where the mask is TRUE, **A** gets 1.0, and **C** gets B+1.0. In the ELSEWHERE clause, **A** gets -1.0. The result of the operation above would be arrays **A** and **C** with the elements:

```
 A =  1.0   -1.0        C =  2.0   5.0
     -1.0   -1.0             1.0   5.0
```

Again, no order is implied in these conditional assignments, meaning they can be done in parallel. Certain types of parallel computers can take advantage of this and process perhaps thousands of conditionals simultaneously, as we'll see in Chapter 15.

Loops now have optional labels, a DO WHILE construct, a CYCLE statement for escaping from the current iteration, and an EXIT statement for jumping out of the loop altogether. The DO/ENDDO combination, borrowed from VAX FORTRAN and commonly supported by other vendor's compilers, is an official part of the language too. Here's a strange looking do-loop, that uses most of these features to print the odd integers between one and ten:

```
    I = 0
    LOOP: DO
       I = I + 1
       IF (I .EQ. 2*I/2) CYCLE
       IF (I .GT. 10) EXIT
       WRITE (*,*) I
    ENDDO LOOP
```

It has a label, LOOP, and would go around infinitely if not for the EXIT statement inside. On the even iterations, the remainder of the statements are skipped by the CYCLE statement.

Fortran 90 also features a new C switch-like CASE construct for choosing one from among many possible integer, logical, or single character expressions:

```
    SELECT CASE (ANSWER)
       CASE ('Y')
          CALL DOIT
       CASE ('N')
          STOP 'DONE'
       DEFAULT
          WRITE (*,*) 'You must choose.'
    END SELECT
```

Each of the tests is made until one is found to be true or until the bottom of the construct is reached. At most, one outcome will be selected.

Automatic and allocatable arrays

Every program needs temporary variables or work space. In the past, FOR-TRAN programmers have often managed their own scratch space by declaring an array large enough to handle any temporary requirements. This practice gobbles up memory (albeit virtual memory, usually), and can even have an effect on performance. With the ability to allocate memory dynamically, programmers can wait until later to decide how much scratch space to set aside. Fortran 90 supports dynamic memory allocation with two new language features: automatic arrays and allocatable arrays.

Like the local variables of a C program, Fortran 90's automatic arrays are assigned storage only for the life of the subroutine or function that contains them. This is different from traditional local storage for Fortran arrays, where some space was set aside at compile or link time. The size and shape of automatic arrays can be sculpted from a combination of constants and arguments. For instance, here's a declaration of an automatic array, **B**, using Fortran 90's new specification syntax:

```
SUBROUTINE FOO(N,A)
INTEGER N
REAL, DIMENSION (N) :: A, B
...
```

Two arrays are declared: **A**, the dummy argument, and **B**, an automatic, explicit shape array. When the subroutine returns, **B** will cease to exist. Notice that the size of **B** is taken from one of the arguments, N.

Allocatable arrays give you the ability to choose the size of an array after examining other variables in the program. For example, you might want to determine the amount of input data before allocating the arrays. This little program asks the user for the matrix's size before allocating storage:

```
INTEGER M,N
REAL, ALLOCATABLE, DIMENSION (:,:) :: X

   ...
WRITE (*,*) 'ENTER THE DIMENSIONS OF X'
READ (*,*) M,N
ALLOCATE (X(M,N))
   ...
 do something with X
   ...
DEALLOCATE (X)
   ...
```

The `ALLOCATE` statement creates an M×N array, which is later freed by the `DEALLOCATE` statement. As with C programs, it is important to give back allocated memory when you are done with it, otherwise your program might consume all the virtual storage available.

Fortran 90 summary

Well, that's the whirlwind tour of Fortran 90. I have probably done the language a disservice by covering it so briefly, but I wanted to give you a feel for it. There are many features I didn't discuss. If you would like to learn more, I recommend *Fortran 90 Explained* by Michael Metcalf and John Reid, published by Oxford University Press. In the meantime, full Fortran 90 compilers are becoming available. Two, from NAG and Parasoft Corporation, translate Fortran 90 code to C and FORTRAN 77, respectively. Subsets of Fortran 90 are already supported on machines by Convex, Alliant (recently deceased), Thinking Machines, MasPar, and others.

High Performance Fortran (HPF)

Even given the extent of Fortran 90's additions to FORTRAN 77, there are groups who are interested in yet more language features. One of these, the *High Performance Fortran Forum* (HPFF), is a collaboration of academia (particularly Rice University and Syracuse University) and industry (DEC, Intel, Thinking Machines, and others), seeking to extend Fortran 90. You may ask: "With Fortran 90 barely out of the cradle, why are there already efforts to enhance it?" To answer this question, you have to look at developments in computer architecture.

Fortran 90 is an explicit vector language in a world that has had vector machines for about 25 years. For programming vector machines, it has many features you would want. However, the limelight of supercomputing research has recently shifted away from vector computers and toward parallel and "massively" parallel computers. These architectures can exploit the same kinds of parallelism that make vector machines, among others, fast, but they are more difficult to program and require more language support to program correctly.

Every parallel computer's memory is distributed at some level. Performance is directly effected by the way data is laid out in memory; bad layout leads to bad performance. Users of these machines would like layout directives for describing how to arrange the data—a concept that is missing from Fortran 90. And although Fortran 90's array constructs make it possible to recast many loops as simple parallel expressions, there are other cases where it is difficult to use the array syntax, even though parallelism is still present. HPF adds convenient FORALL parallel assignment constructs and statements. Lastly, it helps to know a little bit about the computer's architecture; if you are trying to break up a problem for execution on many CPUs, it would be nice to be able to ask how many CPUs do you have. HPF augments Fortran 90 to provide similar features. I'll discuss these in Chapter 15, when I describe distributed memory parallel computers.

Explicitly Parallel Programming Environments

Fortran 90 gives you ways to show the compiler where parallelism can be found. However, you are not required to divide and coordinate parallel computations by yourself—you are letting the compiler take care of that. That's good. Being far away from the problem of how parallel computations are managed makes parallel computers easier to use (perhaps at a loss in performance). HPF brings you a little closer to the machine—you can have some say in how the data is apportioned and arranged, without getting tangled in the details of coordinating parallel computations.

There are other, more explicit ways to program parallel machines as well. These allow you to do the same kinds of problems you might do with Fortran 90 or HPF, and you can do other things as well. For instance, you can portion out data less regularly to level the computational load across the machine. You could even run different things on different processors (provided the hardware allows you to). The downside is that you have to become much more involved in interprocessor communications and the synchronization of different parts of the program. It also means that you have to write some additional code (sometimes a lot) that has nothing to do with your algorithm, and everything to do with making it run on a parallel machine—often at a loss of portability.

The most basic of these parallel environments is called a *message passing language*. This is a set of function and subroutine calls for C or FORTRAN that give you a way to split up an application for parallel execution. Data is divided and passed out to other processors as messages. The receiving processors unpack them, do some work, and send the results back or pass them along to other processors in the parallel computer.* The contents of the messages depend on the program. They might be large portions of arrays or they could be single datums.

---

*I illustrate with an example of this in Chapter 15, "*Programming a Distributed Memory MIMD Machine.*"

Message passing languages come bundled with certain kinds of parallel computers (MIMD machines, such as the NCUBE and the Intel ipsc860). They are also available for networks of workstations, making it possible to treat many workstations as a single parallel machine. An example of a commercial message passing package is *Express*, from Parasoft Corporation, Pasadena, Ca. It provides a whole, portable, message passing environment, complete with analysis tools and debuggers. Lately, a free package called *PVM* (*P*arallel *V*irtual *M*achine) from Oak Ridge National Laboratory has gained a large following.* *Linda*, from Scientific Computing Associates, New Haven, Ct., provides an interesting and different parallel computing environment. It is based on an abstraction called *tuple space*, illustrated in Figure 12-1. Tuple space is like a bulletin board, read by both processes

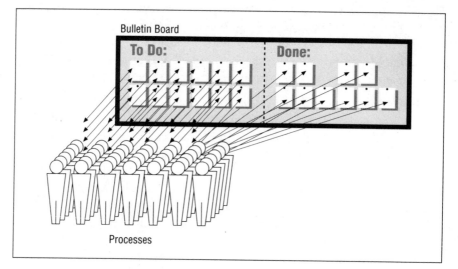

Figure 12-1: Linda's Tuple Space Bulletin Board

with work to do and processes willing to do it. The former posts something up on the bulletin board—a tuple—and expects that some other process will come by and remove it. This process—the worker—will do something with the tuple and post a response back up on the bulletin board, where it can be retrieved by somebody else. You can have many processors working together on one problem, coordinated solely by exchanging tuples through this bulletin board.

---

*PVM is available from *netlib*. To learn more, send this message to *netlib@ornl.gov*: send index from pvm

The implementation details of tuple space are hidden from the programmer, and may vary considerably on different types of machines. This is good because it helps distance the programmer from the details of bundling and passing messages, though it still gives him or her the freedom to explicitly apportion jobs—sometimes different kinds of jobs—between multiple processors. Like *Express*, *Linda* comes with a good set of debugging and monitoring tools.

Closing Notes

In this chapter, I talked about object libraries, vectorizing preprocessors, compiler directives, and parallel languages. We covered a lot, and it may have occurred to you that it all seems pretty complicated. Part of the challenge, particularly in numerical computing, is that the target is moving. There are lots of new and different types of computers to support, some of which are very difficult to program. And though every program runs faster these days, the precipice between promised performance and lousy performance is very steep, and you can fall off very easily. It takes concentration to get that last 90%!

For vendors, the danger is that without good tools, parallel computers will always be oddities. Users will give them a sniff and go find something else to do. That's not what the vendors want. They want you to buy their parallel computers, so they are trying to make them easier to program. Currently however, with thousands of people working on very difficult problems and hundreds of "right" ways to go, the resulting selection of tools can be overwhelming.

III

Evaluating
Performance

13

Industry Benchmarks

Wouldn't it be great if I could simply tell you which is the world's fastest computer? Unfortunately, I can't. That would be like trying to identify the world's fastest runner: although (insert athelete of your choice—any sport you like) may be the fastest sprinter, she may not be the fastest long distance runner. And don't forget about hurdlers and relay racers.

Similarly, computers have their strengths and weaknesses. If you want to understand these strengths and weaknesses, you need to see them "run" in competition (sorry about the pun). Fortunately, the computer business has a good selection of *industry benchmarks*. These let everyone take an initial look at performance without investing any effort of their own.

Who sponsors the benchmarks and who runs them? Are there referees? It's going to make a big difference if users, rather than vendors, decide on objective measurements of performance. And it's certainly a leap of faith to accept benchmark quotes at face value from a salesperson who doesn't understand them. It would be nice to shed the uneasy feeling that comes from relying on someone else's judgement when you are spending so much money.

Most industry benchmarks are application codes or synthetic applications that were written by users for their own purposes, adopted by others, and eventually promoted to legendary status. This is good because it helps keep the vendors from deciding what's important. True, they are usually reporting the results that *they* got. However, because the benchmarks are readily available, the computing community eventually catches on if the vendors are exaggerating. The downside to popular benchmarks is that they lack "orthogonality." Rather than being targeted at a particular feature, such as instruction cache performance or square roots, they test lots of things at once. It is sometimes difficult to say what a benchmark tells you about a given machine, aside from that it is slow or fast.

In this chapter, I'm going to describe a few of the common industry benchmarks and explain what it is that they measure. This will make it easier for you to relate them back to the kinds of applications you run on a daily basis. I'll also tell you what to watch out for when looking at benchmark quotes—the vendors sometimes play tricks with the numbers. Of course, there's no substitute for taking a computer for a test drive. However, understanding benchmarks will help you to quickly narrow the field of possibilities. I will discuss only CPU benchmarks; there are other kinds of benchmarks around (I/O benchmarks, graphics benchmarks, transaction processing benchmarks, to name a few), but we won't cover them here.

What is a MIP?

When pie-eating champions gather together, they probably boast about how many competitions they have won and how many pies it took to win them. They trade stained T-shirts and comment on the unruliness of each others' beards. Newcomers with unsubstantiated claims of great pie eating victories are greated with skepticism. They say: "Oh Yeah? How big were the pies?"

"This big."

"Oh yeah, what were they made of?" (A true champion knows that you can get down a lot more lemon meringue than you can pecan or pumpkin.)

Computer performance metrics such as millions of instructions per second (MIPS) are similar to numbers of pies consumed. The figures are commonly quoted, but as with pies, you have to be sure that the same things are being measured. If you think you are interested in the actual number of instructions the machine can execute per second, remember that not all instructions take the same amount of time (particularly true for CISC machines). A figure that describes how many no-ops your computer can perform is going to be less valuable than a measure of the number of instructions from a real program. And as we saw in Chapter 2, instruction sets can be very different among brands of computers. A complex instruction on one machine may be able to perform the work of ten instructions on another.

So how do we compare machines if instruction rates aren't good enough? We really have no other choice than to take programs and compare their execution time on two different computers. This will give us a brand **A** versus brand **B** comparison. If enough people compare to brand **A**, then we might forget that brand **A** ever existed at all and just assume that its perfor-mance equals unity (1) and that all other brands are **n** * 1.

VAX MIPS

The forgotten brand, in most cases, is the DEC VAX 11/780, introduced in 1978. Through time, people have adopted it as the standard "one MIP" machine. It's a practice that persists today. The funny thing is that the 11/780 isn't a one MIP machine at all—at least not in a pure sense. DEC published figures stating that for a reasonable job mix, the 11/780 executes at a rate of 470 thousand instructions/second—less than half of 1 MIP. This means that any MIPS benchmarks based on a 1 MIP 11/780 have actually been exaggerated by more than a factor of two. So if somebody says that they have a 10 MIPS machine, by comparison with the 11/780, they actually have a 4.7 MIPS machine, though it *is* presumably ten times the speed. You sometimes hear the expressions *VAX MIPS* or *VUPs* (VAX units of process-ing) to make the comparison clear.

Anyway, it probably doesn't matter what one MIP is, as long as everyone agrees on the same thing, and in most cases this is the performance of a VAX 11/780. Note, however, that by choosing the 11/780 as the *standard* standard, people are unintentionally suggesting that its performance is bal-anced. When you compare it with a new machine that has greatly improved performance in one particular area, say memory access, the new machine may look unbalanced by proportion. Is it the new machine that's unbalanced, or the 11/780?

Dhrystones

Now we've agreed to measure MIPS (whatever MIPS may mean), and we've agreed on a standard platform for comparison. Still, we have another prob-lem. Not all programs are going to scale up in speed by the same ratio. If we want to make comparable comparisons, we are going to need to run the same benchmark on every platform too.

In the past, vendors would pick their own collections of programs as a basis for MIPS ratings. Today, vendor MIPS suites have been almost univer-sally replaced by *Dhrystone*, a synthetic* benchmark written in Ada by Reinhold Weicker of Siemens AG, and later rewritten in C by Rick Richard-son. Dhrystone exercises fixed point computations, similar to those you

*Synthetic benchmarks are designed to model real workloads.

would find in compilers or system programs. It does not exercise floating point capabilities; these are addressed by other benchmarks which I will discuss later. When run, it returns a figure called "Dhrystones per second." By convention, 1657 Dhrystones/sec (version 2.1) is taken to equal 1 MIPS, another figure derived from the 11/780.

When crafting a synthetic benchmark, such as Dhrystone, the author tries to model the activities of a typical program. This is a challenge because:

- What is typical depends on what kinds of programs you run.
- Even if you know what typical is, it's difficult to model typical faithfully.

Though Dhrystone does capture some of the qualities of fixed point applications, it has been accused of missing the mark in several places. For one, it spends an inordinate amount of time performing string copies—up to 40% overall. Furthermore, the length of the average string comparison is longer than you would typically find in a real application; most string comparisons either succeed or fail after two or three characters, not ten or so. Additionally, the call-tree depth is shallow—only three or four routines deep—and subroutine calls occur more often than in most real programs.

And whether you believe it is a realistic simulation or not, Dhrystone fits completely within most machines' instruction and data caches, meaning it will not give you an indication of how the memory system responds at large. It is also tremendously sensitive to compiler optimizations. Some of these optimizations are prohibited by the benchmark's rules, but you would want to use them if they were available. For instance, subroutine inlining is not allowed; when you run this benchmark you are supposed to turn inlining off. However, if you are a vendor with a compiler that automatically inlines subroutines, you may think it unfair to cripple compilation for the sake of measuring Dhrystones.

The latest revision, 2.1, was released in the Spring of 1988. If you are comparing results, be sure that they come from like versions. If the version is not specified, then the numbers probably come from version 1.x. Earlier copies of the benchmark had some unused variables and sections of code that clever compilers could discover and discard. This meant that, based on the compiler, one brand of computer might run a reduced binary version, and thus do less work. The latest version is less prone to having sections optimized away.

As you can see, I've presented Dhrystone with a number of cautions. You might wonder why it is quoted at all. You're not alone.* Vendors have

---

*To paraphrase one reviewer, "Friends don't let friends quote Dhrystones."

picked up on it, however, so it is often one of the first figures you will hear spilling from a salesperson's mouth (that or MIPS, which is derived from Dhrystones anyway).

Even with its warts and blemishes, it serves a purpose by giving us *something* to compare against. Besides, for our purposes, the warts help drive home the point that you should make your judgements based on a combination of benchmarks. In fact, consider ignoring Dhrystone MIPS in favor of SPEC integer performance figures (below), or better yet, run your own benchmarks. You will get a broader view of a computer's fixed point processing capabilities than if you consult Dhrystones alone.

Floating Point Benchmarks

Floating point benchmarks sit at the other end of the spectrum, across from MIPS and Dhrystones. Floating point performance is often measured in terms of millions of floating point operations per second, called *megaflops* or *mflops* for short. By the least controversial definition, a *floating point operation* is one that executes on floating point hardware. This would include floating point additions, multiplies, comparisons, format conversions (between fixed and floating point form, for example), and perhaps divides and square roots, if they too are implemented in hardware. Unless otherwise stated, most megaflop figures report the rate at which the hardware can perform some mix of additions and multiplies. Square roots and divides take longer to execute, are less common in most codes, and often can't be pipelined to the same extent as additions and multiplies (they might even be software functions), which makes them less valuable in predicting general performance. You are going to have to dig a little if you are interested in divides or square roots (see the SPEC benchmarks, below).

Just like MIPS, megaflops are sometimes reported in terms of machine peak speeds and sometimes in terms of benchmark speeds. However, while it is considered misleading to talk about peak MIPS ratings as a multiple of the clock speed, vendors regularly quote peak megaflop rates. Peak megaflops for current workstations are usually twice the clock rate. This is because at the heart of many new machines' instruction sets is a floating point multiply-add operation that can perform to two "flops" in the space of one (under optimal conditions). This multiply-add is perfect for accumulating a running sum of vector elements, as in a dot product.

In Chapter 10, we saw some code that can reach near-peak performance. A matrix multiply can be organized so that it has a dot product at the center. If some of the dot product's operands can be retained in registers, the compiler may be able to issue a multiply-add instruction each clock cycle.

Linpack

The most famous floating point benchmark is the *Linpack benchmark*, written by Jack Dongarra, formerly of Argonne National Laboratory, but now at the University of Tennessee. You hear "Linpack" so often that it is easy to believe it is the name of the benchmark. It is actually the name of a library of linear algebra subroutines. The Linpack benchmark uses a handful of those routines to measure the time it takes to solve a dense system of linear equations using Gaussian elimination. The benchmark reports average megaflop rates by dividing the total number of floating point operations by time. Sometimes people just call the Linpack results *Linflops*, for short. The Linpack benchmark's results are publically available via Internet mail. Send the following message to *netlib@ornl.gov*:

```
send performance from benchmark
```

Netlib will then mail you a Postscript copy of the latest Linpack benchmark report.

There are several versions of the Linpack benchmark, differing in size, numerical precision, and ground rules. Workstation vendors usually quote the 100×100 matrix double precision results, strictly compiled FOR-TRAN—no hand optimizations. You are allowed to use whatever compiler optimizations you have at your disposal, like automatic loop unrolling, but you cannot modify the code yourself.

In addition to the 100×100 benchmark, there is also a 1000×1000 "anything goes" Linpack benchmark. Vendors are allowed to solve the system of equations using any method they choose, just as long there isn't an appreciable loss of precision over the original. 1000×1000 Linpack is an important metric because it better predicts the performance on big vector/parallel machines. However, be aware that the larger benchmark may barely resemble the smaller one after the vendor finishes hacking it, and the higher average mflop ratings cannot be compared with the 100×100 figures.

The heart of the 100×100 all FORTRAN Linpack benchmark is a routine called *daxpy*. Daxpy scales a vector by a constant and adds it to another vector:

```
      do 30 i = 1,n
         dy(i) = dy(i) + da*dx(i)
  30 continue
```

Looking closely at the loop, you can count two floating point operations (a multiply and an addition) and three memory operations (two loads and a store). As I discussed in Chapter 10, memory operations will limit this loop's performance on most architectures, though it is the perfect mix for some vector supercomputers. Because most workstations are limited to one memory operation per clock cycle, and because the ratio of floating point operations to memory operations in daxpy is 2:3, you will not see 100×100 Linpack results showing more than 2/3 times the clock rate.

The 100×100 Linpack benchmark was originally written as a test for both floating point performance and for the memory system. It carves a 100×100 piece from larger 200×200 or 201×200 matrices (the test is repeated several times). This breaks up the data so that it is "patchy" within main memory—100 elements of the matrix followed by a 100 (or 101) element void, repeated over and over. Array accesses proceed along columns, meaning that the benchmark steps through memory in a reasonable fashion—the way you would want to do it if you were writing the code yourself. Linpack should be an exercise for the memory system; however, the whole matrix can often fit inside the larger caches on modern machines. 320 kilobytes will hold the whole thing, which isn't much compared to the 2 megabyte caches available on some workstations.

Because Linpack is the most well-known floating point benchmark, Linpack results are important to computer vendors. This has an interesting feedback effect. When deciding what parts of the compiler to work on next, vendors may forgo some projects in favor of others that enhance Linpack performance. You will be shocked to hear a vendor's representatives referring to a particular compiler optimization flag as the Linpack Switch, meaning that it turns on all the proper optimizations to get the quoted Linpack number.

Whetstone

Where Linpack demonstrates something about the performance of vectorizable scientific and engineering code, the Whetstone benchmark attempts to measure the more scalar forms of floating point computation. Transcendental functions such as sine and cosine, mixed integer and floating point calculations, branches, and the use of scalar variables are measured collectively. It heavily tests the mathematical function library, as well as the compiler and hardware.

Like Dhrystone, Whetstone is a synthetic benchmark. It was written by the National Physical Laboratory in Great Britain to represent the computational mix sampled from a large collection of Algol 60 programs. The authors tried to make sure that optimizing compilers couldn't trivialize or discard portions of the code (with mixed success). The body of the program contains a collection of modules that are repeated and timed to get a measure of kilo-Whetstones per second. You can find Whetstones included in every vendor's benchmark report.

The unfortunate thing about Whetstone is that it is difficult to tell what shape the code was in when the vendor actually ran it. Like a message passed around in the game of telephone, benchmarks can get tweaked here and there as they are copied from place to place, to the point where two vendors are no longer comparing the same thing. Whetstone is prone to this. Furthermore, some reported results are for single precision execution and some are for double precision. As ever, you need to be sure you are comparing apples to apples: the same program, measuring the same thing.

If you have a floating point code that is more scalar than it is vector, then the Whetstone number will be more important to you than Linpack. Because of the way the benchmark branches, exercises subroutine calls, and address arithmetic, it is a good representative of the kinds of "dusty deck" codes (old programs that have been gradually updated over a decade, or two, or three) that are typical of laboratory settings. You can't tell any one thing from the Whetstone number, such as "this machine is good at transcendental functions," but you can tell something about overall floating point scalar performance.

The SPEC Benchmarks

In the late 1980s, a group called the Systems Performance Evaluation Cooperative (SPEC) formed to "establish, maintain and endorse a standardized set of relevant benchmarks that can be applied to the newest generation of high-performance computers." Benchmarks submitted by member computer companies were assembled into the first SPEC suite of codes.* You have probably heard of SPECmarks—measurements of how well computers performed the benchmark suite. These are cumulative numbers for the performance of the suite as a whole.

---

*As you can imagine, computer companies would be inclined to submit benchmarks that they do best on, and that the competition does worst on.

Before I go any further, I want to warn you that there are now two sets of SPEC CPU benchmark numbers in circulation. The first are from the SPEC89 suite of codes and the second are from the recently revised SPEC92 suite, released in January, 1992. Look for SPEC92 numbers when comparing machines. Also note that there is a SPEC throughput benchmark suite, designed to simulate the kinds of activities of a software development environment. I'll be discussing the CPU benchmarks only.

There are 20 benchmarks in the SPEC92 CPU benchmark suite, up from ten in SPEC89. This includes six integer and fourteen floating point codes. SPECmarks are reported in two summary figures: floating point (SPECfp92) and integer (SPECint92). These are calculated as the *geometric mean** of the run times for the programs in the suite. SPEC89 used to have a single overall figure that combined integer and floating point performance, but no such number is associated with SPEC92.

The single, original SPECmark number was a pre-emptive attempt by SPEC to prevent the vendor community from accumulating the ten benchmark numbers into their own, possibly biased, summary result. The new, separate integer and floating point numbers serve the same purpose. The reason that the overall SPECmark figure has been eliminated is that it cloaked the differences between fixed and floating point performance. For instance, a machine with good floating point performance and mediocre fixed point performance could come up with a similar SPECmark as a machine with the reverse situation. By having two numbers, the distinction between floating and fixed point performance will be clearer.

Of course, the trouble with summary results is that they smear performance across different types of applications, which can be bad if you plan to spend most of the time doing one thing—such as inverting matrices. For that reason, SPEC regularly publishes the results for each individual benchmark contributing to the SPECmarks, as well as the SPECmarks themselves. Excerpts often appear in the trade press and in vendor literature.†

---

*The geometric mean is the *n*th root of the product of *n* numbers. A geometric mean is effected by the worst benchmarks in the suite, more than an average would be.

†Subscriptions to SPEC's newsletter, or copies of the SPEC benchmarks themselves, are available through SPEC for a fee. Contact SPEC at (703) 698-9600, ext. 318 for more details.

Indivdual SPEC Benchmarks

The benchmarks that make up the SPEC suite are, by-and-large, real applications. A few are kernels—the "core" of applications—but in general, SPEC has been steering itself away from synthetic benchmarks. This avoids some of the problems I discussed above.*

Of the twenty constituent benchmarks, eight are written in C, and the rest in FORTRAN. Five of of these are single precision floating point codes, nine are double precision floating point codes, and six are fixed point (integer). All told, that's 124K lines of integer programs and 65K lines of floating point programs. None of the benchmarks goes out of its way to test disk I/O or other non-CPU intensive operations; all are intended to stress the CPU or memory.

I am now going to take you for a tour of the benchmarks so that you will know what each does. If you recognize some of them as similar to the kinds of work you perform on a daily basis, you may be able to project how they will predict your performance on different workstations. Where possible, I have tried to point out what is unique about each (if anything). The fact that they are samples of real applications makes this sort of a stretch because real applications aren't designed to test one thing; they are written to solve a problem. This means that certain groups of benchmarks are as similar as they are different.

052.alvinn

052.alvinn† is a neural network trainer. It's a floating point C application, written in single precision. It has a very low cache miss rate, yet a very high number of memory references.

026.compress

This is a benchmark of the UNIX compress utility, compressing and decompressing a 1 MB file 20 times. Common substrings in the input are reduced to more compact representations under the direction of tables that the program populates in memory as it goes along. Because the tables are constructed dynamically, and because the program is repeatedly hashing

---

*The use of kernels and applications has a secondary effect: It forces compiler developers to focus on speeding up real codes.

†Although they look significant, the numbers that are in the benchmark names don't mean anything in particular.

into those tables, *026.compress* is a good cache exerciser. It also performs a little bit of I/O.

The performance of *026.compress* predicts how the machine will behave with other programs that have unpredictable memory access patterns and do a little I/O. Linkers and assemblers tend to have these characteristics.

015.doduc

015.doduc is a non-vectorizable, double precision, Monte Carlo kernel written in FORTRAN. Monte Carlo simulations are used where you want to model complex systems as a sequence of individual events with assumed probabilities or properties. For instance, you might want to model the path of a neutron in a nuclear reactor. Of all the neutrons that are released, only a handful collide with other atoms with the correct energy needed to cause a chain reaction. It is easy to follow the neutron through different discrete stages with assigned completion probabilities, but difficult to model the problem in closed form.

Many Monte Carlo simulations, including this one, have flat profiles, many branches, and short loops, though some are dominated by random number generating routines. The most significant routine in *015.doduc* takes less than 10% of the time on many machines.

056.ear

056.ear is a human ear simulation, written in single precision in C.

008.espresso

008.espresso simulates the behavior of high-pressure Italian coffee makers. It is also part of a set of tools used for the optimization of Programmable Logic Arrays (PLA). Like a discretely wired chain of logic gates, a PLA can be programmed to return certain outputs in response to certain inputs. You specify these via a boolean equation. The trouble is that the equation you give may not be optimal—it may waste components within the array. For instance, a C representation of a boolean equation involving logical variables A, B, and C given as A&&B||A&&C would be equivalent to a simpler expression A&&(C||B) (trivial example, of course). *008.espresso* takes the input equation in the form of a truth table and outputs another, optimized truth table. Like *015.doduc,* this program exhibits a fairly flat profile, though floating point operations are not involved. This code performs lots of pointer arithmetic and boolean bit operations.

023.eqntott

023.eqntott is a C benchmark that makes heavy use of integers and pointers. It translates a boolean equation into a truth table. It has a very sharp profile, completely dominated by the C library sort routine qsort. Hence, if you were trying to tune this code, you would spend most of your effort on improving qsort. The presence of *023.eqntott* in the SPEC benchmark suite has an interesting implication: anyone who needs qsort for their own application will find it well optimized by the vendor!

094.fpppp

094.fpppp is a quantum chemistry benchmark taken from Gaussian88. The most heavily used routine is an enormous extended basic block of scalar floating point arithmetic. Processors that can pipeline a random collection of floating point operations (superscalar) will perform well, whereas a vector processor will be unable to do anything useful with it at all. Additionally, it has a high ratio of memory operations to floating point operations. The SPEC92 version of *094.fpppp* runs a larger problem than SPEC89.

085.gcc

The *085.gcc* benchmark is part of the GNU C compiler from the Free Software Foundation. It generates Sun-3 assembly language output from preprocessed C source. It has a very flat profile, hiding a lot of procedure call overhead. There is also a large amount of data cache activity and a smidgen of I/O.

Of course, this benchmark says nothing about how fast your native compiler will execute, but it does predict the performance of gangly system codes. Again, it is a C program with little in the way of floating point operations.

090.hydro2d

090.hydro2d simulates galactic jets using Navier-Stokes methods. It is a small memory benchmark with low cache miss and a high floating point throughput rate.

022.li

The *022.li* benchmark is a small lisp interpreter called *Xlisp* (written in C), solving the nine queens problem. The program tries to find a way to place nine queens on a chessboard such that none of them can attack any of the others. This was an eight queens problem in SPEC89, but the size was increased to lengthen the run time.*

022.li offers little in the way of fine-grained parallelism, meaning that it will benefit little from overlapped execution. Much of the run time is spent traversing linked lists. There is also a fair number of procedure calls, extending to a greater depth than for many of the other benchmarks. This is because the program is written so that subroutines are called recursively.

034.mdljdp2

034.mdljdp2 is a quantum chemistry simulation that solves the equations of motion for the interaction of 500 atoms. It is a small memory problem.

077.mdljsp2

077.mdljsp2 is the same problem as above, except that the 10,000 floating point values are in single rather than double precision. You can compare the two to see the difference (if there is any) in single precision versus double precision floating point performance for a given machine. However, because both have a relatively low number of memory references, you will not see a contribution from access speed differences for doubles versus singles.

093.nasa7

The *093.nasa7* is a (synthetic) benchmark suite in itself, consisting of seven vectorizable double precision floating point kernels. There is a matrix multiplication, two-dimensional complex Fast Fourier Transform, a parallel Cholesky decomposition, block tridiagonal matrix solution along one dimension of a four dimensional array, a couple of fluids codes, and a parallel matrix inversion. Its performance is a predictor of a general mix of numerically intensive computations.

093.nasa7 has been reworked since the original SPEC89 issue to change the way data is initialized. Previously, the benchmark's input was hardcoded into the program. The trouble was that clever compilers could locate

---

*How *do* you fit nine queens on a chessboard?

and identify some of the variables as constants, and propagate them down to the places they were being used. This changed the benchmark—it wasn't meant to be a test of copy propagation (a copy propagation benchmark wouldn't be a very important predictor of real world performance). The new benchmark initializes data outside the program.

048.ora

048.ora is a ray trace program written in double precision FORTRAN. Floating point operations (many square roots) outnumber memory references by a factor of four, and the memory size is small, meaning that this code will work the floating point hardware heavily, even on processors that can only issue one instruction per clock.

072.sc

072.sc is a spreadsheet, calculating budgets, amortization schedules, and SPECmarks. It is pretty unremarkable as a benchmark.

013.spice2g6

Spice is an analog circuit simulation program, written at Berkeley in the early 1980s. It can model non-linear DC, non-linear transient, and linear AC circuits constructed from a number of devices including inductors, resistors, capacitors, diodes, and transistors. There are several versions in circulation, supported and unsupported, coded both in C and FORTRAN. Version 2g6 is double precision, written in FORTRAN.

Like any general purpose application program, the input file determines the program execution pattern: one input deck may cause a flat profile, where another might cause the run time to be dominated by a particular routine. When running the SPEC benchmark, *013.spice2g6's* profile is fairly sharp. The lead routine performs an in-place LU decomposition. Normally you would think LU decomposition as "vectorizable;" however, in this case, elements are stored indirectly and there are quite a few branches, making it a poor vector candidate with relatively low floating point activity. Overall, *013.spice2g6* predicts the behavior of scalar programs with heavy memory activity.

089.su2cor

089.su2cor is a quantum chemistry benchmark that solves for the masses of elementary particles. It is a double precision FORTRAN code that uses an even mix of instructions.

078.swm256

078.swm256 is a single precision finite difference model used for weather prediction. It has very good memory access patterns and a correspondingly low cache miss rate.

047.tomcatv

This benchmark is characterized as a two-dimensional vectorized mesh generation. It has good memory access patterns and a wealth of vectoriz-able constructs, so it should do very well on every machine, particularly those that can issue more than one instruction per clock. From *047.tom-catv,* you can get a sense of how a reasonably constructed vector code will run.

039.wave5

039.wave5 solves Maxwell's equations and particle equations to simulate a plasma. It is written in single precision FORTRAN. It has the largest mem-ory requirements of the SPEC benchmarks.

030.matrix300 Was Deleted

030.Matrix300 is a synthetic FORTRAN benchmark using some routines from Linpack (the library, not the benchmark) to perform eight different matrix multiplications on matrices and their transposes. It is interesting because it forces non-unit strides through memory on seven of the eight cases. Furthermore, the matrices are each declared with different first dimensions, making life extra hard on some types of memory systems. It's a test of how the compiler, CPU, and memory system can work together to handle strided, albeit predictable, memory references.

030.Matrix300 was deleted from SPEC92 because, as we demonstrated a few chapters ago, automatic loop interchange and blocking (by a vectoriz-ing preprocessor) were able to alter the memory reference patterns—the most important feature of the benchmark. This trivialized the program, skewing the results for those vendors that had a preprocessor.

Transaction Processing Benchmarks

For some applications, you are more interested in the interactive response than raw compute power. Interactive applications often demand that the computer and operating system be tuned to respond quickly to outside events, and be able to handle a large number of active processes simultaneously. An appropriate model might be a banking application, or an office environment, where there can be many people sharing time and I/O bandwidth of a single computer. Each interactive request and response can be considered a transaction.

Just as there are CPU benchmarks, there are also *transaction processing benchmarks*. TPC-A and TPC-B are two commonly used industry benchmarks that measure interactive throughput in a database application. TPC-C is a newer transaction processing benchmark, seldom quoted by vendors.

In these benchmarks, users are simulated by another program or another computer* that makes transactions, filling the role of many people signed on to the machine. Performance is measured by the amount of time it takes the computer to complete transactions under various loads.

TPC-A

TPC-A is a benchmark of credit-debit transactions being performed by a second computer simulating bank tellers, each issuing one request every ten seconds. To obtain a 1 TPS rating, ten tellers issuing one request every ten seconds must see transaction completion within two seconds, 90% of the time. There are also some requirements on how the data is distributed throughout the database. High-end servers today achieve over 100 TPC-A transactions per second. Massively parallel machines can surpass 1000 transactions per second.

TPC-B

TPC-B is the same as TPC-A, except that the transactions are generated by other processes on the same computer(s), rather than being initiated across a network. This makes TPC-B less of a terminal I/O test and more of a database stress test. TPC-B numbers will always be higher than TPC-A.

---

*This is called a *remote terminal emulation benchmark*, when one computer drives another through the terminal ports, or across the network. See the next chapter.

TPC-C

TPC-C is a a newer, more complex simulation, modeling the transactions of a company that sells a product or service. Transactions are orders, payments, inquiries, and even (intentional) mistakes that need correction.

All three benchmarks are sponsored by the Transaction Processing Council (TPC), representing 40 computer system and database vendors. The performance criteria for a given TPC rating are spelled out by the council; however, choice of database engines is left to the vendor conducting the test. This means that results can vary between platforms based on the choice of software tested and how well the software is tuned for the machine.

Closing Notes

As you may have noticed, I've given a luke-warm endorsement to many of the benchmarks described in this chapter. Why describe them at all? Because they are the benchmarks you are most likely to hear about, or see quoted in vendor literature.

Industry benchmarks help us compare performance between platforms. Use them as a performance barometer, but remember: there is nothing like benchmarking your own code. In the next chapter I talk about how to do this so that you will have faith and reproducibility in your results.

14

Running Your Own Benchmarks

There is no substitute for the test drive:

• Your application may exercise some feature of the compiler or hardware that wasn't revealed in the industry benchmarks.

• Your code may be "large," whereas most industry benchmarks are "small."

• Your program may require some support in the form of libraries or language features that aren't present on the machine.

• Your application might run (unexpectedly) slowly.

• Your program may expose a horrible bug.

Besides, no benchmark I know of measures how well the keyboard is laid out, how forgiving the compiler is, or how far the vendor deviates from what you expect. You are only going to learn these things by sitting in front of the machine.

This chapter is about benchmarking. It won't be so much a discussion of the mechanics of benchmarking, such as using the timing facilities—I covered most of that in Chapter 7. Instead, I'm going to discuss benchmark preparation and policies that will give you confidence in your results. I mean to address this to people who have source code and people who don't, and I'll show you how to set up both single-stream and throughput benchmarks.

Choosing What to Benchmark

I have seen groups scoop together a fairly random collection of programs and pass them out to vendors as a "benchmark suite." This usually happens when they're pressured to justify their choice for a computer, and helps to satisfy the purchasing department's requirement for a fair and honest evaluation. The trouble is that though these suites may provide general insight into a machine's performance, they don't say much about whether the machine will be good for its ultimate purpose. By picking user benchmarks that reflect what you do every day, or intend to do in the future, you can steer the purchasing justification in favor of the "right" machine.

Some orthogonality in your choices is a good idea. To take an example, say that you do structural analysis for a living. It might be wise to pick problems that represent different types of analyses, rather than several different examples of the same thing. For instance, a suite consisting of one dynamic, one static, and one modal analysis would tell you how the machine (and perhaps a third party software package) performs in three areas. If you do more of one thing than another, that's OK. Estimate the relative importance of each as a percentage of the work you do and use it as a weighting factor when it comes time to tally the benchmark results. This way, the most important things you do influence the outcome to the greatest extent.

Benchmark Run Time

Of course, you don't know how long benchmarks are going to run if you haven't run them yet. Even so, it's worth trying to project the run time so that you can keep the total for the collection to a reasonable level. Each code should execute for more than a few minutes, but less than 15 or so. All told, it should take less than an hour to do the whole thing, if for no other reason than that you are going to end up running it over and over. If benchmarks are too short, performance may get buried in the startup costs. If benchmarks are too long, you'll get bored.

How do you estimate the run time? Use MIPS and mflops! If your last machine was rated at 3 MIPS, and the workstation you are looking at today is rated at 60 MIPS, then everything should run 20 times faster, right? (Well, let's just hope so). Notice that this will take a significant twenty minute job and turn it into an insignificant one minute benchmark, which brings up a good point. You need to choose benchmarks that are representative of what you are going to do in the future, when you get the new machine. This is not only true for run time, but for memory requirements (and I/O) as well. After all, if the old machine was adequate you wouldn't be looking for a new one.

Benchmark Memory Size

Benchmark memory size is one of the most important areas to consider when pulling a suite together. New workstation caches and memory systems are much bigger and faster than those of machines a few years ago. But as we saw in Chapter 3, the relative gap in memory system performance versus CPU performance has widened. This means that one program, running two different sized problems, can test two completely different things:

- CPU performance for small problems
- Memory system performance for large problems

For this reason, it is a good idea to size the benchmarks realistically, or make them representative of the kinds of problems you will be running down the road. Your own benchmarks are probably one of the few places you will get to see figures for the performance of large problems anyway. Many of the benchmarks that used to exercise the memory system (i.e., Linpack) now fit in cache.

Be careful, of course, that the machines have sufficient memory for whatever benchmarks you plan to run. Otherwise, your programs will page (or swap), giving you useless performance data. (You should never plan to page or swap on purpose.) If you need help determining the memory sizes of your programs, see Chapter 11.

Kernels and Sanitized Benchmarks

In some cases, the sheer bulk of an application makes it unsuitable as a benchmark. There may be hundreds of thousands of lines of code or it may require data or resources that are difficult to port. Still, if the application is an important example of the work you do, you might want to construct a *kernel*—a subset of the code that represents the computations where the time is spent. Usually you would extract the central routines and give them their own main or *driver* routine. Data can be hardwired into the source or read into the program at startup.

There are also cases where code is sensitive or proprietary and needs to be *sanitized* before it can be released or reviewed by others. Again, the idea is to extract the essence of the computations while leaving out the peripheral work, including setup, interaction, and output. Comments can be removed with an editor, and variable names can be disguised if necessary. As with a kernel, a sanitized benchmark can have its data hardwired.

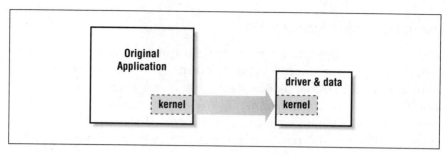

Figure 14-1: Kernel benchmark

A word of warning: when setting up the data for a kernel, make an extra effort to be sure that you haven't left the code open to over-optimization by a clever compiler. Initialize values from a file, a separately compiled block of data or externals; hide the ultimate fate of variables from the compiler by placing some of the results in common or external variables; or print out the values at the end. These steps will help guard against dead code removal or constant propagation that wouldn't have occurred in the original application. If one vendor's compiler recognizes an opportunity to remove unnecessary code, and another doesn't, then you are no longer running the same benchmark across machines.

Benchmarking Third Party Codes

With third party codes, you have little control over the performance on different hardware platforms. The company that owns the code ported, tested, and perhaps tuned it slightly (though not always), and shipped it out in executable form. You may have some control over the amount of memory used (which can effect the performance), but beyond that there is usually little you can do if it runs slowly.

You might expect that the application's speed on various machines would roughly track SPEC, MIPS, and mflops, but it may not! To understand why, consider the potential problems a small to medium-sized third party software developer may face. Each new release incorporates bug fixes from previous releases and perhaps some enhancements—sometimes major enhancements. Developers get into real trouble if they start maintaining separate versions of the code for different platforms, so they work with one and periodically distribute the changes.

Assume that you are Mr. Software Developer. You have ten Brand X computers, one (old) Brand Y, and know where you can borrow time on a

Brand Z. On which platform will you develop? Brand X, naturally, because that's what you own.

Now say that you have finished a release for Brand X—it passed 98% of the QA suite (and the other 2% could be explained)—and now you are migrating the code to Brands Y and Z. It gets through the QA suite with results in the neighborhood of 92% correct. You find that by shutting off optimizations that you can bump it up to 96%. "Hmmm . . .," you say, "I have to get this release out on time. I'll ask Mr. Computer Vendor to look into this later." And you ship the code with compiler optimizations reduced or shut off altogether! By sacrificing performance, you saved yourself development time.

Assuming the scenario is true (and even if it's not in your case), there is an extra step you will want to take when planning a platform for third party codes: ask the people who own the code what platform they recommend. The brand(s) used for development will get the earliest software releases and perhaps the best relative performance. See if they have opinions about the other brands, and whether they have run benchmarks between them. They may even say "Gee, our code sure runs well on Brand Z. If we could choose all over again, that's what we'd buy."

As ever, you will want to run your own benchmarks on various platforms, if possible. It gets a little tricky here because now you have to arrange with both the hardware vendor and the supplier of the third party package. In the case of well known applications, try convincing the hardware vendor to borrow the software for you. They may already have it, or they may have someone in the company who is responsible for the communication with the software supplier. For less popular packages, you will probably have to approach the software vendor yourself.

Types of Benchmarks

There are two components to every benchmark: the system under test, and the quantity for which you are measuring. In this book I have talked primarily about CPU/memory system performance. Accordingly, the benchmark techniques I am describing are aimed at CPU performance, though you can borrow some of them for I/O and graphics tests, too. On the outside, the tests are simple: measure the time it takes to do something.

The way the benchmarks are conducted should mimic the way the machine will ultimately be used. Will you be running one job at a time, or will there be many? Are you more interested in interactive response than CPU performance? How will you compare your measurements between plat-forms? These are some of the questions that you need to ask when planning a benchmark.

Single Stream Benchmarks

In the simplest kind of benchmark, *single stream*, you measure how long it takes the computer to execute a collection of programs, one at a time. Usually the machine is booted "multiuser," running the normal selection of daemons and background processes, but without any other demanding jobs to do, aside from your benchmark. Generally, two important sets of numbers result:

* The elapsed time for the whole collection, and
* The elapsed time for each individual piece.

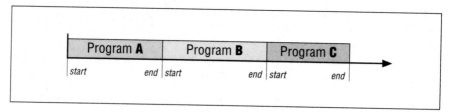

Figure 14-2: Single stream benchmarks

Often the pieces are contributed by different groups within your organization, meaning that there are going to be people who are just as interested in how their portion ran, as how things went overall. To make an objective measurement, you are going to have to gather estimates of the importance of each piece, and use those estimates as weighting factors for tallying the results. Also, you will want to normalize the results because the time it takes to run a particular program may not correspond to its importance.

To illustrate, say that you got the following results from running programs A, B, and C on brands X, Y, and Z:

	Brand X	Brand Y	Brand Z
Program A	322 sec	369 sec	310 sec
Program B	694 sec	801 sec	714 sec
Program C	440 sec	484 sec	441 sec

Taking the same table and normalizing the times in each row by the best time obtained, we get:

	Brand X	Brand Y	Brand Z
Program A	1.04	1.19	1.00
Program B	1.00	1.15	1.03
Program C	1.00	1.10	1.00

Now we need to apply weighting factors. Using whatever yardstick is appropriate, rate the applications by their relative importance. For example, if you run Program A most of the time, you might say that it should contribute 65% of its normalized run time to the answer. Likewise,

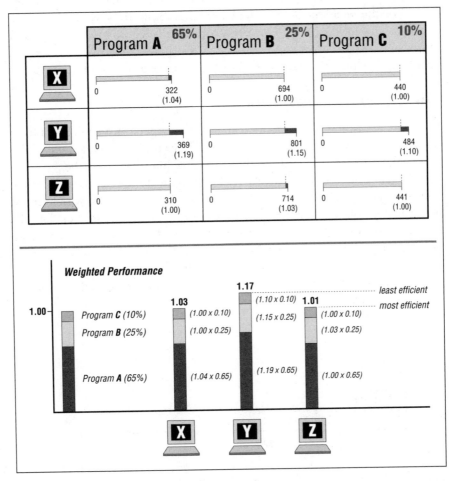

Figure 14-3: Computing an overall benchmark score

Programs B and C might contribute 25% and 10%, respectively. This means that, taking Brand X for example, the accumulated benchmark time would be:

```
1.04 X .65 + 1.00 X .25 + 1.00 X .10 = 1.03        Brand X
```

Brand Y and Brand Z benchmark results would be:

```
1.19 X .65 + 1.15 X .25 + 1.10 X .10 = 1.17        Brand Y
1.00 X .65 + 1.03 X .25 + 1.00 X .10 = 1.01        Brand Z
```

Brand Z wins (though not by much)! This outcome isn't immediately obvious from the raw data. Brand X won two out of the three benchmarks, but Brand Z won the most important of them. How much of a difference is significant? If I were buying the workstations, I wouldn't let 2% or even 10% or 20% be the deciding factor. There are other things to be concerned with, like cost and ease of use. However, a performance difference of 30% or more starts to become important. Still, the hardest part of choosing is deciding the value of the unquantifiable features of a workstation.

Throughput Benchmarks

If you are shopping for a server on which you expect to run several jobs at once, you will want to select a mix of codes to be benchmarked all at the same time. This will show you how the machine handles a heavy load, with a higher number of context switches and greater demands on memory and I/O. For a multitasking multiprocessor, this is the only way you are going to be able to compare between brands; single stream benchmarks will use just one CPU at a time whereas you need to see them exercised all at once (including an increased demand on the memory system). Again, you need to be conscious of your total memory requirements. If the programs don't fit altogether in memory, then the benchmark may become a disk bashing test (because of paging).

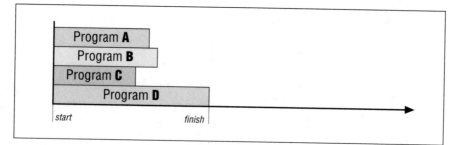

Figure 14-4: Wrong way to run a throughput benchmark

Different programs take different amounts of time to run. If you start them all at once, the last benchmark to finish will have spent some time executing all by itself as Figure 14-4 illustrates.

This is not what you want from a throughput benchmark; you want to see each application run against a steady background load. One way to do this is to construct a "stone wall" of programs as in Figure 14-5. When one of the programs completes it is immediately restarted, making for a (nearly) continuous contribution to the load.

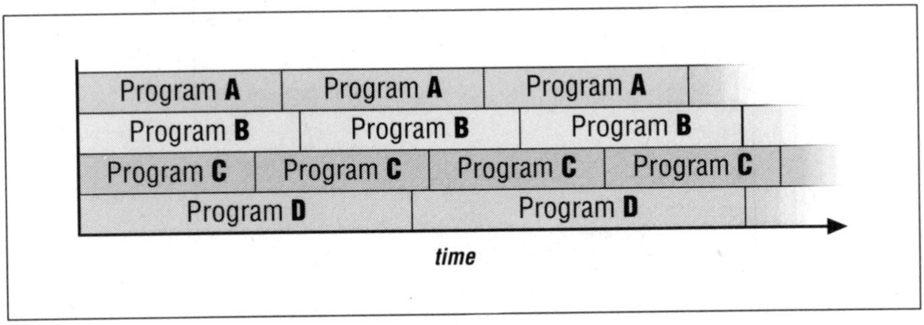

Figure 14-5: Benchmark stone wall

After a little while, you will have gathered one or more times for each benchmark, depending on how long you let them run. Average these together, if appropriate, and add the run times for A+B+C+D+E . . . to get a throughput figure for collection. Be sure to discard any contributions that were not run against the full background load. The proportionate run time for the different pieces will vary between machines, so again you may want to normalize the times for A, B, etc., before adding them together.

Interactive Benchmarks

If you are interested in more than "crunching"—if you are interested in knowing how a group of programmers playing Hunt the Wumpus will slow down a computer—you are going to want to run interactive benchmarks. Interactive response involves components of a computer—I/O system, operating system, networks—that are outside the scope of this book. Nonetheless, interactive response benchmarks may be important for your application.

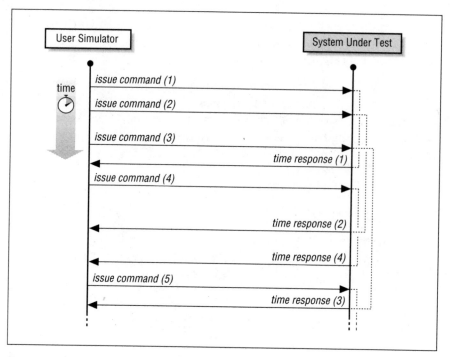

Figure 14-6: Interactive use benchmark

Figure 14-6 shows how an intereactive benchmark is constructed; you need two systems. One plays the part of users running interactive programs (shells, editors, word processors, etc.), while the other (the one being benchmarked) provides the services. As far as the system under test is concerned, there *are* real users on the machine; they log in through the network or serial ports and hammer away. By "playing" more and more users, you can see how performance drops off as interactive demands increase. Usually you measure this as the fraction of a second it takes to get response from a command.

Constructing an interactive benchmark (often called a *remote terminal emulation* or RTE benchmark) is more challenging than constructing a CPU benchmark. Development of the simulator portion is a big project by itself. You might want to look into a commercial product instead, such as Empower, available from Performix, Vienna VA. Or you could have the benchmark run by a third party, such as Neal Nelson & Associates of Chicago, IL. There are others as well.

Preparing the Code

Nothing fouls up a benchmarking effort more than discovering part way through that something is wrong with one or more of the benchmarks, and that they have to be tossed out. The time to look into portability is before you start. You will also want to package your benchmarks into a little kit so that anybody who runs them will get the same results; you don't want misunderstandings about how the code is to be handled to effect the answers.

Portability

Portability is important in a benchmark because it helps ensure that the same thing is being run on each system. Just as importantly, it frees you (and anyone else) from having to go into the code and hack it up as it migrates from platform to platform. A small mistake here or there and suddenly it's a new benchmark. To give yourself a good feeling that the results are reproducible, you have to be able to move benchmarks from machine to machine *without modifications*.

The best way to check for portability in a benchmark is to port it. If you have the luxury of extended access to the machines you want to benchmark, you should make a preliminary pass through each with the same code, tweaking it for portability as you go. That way, when you get to.the end, you will (most likely) have programs that compile and run on all the platforms. Then you can start the benchmark.

If, on the other hand, you don't have ready access to the machines being benchmarked, then port the code to anything! This will expose a fair portion of the portability problems anyway (i.e., namelist support is needed, you can't assign Hollerith strings to reals, alarm(3) behaves differently, etc). It's going to take you longer to port the code than to benchmark it anyway, and you certainly don't want the code to be modified as the benchmarks proceed, so porting ahead of time is important.

Aside from shoe-horning the code through the compiler, you also have to think about how properties of the algorithm will effect the run time. For example, say that your program characterizes the properties of an airfoil by starting out with some initial conditions and iterating until reaching a steady state. How are you going to account for numerical differences that actually effect the number of iterations? One machine may finish in 400 time steps whereas another may execute 420 time steps. You have to decide whether you think that the 420 timesteps is a bug, or whether it is acceptable, and exactly how you want to measure performance. As an alternative, you might plan to measure time per iteration, rather than total time.

Another thing to think about is data files. Does your program require unformatted data as input? If so, you are going to need to create some auxiliary programs to port the data, too; you can't assume that the unformatted files will be good on every machine. And what about interaction with the user? You will want to "hardwire" any dialog so that time spent waiting for keyboard input doesn't figure into the benchmark time. Basically, you want your benchmarks to run without help from you.

Making a Benchmark Kit

As I said at the start of this chapter, it's important to have confidence in your benchmarks. Chances are that a lot of money is going to be spent, partly on the basis of benchmarks. It would be good to feel that the benchmark results are reliable and reproducible. Furthermore, you want them to be as self-documenting as possible. I'll say more about increasing benchmark reliability in a little while. Right now I want to talk about making the results reproducible.

The best way to make a benchmark reproducible is to put a wrapper around it so that it compiles and runs with a single command. Any compiler options used and the exact measurements taken are part of the wrapper, making it easy for anyone to understand where your results came from. You will probably need separate wrappers for each machine—compiler invocations, options, etc., may differ. The wrapper itself can be a *script* (command file) or a *makefile*. Once you have prepared the benchmark—wrapper, code, and data files—you will want to save it into a *tar* (tape archive) file and stash it away. To run the benchmark on a Brand X computer, you should only need to unpack the archive and type **make brandx >& brandx.out**.

Arrange the makefile so that when the benchmark runs, everything written to *stdout*—compiler messages, and timing numbers—is recorded into a file. This file should be tucked away for reference, in case you want to go over the raw data again in the future. If a vendor runs your benchmark, ask for a copy of the output. Place some commands in your script or makefile that list all the files with their respective sizes so that if something has changed (if someone hacked the code), you will know about it.

I would almost be willing to guarantee that you are going to have to run the benchmarks again, down the road. New platforms will come out, and people in your organization will want to compare them with the ones you purchased. Also, keep in mind that compilers are constantly improving. Benchmark times can improve significantly over the life of a workstation, perhaps as much as 30%. If you have a nice benchmark kit, then you can resurrect it without giving up too much of your time.

Benchmarking Checklist

Just so we both sleep a little better, I've written down a list of steps to remember. These will help make your benchmark results reliable—good indicators of performance. Some of these may appear obvious to you, but perhaps one or two will have slipped your mind.

Compile with optimizations turned on

Don't forget to turn on compiler optimizations. The performance difference between optimized and unoptimized code can be great—often more than a factor of two. You will find that there are usually several optimization levels to choose from; however, without a degree of care, the higher ones can cause your program to run slower. And you don't necessarily want to go with the default, -O, flag. Check the manuals and ask the vendor representative to determine the best optimization level for your kind of program. Perhaps you will want to experiment with other optimization flags as well.

Check the memory size

Be sure the machine has enough memory to run your job. With too little memory, your program will page or swap, reducing the performance by as much as 20 times.

Check for other processes

There will always be a bubbling sea of daemons running in the background, but they don't generally take much time. What you are on the lookout for is other processes soaking up lots of cycles in competition with yours. Sometimes they are other "real" programs, but they can also be stuck processes.

Scrutinize the timing output

It is particularly important to pay attention to both CPU time and elapsed time. If they are not close, then look for an explanation. Perhaps your program is performing a lot of I/O. Could there be a memory problem? You would find evidence in the number of page faults.

Check the answers!

The last step is to check the results. You should be especially scrutinizing of the output when a program completes unreasonably quickly or slowly. It would be convenient if you could automatically *diff* the output from different machines, but this generally doesn't work. The problem is that vendors round numbers differently, represent them with different internal precisions and take liberties at compile time. Also, the output formats may vary slightly; the result may be `1.0e-6` rather than `0.10E-5`. Although these are the same number, a tool like *diff* doesn't know this. If the answers are just plain wrong, or the program seems to be producing correct results, but at a snail's pace, you might want to check for non-portable constructs. You could have a memory alignment problem or uninitialized variables as explained in Chapter 6.

Remember to benchmark your own computer

I'm not suggesting that you buy another of the brand you already own, but applying the same procedure to your present machine can be revealing. You may find that you are not using the machine correctly, or that the run time isn't as long as you thought it was. At any rate, you want a standard time to compare against.

Closing Notes

Profit margins on workstations have dropped significantly. Analyst/sales teams are being encouraged to reduce the cost of selling. This means that they are going to be less interested in helping you run a benchmark for the sale of just one or two workstations than they would have been five years ago. That's not to say they don't want to sell them to you, but where benchmarks are concerned, they just can't afford to get too involved. You will probably have to (and want to) run them yourself, perhaps at their office, with consulting access to the analyst.

If you are buying 100 workstations, on the other hand, they just might be able to give you some dedicated benchmarking assistance. Perhaps they will want to drag your code down a hole and hack at it for a while. Inevitably, the process will end with the analyst presenting fabulous results on overheads to a small crowd in a darkened room. The salesperson will be a well-dressed shadow with words of good will and support to put the kabosh on any technical questions. Be careful with the numbers they give you. If you looked at Chapters 9, 10, 11, and 12, you saw what goes on behind closed doors. They probably have a copy of this book!

One more thing: keep good notes. The reason to run a controlled benchmark is so you can live with yourself.

IV

Parallel Computing

15

Large Scale Parallel Computing

Many mathematical models are computationally parallel. Proponents of parallel computing like to point out that there is a very good reason for this: nature itself is parallel. Simulations of molecules, weather systems, economies or fluid flow all have a parallel quality to them, like the systems they represent. Atoms don't take turns interacting, as in a computer program running on a serial computer. They all interact with one another, all at the same time.

Whether running on a parallel computer or not, nearly every program has a mixture of parts that are serial and parts that are parallel. An engineering analysis is a good example. The setup portion may be very serial—data is read in, a matrix is populated. If there is little opportunity to overlap execution, then the setup portion can't benefit from having multiple CPUs at its disposal. The solution phase, on the other hand, will often be highly parallel. So far we have talked about applying this parallelism to vector units or general purpose floating point pipelines, but very often those programs that are vectorizable are also easily divided for execution on multiple CPUs.

Other types of problems are also very parallel, yet aren't as regular as vectorizable code. Sorting and searching are examples; if you have many searches to run, and many CPUs available to do it, you can split the work up so that the searches run concurrently.

Often, running a program on multiple processors requires a fair amount of extra work, if you want any speedup. Programs usually have to be structured specifically for parallelism, so there is enough to do to keep multiple processors busy without spending an inordinate amount of time coordinating or passing information between them. The job of splitting out the parallel parts for execution on multiple CPUs is called problem *decomposition*.

Once a problem has been decomposed for multiple processors, people say it has been *parallelized*.

An application may be parallelized with a particular architecture in mind. For instance, it may be a massively parallel machine containing thousands of small processors, a traditional multiprocessor with four (or so) CPUs, or a network of workstations. In many cases, the effort spent parallelizing an application for one type of machine is transferable to another. The difference is often the granularity of the decomposed parts: the amount of work each processor does before it completes, communicates, or goes back to the well for more.

The bigger question of recognizing parallelism, or training yourself to think in parallel, is another matter. Some models are clearly parallel, both in concept and in code. Others may have a parallel nature that is buried or obscured by the method used or the kind of coding techniques the programmer preferred. Still others have little innate parallelism. Naturally, identifying a fair portion of parallelizable code is important if you want to benefit from a parallel machine. Time spent running serially, using a single processor between patches of parallelism, can easily dominate your run time. And interprocessor communication often limits the effective parallelism in parallel computers. Again, Amdahl's Law comes in to play. The serial portions of the program can contribute heavily to the run time.

The field of parallel computing, though several decades old, is still struggling to reach maturity. Questions about how people should express their models haven't been settled. Nor is there any kind of agreement on what architectures are best. So in a sense, this chapter is less a statement of the way things are and more a tour of the battlefield.

Problem Decomposition

There are two main approaches to dividing or decomposing work for distribution among multiple CPUs. With the first, *data decomposition*, you partition the data your program uses into pieces, and distribute the responsibility for each piece to a separate processor. The processors perform essentially the same calculations, but on different data.

The second method for splitting up an application is called *control decomposition*, where different processors are given different kinds of jobs to do, or are assigned jobs as the processors become available. The approach you choose depends on the problem. You may use data or control decomposition, or a hybrid. In some cases, the architecture doesn't give you much of a choice. At any rate, since the subject of decomposition, especially data decomposition, is somewhat independent of computer architecture, we can treat it first, before looking at hardware.

Data Decomposition

Data-parallel problems occur in many disciplines. They vary from those that are extremely parallel to those that are just sort of parallel. For example, fractal calculations are extremely parallel; each point is derived independently of the rest. It's simple to divide fractal calculations among processors. Because the calculations are independent, the processors do not have to coordinate or share data.

A gravitational model of a galaxy is another kind of parallel program. Each point exerts an influence on every other. Therefore, unlike the fractal calculations, the processors do have to share data.

In either case, you want to arrange calculations so that processors can say to one another "you go over there and work on that, and I'll work on this, and we'll get together when we are finished."

Calculation of the area under a curve by numerical integration provides a simple example of an extremely parallel problem.

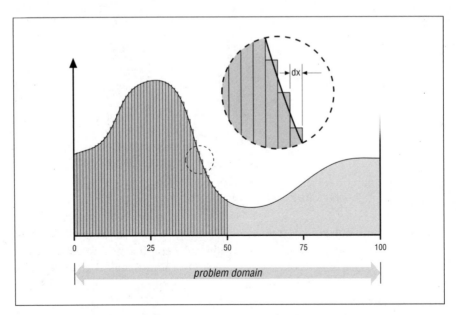

Figure 15-1: Domain decomposition

You compute the area by taking the space under the curve and fitting it with a series of quadrilaterals, each with a fixed width and the height that approximates that part of the curve. The sum of the quadrilaterals estimates the area underneath. The *domain* of the problem can be divided into as many little pieces as you like—the thinner the quadrilaterals, the better the approximation to the area. It's easy to see how to compute this in parallel because the job of generating and summing regions can easily be divided into parts. For instance, if you have four CPUs, the first can handle the region of the domain from 0 to 25, the second can handle 26 to 50, and so on. There is little coordination to be done; each CPU can act independently of the rest until the four partial sums are collected into the final answer.

Problems that offer less independence between regions are still very good candidates for domain decomposition. Have you heard of the "Game of Life?" In its simplest form, you take a Cartesian grid and divide it into cells. You decide whether a cell is alive or dead depending on its environment. For instance, you might claim that the cells represent starfish, and that if they are overcrowded, the starfish die off. On the other hand, lonely starfish don't get to reproduce, and also die off.

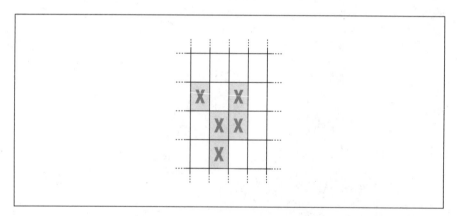

Figure 15-2: Cells with X's have life

We need some rules. Say that a cell is alive if it has precisely two living neighbors—no more, no less. Given this rule and the grid in Figure 15-2, the next iteration will look like Figure 15-3. Some cells that were dead became alive because they had exactly two neighbors. Others died. Some remained as they were.

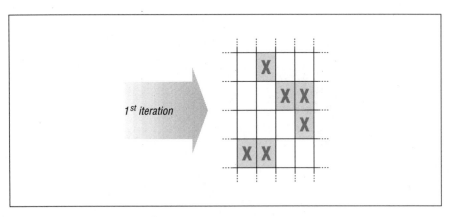

Figure 15-3: One iteration later

You can decompose the cells in the Game of Life so that different processors are responsible for updating different cells. If it turns out that you have one processor per cell, each will need to communicate its state with each of its eight nearest neighbors. The grid may be much larger, of course, perhaps including thousands of cells. With thousands of processors you can still maintain a one-to-one correspondence, if you like, but if you have only a handful of processors, you will need to map groups of cells onto each CPU. How will you go about it?

You could split up the cells randomly; however, this will increase the communication costs. A single CPU can act very quickly on data in its local memory, but when it needs to share information with other processors it always has to go through a slower medium. This is true for every kind of parallel machine.

Careful grouping of the data domain into regions will minimize communication between processors. The processors will have to update one another about the state of the cells on their borders. However, information about internal cells will not have to be shared because it doesn't effect any part of the system outside the CPU on which it lives.

In Figure 15-4 the domain has been divided two different ways—into blocks and strips. When the domain is divided into blocks, CPU 1 has to share border information with CPU 2, 3, and 4. With strips, CPU 1 has to share information only with CPU 2.

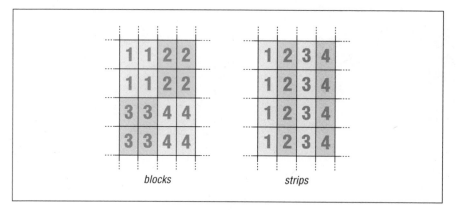

Figure 15-4: Two examples of division of cells between four CPUs

The Game of Life is a simple metaphor for many classes of real applications where data can be divided into cells or groups of cells.* Finite difference problems, short-range particle interaction simulations, and columns of matrices can be treated similarly. If you can divide the domain evenly between the processors, they will each do approximately the same amount of work on their way to a solution.

Other physical systems are not so regular, or involve long-range interactions. The nodes of an unstructured grid may not be allocated in direct correspondence to their physical locations, for instance. Or perhaps the model involves long-range forces, such as particle attractions. These problems, though more difficult, can be structured for parallel machines as well. Sometimes various simplifications, or "lumping" of intermediate effects, are needed. For instance, the influence of a group of distant particles upon another may be treated as if there was one composite particle acting at a distance. This is done to spare the communications that would be required if every processor had to talk to every other regarding each detail. In other cases, the parallel architecture offers opportunities to express a physical system in different and clever ways that make sense in the context of the machine. For instance, each particle could be assigned to its own processor, and these could slide past one another, summing interactions and updating a time step.

---

*For a more detailed description of the "Game of Life" see John Horton, "Computer Recreations," *Scientific American*, March, 1984.

One last thought on data decomposition: perhaps your involvement with a parallel machine is in terms of vectors and matrices—the physical significance may not be immediately apparent to you. Even so, you can still perform data decomposition by dividing up loop iterations across processors. If you think about it, loops merely walk through arrays. These arrays can be thought of as the domain of your application—apart from the physical significance of the problem. By spreading loop iterations across processors, you are parceling out parts of the domain.

Control Decomposition

Sometimes, it is possible to divide the work based on function, rather than data. To give an example, say that you are modeling a sewage plant. Each major functional component—sewer pump, cesspool, annealing pit, river dump, toilet—can be represented as its own computational black box. These same pieces can also be naturally sprinkled among the processors of a parallel machine. Particularly complex sub-models might occupy several processors, but overall you can point to individual processors and say "this one is in charge of that." Breaking computation along functional lines like this is is called *control decomposition.*

For finer-grained tasks, control decomposition is a method for assigning jobs to particular processors based on their ability to handle more work, or their suitability for a given task. The parallel program can be arranged into a master-worker relationship, in which some parts of the program distribute work to others as program execution proceeds. The next section shows an example of control decomposition of a problem based on individual processors' authority over portions of the dictionary.

Control decomposition is less straightforward and less universally applicable than data decomposition. Whereas the notion of data decomposition applies well to every kind of parallel architecture (and many problems), control decomposition requires that each processor be able to act independently. This isn't always possible, as we'll see in a little while. A more fundamental problem is that control decomposition often doesn't scale easily. For instance, how do you take a four processors doing four separate jobs and scale the computations up to eight processors? Unless you add more computational black boxes, it isn't going to be so easy.

Distributing Work Fairly

Simple data decomposition doesn't always provide the most even distribution of work. It could be that the domain is irregular, making it difficult to tell where it should be divided. In other cases, it is difficult to anticipate how much effort will be involved with a particular portion of the data.

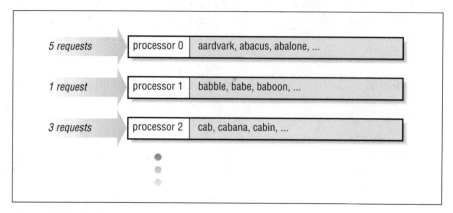

Figure 15-5: Each processor with a piece of the domain

For illustration, say that your domain is the English dictionary. If you have 26 processors, you could give each responsibility for their own letter of the alphabet as in Figure 15-5. The first processor could process requests for definitions of words starting with the letter A, the second could handle B, and so forth. Knowing the English language, you might expect to handle more requests for letters like R than for letters like Z. This means that some processors will be idled while others work through a backlog. In a worst case scenario, the system could queue up 2000 requests for A words, and none for B through Z. Think about how you would prepare for this.

One approach might be to make each processor responsible for the whole alphabet, and to parcel lookups to them like bank tellers (Figure 15-6). However, we are immediately faced with a logistics problem: because each processor has to be able to handle a request for *any* letter, they either have to share information from their portion of the dictionary with other processors, or each CPU has to have a complete local copy of the whole domain.

Depending on the architecture of the parallel computer, a choice for either dividing or replicating (portions of) the domain may add unacceptable overhead or cost to whole project.

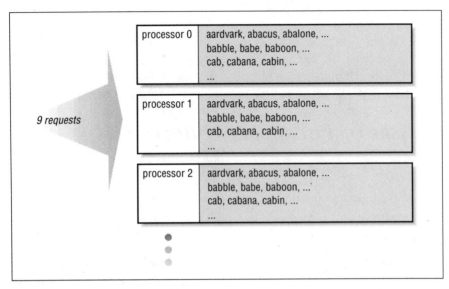

Figure 15-6: Duplicated data domain

For a large problem, the dollar value of main memory may make keeping separate local copies of the same data out of the question. In fact, a need for more memory is often what drives people to parallel machines; the problem that they want to solve can't fit within the memory of a conventional computer.

By investing some effort, you could allow the domain partitioning to evolve as the program runs, in response to an uneven load distribution. That way, if there were a lot of requests for A's, then several processors could dynamically get a copy of the A piece of the domain. Or the A piece could be spread out across several processors, each handling a different subset of the A definitions. You could also migrate unique copies of data from place to place, changing their home as needed. In fact, as long as nobody adds words to the dictionary or changes definitions, it will be possible to keep multiple copies. This would be a form of data caching, much like we talked about in Chapters 2, 3, and 11, except that now there is the challenge of maintaining many copies of a given portion of memory. I'll have more to say about this later.

The dictionary example illustrates a problem that programmers of large scale parallel machines often face. When the data domain is irregular, or changes over time, the parallel program encounters a load-balancing problem. Such a problem becomes especially apparent when one portion of the parallel computations takes much longer to complete than the others. A real world example might be an engineering analysis on an adaptive grid. As the program runs, the grid becomes more refined in those areas showing the most activity. If the work isn't reapportioned from time to time, the section of the computer with responsibility for the most highly refined portion of the grid will fall further and further behind the rest of the machine.

Classes of Parallel Architectures

There are three major types of parallel architectures you are likely to encounter:

- SIMD (*S*ingle *I*nstruction, *M*ultiple *D*ata) with distributed memory
- MIMD (*M*ultiple *I*nstruction, *M*ultiple *D*ata) with distributed memory
- MIMD with shared memory

Examples of SIMD machines are the CM-2 from Thinking Machines Corporation, the MP-2 from MasPar Corporation (also available from DEC), and the Wavetracer.

The distinction between distributed memory MIMD machines and shared memory MIMD machines is significant. In the first case, memory is partitioned between processors, meaning that you (or the compiler or operating system) have to explicitly arrange for data transfer between CPUs if they are to work together on a single problem. In the shared memory MIMD model, all machines see the same main memory as one global pool. Examples of shared memory MIMD machines are the Power Series machines from Silicon Graphics, the Convex C3, and the Sun SPARCcenter 2000. Examples of distributed memory MIMD machines are the Intel iPSC/860 Parallel Supercomputer, the Intel Paragon, Thinking Machines CM-5, the nCUBE 2, and, to some extent, any network of workstations (!). We talked about this briefly in Chapter 12. There are software tools available for treating networks as a single parallel processing pool.

In the next two sections, I am going to explain the differences between distributed memory SIMD and distributed memory MIMD machines. All of Chapter 16 is devoted to shared memory MIMD.

Single Instruction, Multiple Data

A SIMD (pronounced *symdee*) machine is a collection of processors, usually thousands, that all perform the same operation at exactly the same time as every other, yet on different data.* Each processor has a little bit of local memory and some communications paths to its "neighbors." They don't share any memory, so if you want more than one processor to see the same value of a particular variable, you have to transfer it across the communications path.

At first glance, this seems like a peculiar idea. But think about a do-loop. If each iteration is independent of the rest, then you are free to execute them all at the same time. Furthermore, the math for each iteration is the same (or nearly so). The only difference is that you are working with a different value of index variable: I=n in one case, and I=m in another. Same instructions, different data—this matches the concept of a SIMD machine very well. Iterations can be spread across the available nodes and executed all at once. If there are more iterations than nodes, they can be doubled-up so that each processor handles several calculations. Figure 15-7 shows how you might map the following loop onto a SIMD machine:

```
      DO 10 I=1,N
         A(I) = B(I) + D(J) * ....
10    CONTINUE
```

Communications between nodes can be replicated as well. Returning to the Game of Life, each cell could check its neighbor to the North, North-East, East, etc., in lock-step with the rest.

Keeping communications to a minimum is key. If you are adding a vector **A** to a vector **B**, for example, and corresponding elements exist in each processors' local memory, then the addition will be very fast. That is, if A(I) lives on the same processor as B(I), and the loop says A(I)=A(I)+ B(I), then there will be no inter-processor transfer of data.

However, if the loop says something else, for example, A(I)=A(I)+ B(I+1), then each processor will have to send its value of B(I+1) to the neighbor performing the addition. The communications will all take place

---

*Here's an illustration: The largest SIMD machine in the world runs every weekday around noon, when the aerobics and exercise programs come on the air. The hostess calls out the instructions: "left, and down, and up, then right...," while thousands follow along in lock-step.

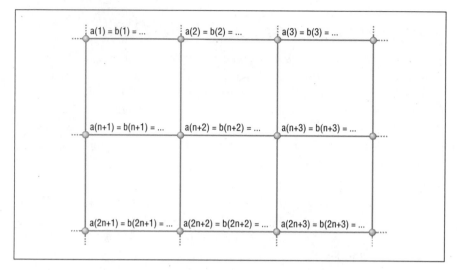

Figure 15-7: Iterations mapped onto SIMD nodes

in parallel, so they won't be show-stopping, but they will have an effect. You can see that the layout of data among the processors matters. In the first case no data needed to be transferred. In the second, all the B(I+1)'s did.

Other constructs contain greater potential communications overhead. We spent much of Chapter 11 looking at examples: strided references, permutations, etc. These will necessarily cause communications between nodes; there is no way to lay out the data so that only local memory is used. With a permutation, for instance, a node may need to talk to its next door neighbor or one all the way across the machine. Generally, there isn't a regular pattern to the communications. The resulting bustle of activity will be reminiscent of flies being shooed and redescending on a plate of hamburger.

Vector reductions, such as MAX, MIN, dot products, etc., need special treatment on SIMD machines. Each requires that all nodes cooperate in coalescing a single value from many. For instance, if you are looking for the largest value A(N) from a vector A, eventually all values A(I) will have to be compared. Hand-crafting such operations would be possible, but SIMD machines generally come with very efficiently implemented vector reductions, transpose functions, matrix multiplies, etc. These overlap transfer of operands with computation.

There are times when you want to prevent a portion of the nodes from participating in some computations. You need to be able to do this in order to simulate branches. Imagine for instance that you want to make a conditional assignment, for example, the assignment expressed by the Fortran 90 WHERE statement shown below:

```
WHERE (A .LT. 0) A = A + B * C
```

None of the nodes on a SIMD machine can act independently. Therefore, the idea of a branch is difficult. You can't have a situation where some of the nodes take a branch and some don't. Conditional computation is handled by masking out those nodes for which the conditional is false, and computing on those where it is true.

SIMD Architecture

The individual processors of SIMD machines are not particularly fast or powerful, but there are usually thousands of them, which makes the whole machine, taken together, quite powerful. Each processor will have a small amount of local memory, some neighbors, and a mechanism for sharing data with other processors.

For a node to talk to another which is several hops away, it either opens a connection through a router or passes a message through intervening nodes to its final destination. Opening a connection is like placing a phone call. One processor tries to get a circuit to another. If the circuit is tied up, the processor gets a busy signal and has to try again. A message, on the other hand, is more like a letter. It gets routed through from one processor to another, but doesn't tie up the path between them. Circuits potentially cause more contention for communication, but they allow processors to pass a lot of data once the circuit is established. Messages are generally limited in length, so the processor may need to issue several to complete one transfer. You don't get to choose which it will be; the technique for communicating between nodes is a function of the brand of parallel machine you bought.

The processors or nodes are wired together in either a mesh or a hypercube configuration—perhaps a little of both. A mesh is easy to visualize: it looks like a window screen extending in two or three dimensions. Each node has four or six directly-connected Cartesian neighbors, depending on whether the machine is two-dimensional or three-dimensional.* To move data from node A to node B, you map a Cartesian route through the mesh.

---

*The Wavetracer is an example of 3D mesh. The MasPar MP-2 is a 2D mesh.

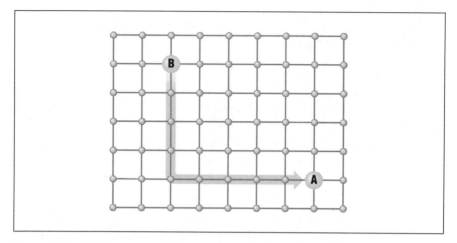

Figure 15-8: Mapping a route through a strictly Cartesian mesh

The question is: If you want to move data between any node A and any node B, what is the longest path you will have to take? That is, if two nodes located in the extreme opposite corners want to talk, how far does the data have to go? The question is significant because each node along the way is involved in routing your data to its final destination, so it takes time to get there. In the case of an M by N mesh, the longest path is $(M-1)+(N-1)$. *

A hypercube is a little more difficult to envision, so I will take you through the reasoning behind it. Imagine that you want to glue a large number of processors together in a manner that gives you the highest degree of connectivity for the least number of physical wires (and associated circuitry). Let's start with four nodes (Figure 15-9).

If you arrange them in a straight line, the worst case transfer (from node 1 to node 4) will take three hops $(n-1)$. That may not seem like too much of a penalty, but it doesn't scale very well. With 1024 processors, it will take 1023 hops for the worst case transfer. However, the wire count is very low—two connections per processor, 1023 total—so it will be cheap to build.

---

*SIMD machines also feature a *router*—a facility for getting from any node to any other by stepping outside the mesh for an instant. It's good for sending limited amounts of data far away.

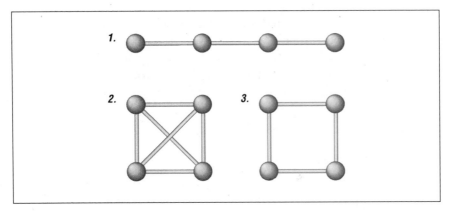

Figure 15-9: Four nodes

In the other extreme, if you attach every processor of a four node configuration to every other, the worst case transfer will be just one hop and the number of physical connections will be three per processor, or six total. This degree of connectivity may be manageable for four processors, but for 1024, it scales to $N*(N-2)/2=523,776$ connections (yow!). That's 1023 per processor. This is a ridiculous number of connections. There would be far too much hardware and no one would be able to afford it.

A good compromise is to arrange the processors into an *n*-dimensional cube. For instance, with four processors you could build a 2-cube (the number of nodes, N, is 2^n). A 3-cube would be a volume composed of eight processors. The longest path from any node to any other is n hops—two in the case of a 2-cube. This turns out to be a reasonable number of connections, and it scales well.

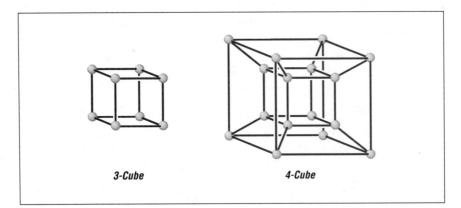

3-Cube   **4-Cube**

Figure 15-10: A 3-cube and a 4-cube

Higher dimensional cubes are formed by cementing two lower dimensional cubes together. For instance, you can build a 4-cube by combining two 3-cubes. If you scale it to 1024 processors (this is a 10 cube), the longest path between any two nodes is ten hops, and the total number of connections is $2^{(n-1)*n} = 5120$.

Table 15-1: Worst Case Communication

Number of Nodes	Cartesian Mesh	Hypercube
16	6 hops	4 hops
256	30 hops	8 hops
1024	62 hops	10 hops
2048	126 hops	11 hops
16384	254 hops	16 hops

You can see that as the number of processors goes up, a hypercube has an increasingly low communications cost, relative to the Cartesian configurations. In the case of 1024 nodes, for example, the worst case transfer length is less than 1/6 that of a mesh. However, you aren't always sending data all the way to the other side of the machine, so the worst case transfers don't always matter. Hopefully, most communications take place between neighbors, and are being conducted between many processors all at once.

As far as matching the machine topology (mesh or hypercube) to your program, it generally isn't a problem that you have to be overly conscious about. You would prefer to distribute the data in a way that makes sense in the context of your problem. In fact, you'd like to imagine that the SIMD machine's nodes take the shape of your data. This often turns out to be a mesh. But since there is total connectivity anyway, the significance of the node interconnection isn't as important as you might guess at first. A mesh can be easily emulated by a hypercube.*

The SIMD mesh or hypercube is connected to a front-end—a workstation or a VAX—as though it were memory or a peripheral of some sort. The front-end will sit on a network like any other machine. You log into it to get

---

*The Thinking Machines CM-2 is organized as a hypercube of clusters containing 32 nodes apiece. Topologically it is arranged as a hypercube, but software primitives treat it like a mesh.

access to the parallel machine. There may be a fast scalar processor pack-aged with the parallel processor, or perhaps the front-end itself is responsi-ble for the non-parallel part of the computations. In either case, it is a more traditional machine that handles serial execution. Other peripherals, such as disk drives, input devices, or data switches, may hang off the cube or mesh.

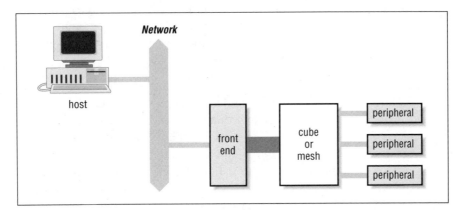

Figure 15-11: Front-end and SIMD machine

Mechanics of Programming a SIMD Machine

How do you write a program for such an oddball architecture as this? It looks to be a real to challenge map data onto the nodes and get them to talk to each other correctly. Actually, given a problem with a regular struc-ture, it's pretty straightforward. For less regularly structured problems, it can be difficult. In any case, you can choose from one of several choices in programming languages. Generally, these fall into two categories:

- Languages that explicitly choreograph the movement of data and instructions on each node of the machine

- Higher level languages, where you trust the compiler to decompose the problem and organize computation on the nodes on your behalf

Explicitly programming a SIMD machine

SIMD languages for explicitly programming the actions of the nodes can produce very tight, efficient code. You are free to lay out the data exactly as you please and explicitly pick the computations and data movement you want. Of course, you are coding for all of the nodes at once, so if you say "pass a value to the neighbor on the left," every processor does it at the same time—which also means that you can expect to be receiving one from someone else. In less regular codes, you may be passing data around the mesh or cube arbitrarily, based on pointers or permutation indices, in which case the data can go to and come from any other node.

The front-end machine treats programs written for the SIMD nodes as subroutines. Depending on what your application does, you may alternate between patches of execution on the serial front-end and the parallel SIMD machine. Data can be passed back and forth as you please, though you want to minimize data movement whenever possible.

What do these node level programming languages look like? On the MasPar MP-2 and the Wavetracer, the language of the mesh looks just like C, with extensions for the SIMD environment. You write and compile subroutines to be run on the mesh and invoke them from the main program running on the front-end. One significant difference between normal C code and an extended C is that the parallel language typically has several new data types. Variables can be declared as replicated or unique, depending on whether there are individual copies on each node or a single copy residing on the front-end. In addition, there are functions or variables for explicit communications with neighbors in the mesh.

Like the Wavetracer and the MP-2, the CM-2 also has a parallel C language (in fact, they had one first), called *C** (pronounced C-star); however, it is not the lowest level user language for the machine. There is another, called PARIS (*PAR*allel *I*nstruction *S*et), that has opcodes like an assembly language, except that the operations can be very sophisticated, and include communications and transcendental functions. Though PARIS is probably not going to be the programming language of choice for most CM-2 users, it does have its history. As you can imagine, compiler efficiency gains for parallel machines are asymptotic (and will be going on forever), so the absolute best performance is still going to come from hand-coded routines.

Languages that apply to the whole environment

Writing code explicitly for the cube or mesh is akin to hand-coding for a supercomputer vector unit. People usually like to avoid that level of detail. Just as there are vector compilers for identifying and generating vector instructions, there are also compilers for identifying and generating code for SIMD execution. In fact, the environments have a lot in common. Something that is vectorizable generally runs well on a SIMD machine.

However, unlike the developers of vector compilers, the authors of SIMD compilers have generally adhered exclusively to higher level languages that feature *explicit* array constructs, like those found in Fortran 90 and High Performance Fortran (Chapter 12). Many vector compilers are designed to derive vector constructs from FORTRAN 77 or C; no such compilers exist for SIMD processors. Rather, Fortran 90-based SIMD compilers take their cues exclusively from the explicit array constructs. Those portions of the program that are written using Fortran 90 array constructs execute on the cube or mesh. Those that are written serially execute on the front-end.

To illustrate, here are two vector scale and add operations (*daxpy*) from a Fortran 90 application:

```
      PARAMETER (N = 1000)
      REAL A(N), B(N), C
      ...
   C FORTRAN 77; could be vectorized by a competent vector compiler
      DO 10 I=1,N
         A(I) = A(I) + B(I) * C
   10    CONTINUE
      ...
   C Fortran 90: explicit array construct
      A = A + B * C
      END
```

Because of the way they are coded, the first will run on the front-end, the second on the SIMD nodes. The difference, as I described in Chapter 12, is that the first construct implies an order to the calculations, whereas the second does not. A non-ordered instruction is a perfect match for a SIMD machine, since every node can execute it at the same time.

It's not enough just to decide where instructions should be executed. The compiler is going to have to choose where to store an array—to choose where its home is. Typically, you want data near the place where it will be operated upon. The compiler guesses where to store the data by looking at how it is used. If the programmer uses any parallel constructs at all, then the compiler will keep the array on the parallel machine. Otherwise, it will store the array on the front-end.

Laying out the data and choosing its home are things that the programmer needs to think about. If some of the routines lead the compiler to believe that the array lives on the parallel machine, and some suggest that it lives on the front-end, there will be run time disagreement about how the memory should be accessed. Some routines will be looking in the front-end's memory, others will look on the SIMD machine. And as we saw above, there are performance benefits to aligning data to minimize movement. I'll talk more about this below.

SIMD programming offers several benefits over some of the other parallel programming environments we will be looking at. For one thing, a SIMD machine is *synchronous*, meaning that all operations take place in lock-step and proceed exactly the same way every time the program is run with the same input data set. This makes programs on SIMD machines relatively easy to debug. For example, you never have a situation where a slight reordering of the computations (by the machine, not by the programmer) produces different answers. The SIMD programming environment is also more mature than some other parallel programming environments (they are catching up though), in spite of the fact that it is much younger in many ways. The languages are designed for parallelism and the development and debug tools have a finished quality about them.

You can find examples of successes using SIMD computing in fluids analysis, electromagnetics problems, particle simulations, structural analysis, full text searches, and neural networks. One of the biggest applications for SIMD machines so far has been in signal processing, including nose-cone computers for inter-continental ballistic missiles.* But even given some successes, SIMD is still struggling to become part of mainstream computing (and losing to MIMD, lately). Still viewed as specialty hardware, and challenging to use, SIMD computers are by and large research machines.

Multiple Instruction, Multiple Data

Now imagine machines with the same basic layout as SIMD machines, except that each of the nodes is a microprocessor running its own independent instruction stream. Additionally, these processors are quite a bit more powerful than SIMD nodes and there are usually far less of them. Such a machine might be a collection of Intel i860s, as in the Intel iPSC/860 parallel supercomputer, each with many megabytes of local memory. The two types of interconnects still apply (you'll see hypercubes and meshes, though there are other types too), although other features of SIMD machines, such as the router and tightly integrated front end, are missing. Also missing is the concept of keeping part of the data on the front-end and

---

*SIMD Nose-cone computers for signal processing are packed in so tightly that that they are inadequately cooled. That is, after 30 minutes of operation, they'll fail . . . but they only have to work for 15 minutes!

part on the nodes—the nodes are as powerful as most front-ends anyway. Such machines are called Distributed Memory MIMD computers. The term MIMD (pronounced *mimdee*) stands for *Multiple Instruction, Multiple Data*. The distributed memory classification points out that each node has its own local memory (like SIMD), which is not visible to any other nodes in the machine. As with SIMD, if any two nodes wish to share data they must explicitly arrange to send it to one another.

There are also differences in how you program MIMD machines. With MIMD, you have more choices about how to divide your application for execution: you can cut the data domain into pieces or, if the problem lends itself, you can do control decomposition (at a cost of programming complexity). This gives you some additional flexibility over SIMD. For instance, you could conceivably have completely different programs working cooperatively on different nodes of a MIMD machine. One node could be doing I/O while another performs calculations, or you could treat each node as a transaction processor, handling requests as they come in and nodes become available.

If you choose to divide the data domain, much of the same thinking that applies to execution on a SIMD machine applies to MIMD as well: you split the problem into pieces and hand the pieces out to the processors. However, each node may work on hundreds of data points, rather than a handful. Because the nodes are very powerful, a handful of MIMD nodes has the equivalent throughput of a much larger number of SIMD nodes (at correspondingly greater cost). The processors work on their own patches of data and share only that information that other processors will need to complete their calculations.

Division of labor and sharing of data on a distributed memory MIMD machine are things that you code very explicitly. That is, a compiler won't do it for you—you have to decompose the problem by hand.* Recalling the example of integration of the area under a curve, for example, you would need to include a little bit of code to determine the size of the chunk that each processor is going to work on. The choice would normally be a

---

*This is changing. Fortran 90 and High Performance Fortran are coming to MIMD hardware, leaving some of the work to the compiler. Additionally, a new programming model is appearing on the scene—virtual shared memory—where you depend on the hardware to handle data sharing for you. I'll say more about these things shortly.

function of how large the data domain is and how many processors you have at your disposal. For instance, each node would say:

- How many nodes are there?
- Which node am I?
- I will do the *n*th of the work corresponding to my node number.

You would also have to determine what part of the data needs to be shared and you would have to explicitly write the code that packs up messages and sends them to a neighboring processors. The contents of the messages are usually just those portions of the data that reside on the border with neighbors. For the Game of Life, for instance, the state of the cells along the edges has to be shared. To pass information to another node elsewhere on the machine, you have to:

- Pick the destination
- Pack the information into a message
- Pass the message to the destination machine

The transaction isn't complete until the node receiving the message goes to see if it has arrived (it has to be expecting it). It is the passing of messages that synchronizes computation on a distributed memory MIMD machine; cooperative computation doesn't proceed until messages are exchanged.*

Distributed Memory MIMD Architecture

Imagine if you took the major cities in the United States—New York, Los Angeles, Chicago, etc.—arranged them in a hypercube and connected them with two lane highways. This graphically describes the nature of the previous wave of commercially available distributed memory MIMD machines. The individual processors are as powerful as many workstations, but they are connected together by bit-serial connections with transfer rates of just a few megabytes per second. The number of CPUs is generally much smaller than on a SIMD machine—usually no more than 128, although it is possible for them to number in the thousands.

Some examples of hypercube distributed memory MIMD machines are the Intel iPSC/860 and the NCUBE 2. Additionally, there are a few new parallel machines coming on the scene. Intel has announced its *Paragon* machine, using i860s like the iPSC/860, except that it replaces the 1-bit wide hypercube interconnect with a 16-bit wide mesh. This is an improvement over a

---

*Message passing can be asynchronous too.

hypercube because the parallel data paths give faster node-to-node transfers. And if you recall the comparison of the worst case number of hops for a hypercube versus a mesh, the difference is small when you are working with a handful of processors, so the penalty for going to a mesh isn't significant.

Thinking Machines Corporation is shipping the CM-5, a SPARC based MIMD machine featuring the same programming model as the CM-2 (plus it can be programmed as a MIMD machine). That is, you can program it like a SIMD machine, though it is MIMD underneath. Kendall Square Research* is selling a virtual shared memory machine, organized as rings of processors (I'll say more about this later). Convex and Cray Research have both announced plans to offer parallel machines in the future. In Convex' case, the processors will be HP Precision Architecture. Cray will work with both SPARC and DEC AXP.

Each processor of a MIMD machine may have from 4 to 64 MB of main memory. There will also be a fair amount of hardware dedicated to routing messages or establishing circuits through the cube or mesh. This hardware is designed so that a processor doesn't have to get involved in message transfer unless it is sending or receiving the message. Think of it like the phone company building. The basement is full of switches and wiring for routing calls, but the phone doesn't ring in the offices upstairs unless the call is intended for someone at the phone company.

The cube or mesh is often connected to the rest of the world via a front-end, the same as a SIMD machine, except that the front-end doesn't actively engage in the computations. Basically, you download the parallel machine from the front-end, start execution and let go. The front-end then services I/O and keeps control of the parallel machine. Future MIMD machines will likely serve as their own front-ends.

Programming a Distributed Memory MIMD Machine

The most common languages for programming Distributed Memory MIMD machines are C and FORTRAN. If you care to run on only *one* node of the machine, you can take source code that you already have and compile it. Many functions—disk file access, terminal I/O, etc.—will work as you expect. You can even take the same program and run multiple copies on

---

*Located in Waltham, Massachusetts.

multiple nodes (provided that they don't all try to write to the same files). However, if you want them to cooperate on a single problem and share data, you will have to add calls to message passing subroutines. This should change over the course of 1993 and 1994, when Fortran 90 and High Performance Fortran start to become available. For now, however, message passing is the environment on distributed memory MIMD computers.

Let's borrow a few of the subroutines and functions from the Intel iPSC/860 hypercube message passing library to create a simple illustration of how it's done. The calls we need are:

`numnodes ()`
> tells how many nodes have been allocated

`mynode ()`
> tells which node this one is

`csend` (type, `buffer`, `length`, `destnode`, `destproc`)
> sends a message

`crecv` (type, `buffer`, `length`)
> receives a message

The first step in starting a program on a distributed memory MIMD machine is allocating some number of processors (something you do from the command line). This may be all the nodes available on the machine or a *subcube*—a portion of the machine. The function `numnodes` gives you the number of processors you have to work with. Each node will run an identical copy of the program. `mynode` tells you which of those processors you are running on.

The `csend` subroutine sends a message to another processor. Messages have types—arbitrary integers that you assign so that you can tell one type of message from another. For instance, you might be sending two separate messages out and would like to be sure that one is not mistaken for the other when they reach their destination. For some applications, this is important because messages can arrive in an unexpected order. You can be sure of a message's content by assigning the messages a unique `type`. You might choose a type of 1 to indicate that this message contains the contents of vector **B**, and a type of 2 to indicate that another message holds vector **A**.

The second parameter, `buffer`, is a pointer to the array or variable containing the message to be sent. For instance, you might want to send a vector, in which case the `buffer` parameter would be a pointer to the starting element: `A(1)`, perhaps. Sometimes you have to gather data and put it into a scratch area before you send it out. Imagine sending a row of a FOR-TRAN matrix. Recall that FORTRAN matrices are stored in column-major order, meaning that each element across a row is actually stored some distance away from every other. To send the contents of a particular row, you would first have to collect the elements into a scratch area and send that instead; you'd need a loop like this:*

```
      PARAMETER (N = 1000)
      REAL A(N,N), SCRATCH (N)
      ...
      DO 10 I=1,N
        SCRATCH (I) = A(1,I)
  10  CONTINUE
      ...
      END
```

Returning to the `csend` routine, the third parameter, `length`, tells how long the message is in bytes. The fourth parameter, `node`, tells who the message is for. Node 0 might want to send a message to Node 1, for instance, so the value of `node` would be set to 1. The last parameter is used to identify individual processes running on the nodes. We will not be using it.

The `crecv` subroutine synchronously receives a message sent using a `csend` call. The first parameter, `type`, is for choosing what type of message we would like to receive. If a −1 is supplied, any message type is accepted. The `buffer` parameter tells where the message is supposed to go when received, and the `length` parameter tells the size of the destination buffer.

Let's put this machinery to work by writing a simple application for a MIMD machine. We'll take the average of a vector of N real numbers; on a traditional computer, the code would look like this:

```
      IMPLICIT NONE
      INTEGER N,I
      PARAMETER (N = 1000)
      REAL A(N), SUM, AVG
      READ (10) A
      DO 10 I=1,N
        SUM = SUM + A(I)
  10  CONTINUE
      AVG = SUM/FLOAT(N)
      WRITE (*,*) AVG
      END
```

---

*Some message passing libraries have routines that allow you to specify a stride, eliminating this extra step. The CM-5 and Paragon have such routines.

On a single processor, you merely add the numbers together and divide by
N. With a distributed memory MIMD machine, you could cut the domain
into pieces and have each processor sum a portion of the numbers. Each
processor, when done, would return its partial result to one node, which
would collect the results and print the average. Here's the MIMD code:

```
        IMPLICIT NONE
        INTEGER N, NODES, MYID, MSTART, I, J
        PARAMETER (N = 1000)
        REAL A(N), PSUM, SUM
C
C Determine the number of nodes and which node this is running on.
C
        NODES  = NUMNODES()
        MYID   = MYNODE()
C
C If this is node 0, act as a master: send work out and collect the
C responses.  If this is any other node: be a worker.
C
        IF (MYID .EQ. 0) THEN
        READ (10) A
C
C Divide the work fairly among processors.
C
        DO 20 J = 1, NODES-1
           MSTART = (J-1) * N/NODES + 1
           CSEND (1, A(MSTART), N/NODES * 4, J, 0)
 20     CONTINUE
C
C The master does some of the work too.
C
        DO 30 I = (NODES - 1) * N/NODES + 1, N
           SUM = SUM + A(I)
 30     CONTINUE
C
C Collect all the partial sums.
C
        DO 40 J = 1, NODES-1
           CRECV (2, PSUM, 4)
           SUM = SUM + PSUM
 40     CONTINUE
C
C Compute the average.
C
        AVG = SUM/FLOAT(N)
        WRITE (*,*) AVG
C
      ELSE
C
C Workers expect a message containing a portion of the A array.
C Form a partial sum.
C
```

```
          CRECV (1, A, N/NODES * 4)
          DO 10 I=1, N/NODES
             SUM = SUM + A(I)
   10     CONTINUE
C
C Send the results back to the master.
C
          CSEND (2, SUM, 4, 0, 0)
          ENDIF
C
          END
```

There are a couple of points to note. Only the first processor reads in values and populates the **A** array. The rest receive portions of **A** from the messages they were sent. At first glance this can be confusing, but you have to keep in mind that shared memory machines keep private copies of each variable on each node. That means the space used for **A** is duplicated NUM-NODES() times. The master uses the whole **A** array, the workers use just 1/Nth of it. In a real life example, the data may be much too large to fit on one node, all at once.

Secondly, the worker nodes all return their results to node 0 (the master) with a csend and a message type of 2. This means that the master doesn't know which node is sending which message, and isn't concerned with collecting the data in order. We saw in the last chapter how operation order is significant in some calculations. With partial sums being collected in a non-deterministic fashion, the answer can vary slightly from run to run. If it were important, we could have encoded the node number in the message type, for example.

You can see that it took a lot more code to coordinate a parallel computation of the average of a collection of numbers.* Of course, you would normally spread the overhead over many more computations (hopefully). Otherwise, the communications would dominate the run time and it wouldn't be worth the effort.

A Few Words About Data Layout Directives

As we have seen in this chapter, one of the big challenges on all parallel machines—MIMD and SIMD— is mapping data onto the nodes. You want the data to be distributed, so that the whole machine participates in the cal-

---

*By contrast, here's the Fortran 90 (and HPFF) representation of the code in the last example:
AVG = SUM(A)/FLOAT(N)

culations. At the same time, it is important to position data "close" to other data it participates with, because communication is very expensive.

When programming in a message passing environment, you have some control over how the problem is decomposed. You might choose to cut the data into strips or blocks, for instance. In a Fortran 90 environment, on the other hand, you trust the compiler to decompose the problem on your behalf. For many people, this is much more appealing; the code isn't cluttered with the mechanics of parallelization, and the programmer doesn't have to soil his hands. However, because data placement is so important, a compiler that automatically decomposes the data domain can benefit from hints and directives supplied by the programmer. A parallelizing compiler with layout directives would give you the best of both worlds.

Layout directives are already part of the Fortran 90 programming environment for some SIMD computers (i.e., the CM-2). The group promoting High Performance FORTRAN (HPF, see Chapter 12) has proposed a standard set of directives as supplements to Fortran 90 to help the programmer decompose data parallel problems for all parallel machines.* Additionally, they are proposing more library functions and giving some practical interpretations to parts of the Fortran 90 standard dealing with data storage.

Generally HPF will let the programmer:

- Identify scalars and arrays that will be distributed across a parallel machine.
- Say how they will be distributed. Will they be strips, blocks, or something else?
- Specify how these variables will be aligned with respect to one another.
- Redistribute and realign data structures at run time.

There is also be a new FORALL control construct for parallel assignments that are difficult or impossible to construct using Fortran 90's array syntax. There are some new intrinsic functions as well.

Virtual Shared Memory

Now that you have seen an example of how distributed memory MIMD machines are programmed, you probably have an appreciation for why they aren't in every corner drugstore. Porting a code involves a lot more than just pushing it through the compiler. You either have to coordinate

---

*Send mail to *hpff-info@cs.rice.edu*

the activities of the different processors explicitly, through message passing, or become closely involved with a parallelizing compiler to make sure the data layout is correct.

A paradigm that is gaining popularity, and one that you may be seeing in a lot of products in the future, is *virtual shared memory*. It would be nice to treat the distributed memory parallel machine as if every processor was tapped into a single, large pool of memory, and let some portion of the environment—software or hardware—back up the illusion by shuffling the data around transparently. Underneath there would still be separate memories, but the programmer wouldn't have to worry about it—at least not *too* much. As you can imagine, data placement and locality of reference would still be important, though the details of moving data around would be hidden.

Providing the illusion of a simple integrated memory system to a distributed memory computer is a challenging problem. I describe how you manage it for a shared memory multiprocessor in the next chapter. First, each cache snoops on every other, and maintains cache coherence by intercepting memory references or broadcasting directives to the other caches in the machine. It works well, but it doesn't scale to distributed memory computers. Part of the problem is that there is no good way to broadcast, since there is no common communications channel, such as a bus. Second, with potentially thousands of processors, it's a big job to track "who has what."

An alternative is a distributed cache directory, where processors can find out who else is sharing access to the same data. One form of cache directory receiving a lot of attention lately is known as *Scalable Coherent Interface* (SCI), being defined in IEEE standards project (P1596). SCI-based systems would track data ownership with a doubly linked list, stringing together each node holding a copy of a particular piece of data. A processor wishing to modify that data has to coordinate with all other processors in the list, which means traversing that list and possibly adding or deleting itself. The notion of memory systems is back (there are some central memories). However, once the data has migrated out into the caches, it is managed by the caches. A reference to data that is already living out in the caches is answered with a pointer to the head of the list, rather than the requested data, and must be tracked down by the node making the request.

There are other schemes, too. The first commercial virtual shared memory machine is the KSR-1 from Kendall Square Research. Processors are organized in rings of up to 32 processors apiece, as shown in Figure 15-12. The vendor claims that thirty-four of these can be joined together to make a "ring of rings" of up to 1088 processors.

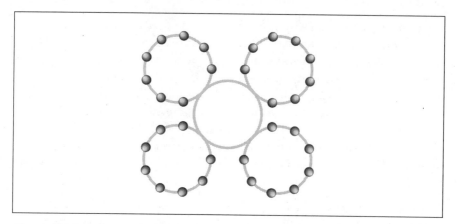

Figure 15-12: KSR-1 ring of rings architecture

The virtual memory illusion is handled by a system they call *ALLCACHE*. Conceptually similar to SCI, it is a data cache hierarchy with an integrated directory that tracks the location and ownership of pieces of data throughout the machine. If one processor needs data that others have, it can find its location by consulting the directory.

As you can see, virtual shared memory changes the MIMD model a little, blurring the line between traditional shared memory computers (next chapter) and traditional distributed memory MIMD machines. Virtual shared memory has a compelling attraction in the scientific and commercial marketplaces; it can run "dusty deck" codes without explicit parallelization. This helps make parallel computers more palatable in the same way that assemblers, compilers, and vectorizing compilers advanced the state of the market in their days. Less drudgery means more applications will be ported.

Likewise, you could argue that a virtual shared memory MIMD machine won't get the same performance as one with an explicit message passing model, and I'd agree with you. However, I'd argue that the comparison is somewhat analogous to the differences between assembly language and higher level languages. Provided that you structure the layout and use of your data for parallelism, and make it explicit, a compiler will be able to apply a good portion of what *you* know about your code to the program at run time.

Closing Notes

Distributed memory parallel machines are the only vehicle for applying hundreds or thousands of processors to an individual problem. Although they have been around for a number of years, they haven't yet been mainstreamed. You can convince yourself of this if you look to see what third party applications are available. Some tools, such as linear algebra libraries, have been ported, but most production commercial packages still run exclusively on single processors.

There are two barriers to general acceptance of large scale parallel machines: the price and the programming environment. It's not that the price is sky high—small machines start at around $200,000. It's that the price is high when you consider what you get: a machine that runs very quickly for certain problems and very slowly for others (depending on the proportion of parallel to serial code), and in either case requires special programming. If you work in a shop where you do one thing most of time, i.e., a particular type of engineering analysis, perhaps the effort of casting your code in parallel form will pay off very quickly. But if you are looking for a general-purpose workhorse, a distributed memory parallel machine probably isn't what you need.

At any rate, it takes a fair amount of manual intervention to get the code to run in parallel. People recognize that this is a painful hindrance to migrating programs to distributed parallel machines. Currently, vendors and consortia are working hard to create compilers which automatically parallelize programs and distribute the pieces for execution on multiple CPUs. It won't be easy. Parallelism in an application is often expressed serially in a fashion that forever obscures whatever parallelism once existed.

Exercises

1. Here's a subroutine that counts the number of times two divides its argument. It returns as soon as the count, n, is found.

```
int ntimes (k)
int k;
{
    int m, n;

    n = 0;
    m = k < 0 ? -k : k;
```

```
        while (m != 0) {
          n++;
          m = m >> 1;
        }
        return (n);
      }
```

Suppose that you want to express the the same function on a SIMD computer, where different points are mapped onto different processors. Recall that because all processors execute identical instructions in lockstep, it's not possible for one to return from the routine as the others continue on. Suggest how you could recode the above routine above for a SIMD computer so that it accommodates different numbers of iterations on different processors.

16

Shared-Memory Multiprocessors

In Chapter 15, I discussed distributed memory SIMD and MIMD machines. In many ways, the biggest challenge presented by distributed memory machines is that they *are* distributed memory machines. They are difficult to program because you have to be concerned about the location of your data, and how it moves from place to place. Furthermore, there are only a handful of them in use in the world, which eliminates the incentive for third party applications vendors to migrate their applications. Lastly, they only do a few things well, though they admittedly do them *very* well. It comes down to this: you might use your SIMD machine for finite element analysis, but when it comes time to play Hunt the Wumpus or to use the text editor, you will be running back to your workstation.

This chapter is about a different class of parallel machines: *shared memory multiprocessors*. They run UNIX (or some operating system) natively; they can execute any kind of application; they have multiple CPUs that share memory. The data in memory looks the same to every processor. If one wants to pass a value to another, it is merely a matter of writing the value back into memory. The other processor will see the updated value as if it spontaneously changed. Such computers are known as *shared memory multiple instruction, multiple data machines*, or just shared memory MIMDs. People also often call them *multiprocessors* for short (though this doesn't completely describe them or exclude other types of machines). For convenience, I'll call them multiprocessors, too. Examples of workstation server multiprocessors are Silicon Graphics' Power Series machines—up to eight processors sharing a common memory system—and the Sun SPARCcenter 2000 machines. Larger multiprocessors are the Convex C3 and the Cray Y/MP.

Think of the processors on the machine as a pool of resources. The number of processors your program uses depends on the way it was coded and compiled. An editor, for instance, will use only one CPU at a time. An engineering analysis may be written to use many. As a user, the difference is nearly undetectable—apart from increased performance. The components of a parallelized program timeshare with the rest of the activity on the machine as if they themselves were independent programs.

You might imagine that this would be an easy environment to program for. It is, relative to the parallel machines of the last chapter. It is also safe to say that you will be seeing much more in the way of multiprocessing in the future. Unfortunately, shared memory multiprocessing has its limitations too. It is not a simple feat to enable more than a handful of processors to have access to the same memory, yet keep them from starving for data. Eight processors, each with an appetite for 64 megabytes of data per second, would need to be fed by a bus with a bandwidth of 512 megabytes per second, for instance. That's not unheard of, but it doesn't come cheaply. The bright side of it is that applications don't always blast through memory in such a manner, so a fair amount of memory bandwidth can be spread around for reasonable performance.

Symmetric Multiprocessing

Picture a typical computer. It runs an operating system which in turn runs user programs. If one of the user programs wishes to use a peripheral, or needs some other non-trivial service, it asks the operating system. On a UNIX machine it works like this: the program executes a special trap instruction that causes the computer to switch from user mode to kernel mode. Lots of changes happen, but basically your program stops executing while the operating system takes over to see why it was awakened. If you are asking for a system service, such as I/O, the kernel performs it for you and returns you to user mode sometime in the near future.

There are also lots of other reasons why the processor might stop running in user mode and switch to kernel mode. A time slice may be up; someone's program may have executed an illegal instruction or caused an exception; I/O may have completed; the clock may have ticked, etc. The kernel deals with each of these accordingly. Since the typical computer has only one CPU, there is never a question about which mode it is operating in; it is either in user mode or kernel mode. A single CPU also means that there is a single *thread* of execution. That is, you never have to suffer the danger that two programs might be rummaging through and updating the same data structures at the same time. This is an important point. With more than one CPU and shared memory you can have situations where they are both reading and writing the same memory locations at the same time.

Operating System Support for Multiprocessing

For analogy, say that you live alone. If you pull the milk out, set it on the counter and forget to put it back, it will be there when you return from work in the evening. There is no chance that someone else will put it back for you. It also means that when you throw your underwear in the corner you'll be able to find them when you need them tomorrow and the next day.

Suppose that you get married. One day a funny thing happens: you pull the milk out of the refrigerator, set it on the counter and turn to search through the cereal boxes. Meanwhile your spouse notices that the milk is out and returns it to the refrigerator. You look over your shoulder and say, "hmmm..., I thought I took the milk out." You stop searching for a second and get the milk out of the refrigerator. Your spouse looks up and sees it on the counter and says, "hmmmm... I thought I put that back." An extremely dull couple could get trapped in that loop for well over an hour. The problem is that you are both updating the state of the milk container at the same time.

One way to fix the problem is to agree that the kitchen is a *critical region*, meaning that you and your spouse can't both be in the kitchen at the same time.* That way, there is no possibility that you will be waylayed indefinitely while preparing a bowl of flakes. By convention, if your spouse wants to enter the kitchen while you are in there, he or she will have to lean against the door jamb until you are through. Of course, if your spouse just wants to come in because the oatmeal is in flames, it would be a shame to make him or her wait until you have had your breakfast and read the paper. For that reason, you might want to subdivide the kitchen into a number of critical regions, such as the toaster, the stove, the sink, etc., so that one person isn't excluded unnecessarily.

The analogy applies to multiple CPUs updating the same memory locations, particularly in kernel mode. You would like any of the processors to be able to perform any of the duties needed to run the machine. This includes

---

*It might save a few marriages too.

I/O, exception handling, etc. To be able to allow all the processors to run in kernel mode (perhaps simultaneously), you need to identify and mark critical regions in the kernel. These are places where a CPU updating a data structure can be guaranteed exclusive access to that structure. With critical regions marked and protected, you can allow more than one processor to run operating system code because you can be sure that what processor A is doing will not damage what processor B is doing.

To take a simple example, imagine that two of a multiprocessor's CPUs are available to take a job off the ready queue and run with it. If the code that manipulates the ready queue is not marked as a critical region, both CPUs might examine the queue, remove the top job and update the queue simultaneously. That is, there is a fair chance that they would both select the same job to be run, each try to remove it, and leave the queue in a damaged state. It is better to leave one of the processors "waiting at the door" than to allow them both in the kitchen together. Once you have done this, you can give all CPUs equal privileges—allow them all to run in kernel mode—because you can be sure that they will not try to simultaneously update the same operating system data structures. A multiprocessor where all of the CPUs can run in kernel mode with equal privileges is known as a *symmetric multiprocessor.*

The kernel and programs that run on a symmetric multiprocessor take the next available CPU when it is their turn to run. This has the interesting effect of causing your program to bounce around between processors as it executes, which generally results in an even distribution of jobs among them. Parallelism comes into play when you code or compile your program so that separate pieces of a single job spawn off as *lightweight processes.** These enter into the mix and get scheduled along with the rest of the activity on the machine. If you have asked for more lightweight processes than there are available CPUs, or if the machine is also busy with other jobs, you may find that several of the parallel components of your program actually end up running on the same processor. By this mechanism, programs can be written for an unknown number of processors, or CPU loads can accommodate themselves to the machine at run time.

---

*Normal process creation can take a long time—page tables and data segments have to be copied as soon as the new process tries to update its variables. A lightweight process shares many of the data structures of the parent, considerably reducing the overhead of process creation.

Multiprocessor Architecture

As you might guess, hardware support is necessary for symmetric multiprocessing. In particular, the individual CPUs need to be able to access all of the resources of the machine, such as the peripherals and memory, meaning that there will have to be some structural backbone allowing total connectivity. Furthermore, they need a facility for deciding among themselves who has access to what, and when, which means there will have to be hardware support for arbitration. The two most common architectural underpinnings for symmetric multiprocessing are *multimaster buses* and *crossbars*.

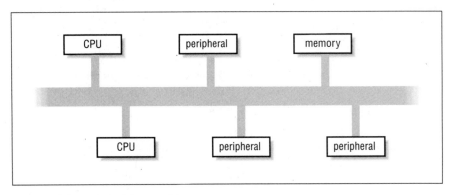

Figure 16-1: A typical bus architecture

A bus can be thought of as a set of parallel wires connecting the components of the computer (CPU, memory, and peripheral controllers), a set of protocols for communication, and some hardware to help carry it out. A bus with multimaster capability has the additional feature of allowing any device sitting on the bus to take control and initiate communication with any other. This is essential for symmetric multiprocessing.

A crossbar is like several buses running side by side with attachments to each of the modules on the machine—CPU, memory, and peripherals. Any module can get to any other by a path through the crossbar, and multiple paths may be active simultaneously. In the 4×4 crossbar of Figure 16-1, for instance, there can be four active data transfers in progress at one time. In the diagram it looks like a patchwork of wires, but there is actually quite a bit of hardware that goes into constructing a crossbar. Not only does the crossbar connect parties that wish to communicate, but it must also actively arbitrate between two or more CPUs that want access to the same memory or peripheral.

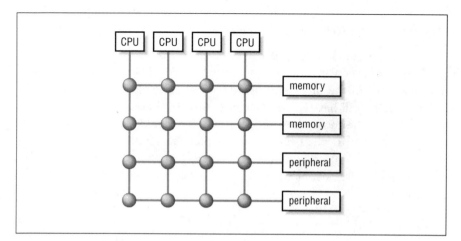

Figure 16-2: A 4x4 crossbar

In the event that one module is too popular, it is the crossbar that decides who gets access and who doesn't. Because of their cost, crossbars haven't yet become part of the workstation market.

Shared Memory

Shared memory machines are easier targets for parallel applications than distributed memory machines. You don't have to go through the bother of collecting domain boundary data and shipping it off in messages to neighboring processors. However, shared memory has its limitations. There is only so much memory bandwidth to go around; four or eight processors drawing from one memory system can quickly use it up. Also, the computer has to do a lot of behind the scenes data shuffling to assure that each processor sees the same values in memory. I'll explain why shortly.

Conservation of Bandwidth

Recall that for a single processor, a cache improves performance. Main memory is slow, relative to the CPU, but caches are fast. If the information in cache is used repeatedly, slower main memory accesses will be avoided and the whole system will perform better. All the same things are true for the CPUs of a multiprocessor—memory caches increase performance—but caches take on a new importance as well: they help reduce the demand on the bus or crossbar, leaving more spare capacity for unavoidable memory references and for other purposes, such as I/O. To understand why, consider what happens when the cache hit rate is very high.

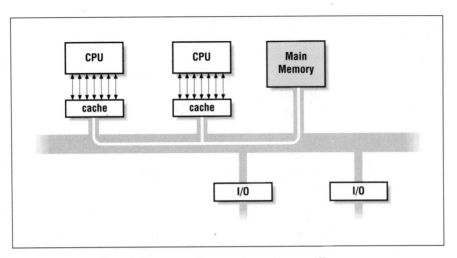

Figure 16-3: High cache hit rate reduces main memory traffic

A high cache hit rate eliminates some of the traffic that would have otherwise gone out across the bus or crossbar to main memory. Again, it is the notion of "locality of reference" that makes the system work. If you assume that a fair number of the memory references will hit in the cache, the equivalent attainable main memory bandwidth will be more than the main memory system is actually capable of. The assumption explains why multiprocessors are designed with less memory bandwidth than the sum of the CPUs can consume all at once. For many applications it works quite well. However, those with an appetite for data will be reduced to the speed of the bus or main memory system, regardless of how many additional processors you throw at them. This is an important point to consider when planning for a multiprocessor.

Many of the microprocessors that go into multiprocessor machines—SPARC, i860, R4000, etc.—have built-in data and instruction caches. But these are generally pretty small—64 KB at most. The main memory system is better shielded when a larger cache is used. For this reason, multiprocessors sometimes incorporate a 2-tier cache system, where each processor uses its own small local cache, backed up by a larger second level cache of perhaps as much as 4 MB of memory. Only when neither of these two can satisfy a memory request, or when data has to be written back to main memory, does a request go out over the bus or crossbar.

Coherency

Now, what happens when one CPU of a multiprocessor changes the value of a variable and another tries to read it? Where does the value come from? These questions are interesting because there can be multiple copies of each variable—and some of them can hold old or stale values.

For illustration, say that you are running a program with a shared variable A. Processor 1 changes the value of A and Processor 2 goes to read it. The question is: where does the new value of A come from?

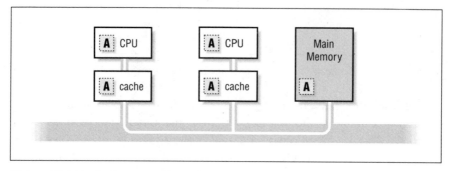

Figure 16-4: Multiple copies of variable A

If Processor 1 is keeping A as a register-resident variable, then Processor 2 doesn't stand a chance of getting the correct value when it goes to look for it. There is no way that 2 can know the contents of 1's registers; so assume, at the very least, that Processor 1 writes the new value back out. Now the question is, where does the new value get stored? Does it remain in Processor 1's cache? Is it written to main memory? Does it get updated in processor 2's cache?

Really, we are asking what kind of *cache coherency protocol* the vendor uses to assure that all processors see the same values. It generally isn't something that the programmer has to worry about, except that in some cases it can affect performance. The most straightforward cache coherency approach is called a *write-through policy*: variables written into cache are simultaneously written into main memory. As the update takes place, other caches in the system can see the main memory reference being performed. If they also contain copies of the data from the locations being written, they may either *invalidate* their copies of the variable or obtain new values (depending on the policy). One thing to note is that a write-through cache still demands a fair amount of main memory bandwidth since each write goes out over the main memory bus. Furthermore, successive writes to the same location or bank are subject to the main memory cycle time and can slow the machine down.

A more sophisticated cache coherency protocol is called *copy-back* or *write-back*. The idea is that you write values back out to main memory only when the last cache housing them needs the space for something else. Updates of cached data are coordinated between the caches, by the caches, without help from the processor. Copy-back caching needs hardware that can monitor (snoop) and intervene in the memory transactions of the other caches in the system. The benefit of this method over the former is that memory traffic is reduced considerably. Let me walk you through it so that you can see how it works.

The first cache to ask for data from a particular part of memory completes a normal memory access; the main memory system returns data from the requested location in response to a cache miss. The associated cache line is marked *exclusive*, meaning that this is the only cache in the system containing a copy of the data, and that it is the owner of the data. If another cache goes to main memory looking for the same thing, the transfer is intercepted and the data is returned by the first cache—not main memory. Once an interception has occurred, the data is marked *shared*.

When a particular line is marked shared, the caches have to treat it differently than if they were the exclusive owners of the data— especially if any of them wants to modify it. In particular, a write to a shared cache entry is accompanied by a broadcast message to all the other caches in the system. It tells them to invalidate their copies of the data. The one remaining cache line gets marked as *modified* to signal that is has been changed, and that it must be returned to main memory when the space is needed for something else. By these mechanisms, you can maintain cache coherence all across the multiprocessor without adding tremendously to the memory traffic.

By the way, even if a variable is not shared, it is possible for copies of it to show up in several caches. On a symmetric multiprocessor your program can bounce around from CPU to CPU. If you run for a little while on this CPU, and then a little while on that, your program will have operated out of separate caches. That means that there can be several copies of seemingly unshared variables scattered around the machine.

Data Placement

There is one more pitfall regarding shared memory that I have so far failed to mention. It involves data movement. Although it would be convenient to think of the multiprocessor memory as one big pool, we have seen that it is actually a carefully crafted system of caches, coherency protocols, and main memory. The problems come in when your application causes lots of data to be traded between the caches. Each reference that falls out of a given processor's cache (especially those that require an update in another processor's cache) has to go out on the bus.

The same techniques that are critical for getting performance from a distributed memory machine deserve consideration when coding for a shared memory machine: you need to try to keep data references localized. The shared memory of a multiprocessor only appears to be shared. It is, in fact, an automatic distributed memory machine—the local memories are the caches, and the interconnection is the bus. If your program operates predominately out of the caches, it will run faster.

Multiprocessor Software Concepts

With shared memory multiprocessors, as with other parallel machines, there are two basic approaches to parallelizing an application across multiple CPUs. We talked about them in Chapter 15: domain decomposition and control decomposition. Domain decomposition entails splitting up the data and making each CPU responsible for a different portion of the same set of calculations. With control decomposition you split up the functions to be performed and make each CPU responsible for (possibly) different calculations, often in a master/worker relationship. And there can be hybrids too. These same approaches apply directly to shared memory multiprocessors. However, there are some aspects of programming for a shared memory multiprocessor that are very different. For instance, synchronization of multiple CPUs through shared memory is a challenge we haven't seen before.

Recall that with distributed memory MIMD machines, message passing synchronizes computations; processors need to share data before the program can proceed. And on SIMD machines, all processors proceed under a single control stream, so it is impossible for computations to get out of step. But with a shared memory machine, the programmer has to be conscious of points in the application where out-of-order execution will lead to incorrect results. There is nothing inherent in the way the machine is designed that will force synchronization—it is the programmer's or compiler's responsibility. However, there are tools and techniques for cooperatively coordinating programs on a multiprocessor, as we'll see shortly.

Fork and Join

The pieces of parallel programs that would run on a multiprocessor have a granularity somewhere between the instruction level parallelism of a superscalar and the large chunks that run on a distributed memory MIMD machine. The outer loop of doubly or triply nested loop is often a good candidate. With parallelization of the granularity of a loop or similar-sized block of code, the most common approach is to repeatedly *fork* off small processes. These later re-rendezvous or *join* with the parent, as the program switches between single-stream and parallel execution, similar to a small school of fish that occasionally spreads out and later regroups into one mass.

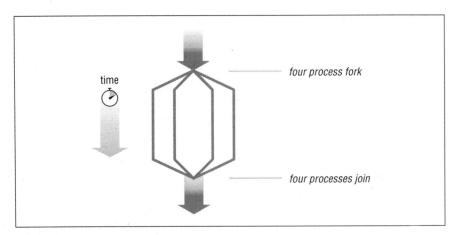

Figure 16-5: Fork and join

Functions for forking and joining are not defined as part of languages like C or FORTRAN. So, for the sake of illustration, I am taking *pfork* and *pjoin* to be the respective functions that fork and join shared memory processes.* I am also introducing a new keyword to the FORTRAN example, *local*, to denote that this is a variable which is not shared between processes.

---

*The actual names on your system (if the calls exist at all), their arguments, and specific effects may be different. However, the basic concepts will be the same.

In the following code, my *pfork* creates the number of processes specified by its argument:

```
program main
implicit none
integer nprocs
local integer itid
nprocs = 4
itid   = pfork(nprocs)
write (*,*) itid
call pjoin
end
```

What happens next is a little confusing: except for the value of `itid` returned, a given spawned process can't tell itself from any other. They all return from the call as if nothing has happened; however, now there are many where once there was one. Upon completion, the variable `itid` contains a *thread ID*—a value from 0 to `nprocs-1`. The processes spawned can use the thread ID to tell which part of the problem they are responsible for. The parent always receives a thread ID value of zero. So, the short program above creates four subprocesses.

Between the call to *pfork* and the call to *pjoin*, there are actually five copies of the program running—the four children and the parent. The output will be the thread ID's of the parent and children. However, there is no telling in what order they will appear. Because these are all separate processes, they are subject to the seemingly random scheduling of the operating system. Unless you take steps to force them to finish in order, they will finish whenever they finish.

Let's look at the simple integration problem from Chapter 15. Assume that you have a multiprocessor with four CPUs. You could write a program to fork three child processes to integrate the four regions of the problem domain along with the parent. When the children have all computed their regions and rejoined the parent, you could sum the subtotals to find the total area under the curve. Here's the code:

```
subroutine integr8 (f,total)
implicit none
integer nprocs, itid, nquads
parameter (nprocs = 3, nquads = 25)
real f, total, sum (0:3)
parameter (quadwdth = 1.0)
local integer itid, i
external f
```

```
itid   = pfork(nprocs)

do 10 i=1 + itid*nquads, nquads + itid*nquads
   sum(itid) = sum(itid) + f(float(itid))
10    continue

call pjoin

total = sum(0) + sum(1) + sum(2) + sum(3)
write (*,*) total
end
```

This subroutine integrates function *f* from 1 to 100, in four sections. For simplicity, I chose the quadrilaterals to be of width *1.0*. Upon execution of the call to *pjoin*, each process waits until all other processes have called *pjoin*. Then, the parent collects the result as the other processes all die.

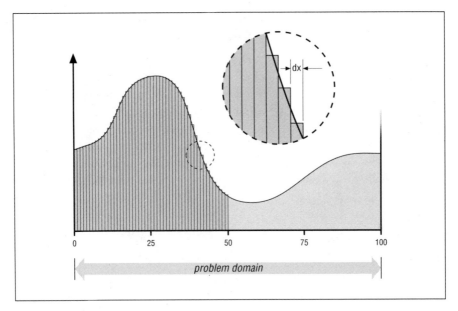

Figure 16-6: Integration

Synchronization with Locks

In the previous example, I declared four separate **sum** variables to keep the subtotals. I didn't collect the area in a single variable **sum** because of the possibility of contention during updates. Two or more processes that simultaneously read and write the value of **sum** could cause trouble. To see why, assume that two processes simultaneously reach the center of the do-loop which I've represented below:

```
      ...
      itid   = pfork(nprocs)

      do 10 i=1 + itid*nquads, nquads + itid*nquads
        sum = sum + f(float(itid))
 10   continue

      call pjoin
      ...
```

After calling some function *f*, they both load the value of sum into a register, add the result from *f* and write the answer back into memory. There is a possibility that their activities will interleave such that they both retrieve the same value of sum and update it independently—which would be incorrect. The contribution of the last process to write its new value into memory will become part of the final answer. The other's will be lost.

To be sure that no two processes attempt to update the variable sum simultaneously, you could place a *lock* around the line where the update occurs. This is the exact scenario we discussed when we were talking about the operating system and critical regions. By placing a lock around the code where contention may occur, you are creating a critical region and preventing two or more processes from updating the same variable at the same time. When a lock is in place, only one process can enter the critical region. Here's how we would rewrite our example using a lock:

```
      local real quadarea
      integer lockword
      ...
      call initlock (lockword)
      itid   = pfork(nprocs)

      do 10 i=1 + itid*nquads, nquads + itid*nquads
        quadarea =  f(float(itid))
        call lock    (lockword)
        sum = sum + quadarea
        call unlock (lockword)
 10   continue

      call pjoin
      ...
```

I created a variable *quadarea* to hold the result of the function *f*, and placed the function call outside the critical region. The goal is to limit the activity in the critical region as much as possible; there is no sense protecting *f* if subsequent calls don't interact.

The *lock* and *unlock* functions may be implemented by the vendor using one of several methods, perhaps the most common being a *spin-lock.* A spin lock works like this: a memory location (*lockword* in the example) serves as a lock. During initialization it is set to an unlocked state—perhaps a 0. The first process that calls *lock* is said to acquire the lock (perhaps setting it to 1), after which it continues on to the next line of code. Another process following right behind will call the *lock* function, but find that the lock has already been acquired. That process will then enter an endless cycle of checking and rechecking the lock—hence the name *spin-lock.*

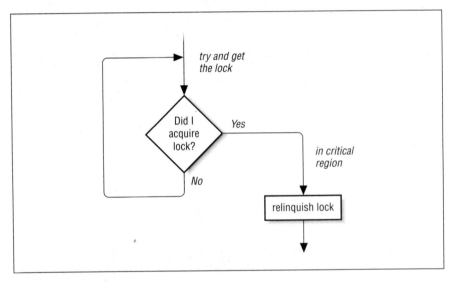

Figure 16-7: Implementation of a spinlock

More than one process may be waiting for the lock to be relinquished. There is no way to predict which process will acquire the lock when it becomes available. That is, there is no ordering—it isn't first-come, first served. If many processes are waiting for the lock, or if one process is waiting for a long time, the CPU will waste cycles. This is because waiting for a lock to be relinquished requires CPU activity. There are often options that allow you to give it a rest after a certain number of tries—voluntarily give up the CPU and let another process run for a while—but this means that it may be some time before you get to try the lock again. In the meantime, it may have become available.

Synchronization with Barriers

Do you remember the last time you took an organized nature walk or hike through woods? I'll bet you hadn't gone very far before the group spread out into little pockets. Soon, the hikers in back lost sight of the those up front. By analogy, a·*barrier* is to parallel processes what the hike leader is to the group when he or she says: "Let's all wait here a few moments for the rest to catch up." All processes wait at the barrier until the rest have arrived.

Barriers are useful when you want to synchronize execution (the same way a join does) without terminating the child processes. Usually you place one just before a point in the program where you want to collect some partial results together: the barrier insures that all partial results are ready before the combined result is formed. Without a barrier, some of the processes might pass through the would-be synchronization point ahead of others, forming incorrect combined results in what is called a *race condition*. Placing a barrier in the program guarantees that they will all stop and wait for each other to arrive before proceeding.

At the risk of beating the integration example to death, let's see how a barrier could fit in:

```
        integer barword
        ...
        call initbarrier (barword, nprocs)
        itid   = pfork(nprocs)

        do 10 i=1 + itid*nquads, nquads + itid*nquads
          sum(itid) = sum(itid) + f(float(itid))
  10    continue

        call barrier (barword)

        total = sum(0) + sum(1) + sum(2) + sum(3)

        if (itid .eq. 0) then
          write (*,*) total
        endif
        ...
```

A call to *barrier* replaces the call to *pjoin* in the original example, but in many ways serves the same purpose: the four subtotals, sum(0..3), are guaranteed to be complete before total is calculated. The difference between the join and barrier calls is that the four processes continue to live afterwards. Also, notice what could have happened if the barrier was not included: the four processes would have been in a race to complete their partial sums before `total` was calculated. Had they arrived at the rendez-vous point at separate times, `total` could have ended up with four differ-ent values.

Automatic Parallelization

We have been looking at the kinds of tools you would need to manually parallelize an application for a shared memory parallel processor. As you might have guessed, precompilers and compilers can do the same things for you. Predominantly, they work on loops. And as with vectorizing com-pilers, they sometimes need your help to decide when it is safe for instruc-tions to be scheduled in parallel.

Loop Splitting

The most straightforward opportunity for parallel execution comes from dividing the range of a do-loop into sections and passing them out for exe-cution on separate processors. Consider the following loop:

```
        do 10 i=1,n
          a(i) = a(i) + b(i) * c
   10   continue
```

Given that n is large enough, this loop could be divided into pieces. If you had four processors, the first could perform iterations 1 through $n/4-1$, the second $n/4$ through $n/2-1$, etc. Of course, if n is small, then the time spent spawning lightweight processes may outweigh any gains to be had by performing the loop in parallel. Below we've used the *pfork* and *pjoin* primitives to parallelize this code for processors. Child processes are forked and remain in existence only long enough to complete execution of the loop:

```
        implicit none
        local integer i, itid
        integer nprocs
        parameter (nprocs = 4)
        ...
        itid = pfork(nprocs)
        do 10 i=1+itid*n/4, itid*n/4 + n/4
          a(i) = a(i) + b(i) * c
   10   continue

        call pjoin
        ...
```

Like a compiler for a vector processor, a compiler splitting loops for a multiprocessor has to determine whether each iteration can execute independently. If you can supply hints in your code about dependencies in the form of assertions and structured comments, you will help the compiler understand the dependencies, and hence increase your performance.

Subroutine Calls in Loops

A multiprocessor's compiler likes to find a subroutine call in a loop, together with a directive stating that it can distribute the loop across multiple processors. That is, it wants to deal with subroutine calls that are completely independent from one another in every way. If the subroutine is meaty, then there will be a great deal of execution overlap.

Your computer may allow you to add a directive that tells is that successive subroutine calls are independent:

```
C$ <directive for overlapping subroutine calls>
      do 10 i=1,n
        call bigstuff (a,b,c,i,j,k)
  10    continue
```

If, on the other hand, the compiler cannot determine the side effects of the call from looking at it, or if you haven't explicitly said that it is OK to run multiple calls concurrently, it will have to be conservative and run the calls serially. Even if the compiler has all the source code, use of common variables or equivalences may mask call independence.

Nested Loops

Doubly and triply nested loops are often great candidates for multiprocessor execution, especially when the inner loop is extremely vectorizable and the outer loop is distributable. Again, it takes some sophisticated dependency analysis to determine when this is the case.

One loop nest that responds well to this treatment is a matrix multiplication, using *daxpy* for the innermost loop:

```
      do 10 i=1,n
        do 20 j=1,n
          c(j,i) = 0.0
  20    continue
  10    continue

      do 50 K=1,n
        do 60 j=1,n
          do 70 i=1,n
            c(i,j) = c(i,j) + a(i,k) * b(k,j)
```

```
70        continue
60      continue
50    continue
```

The outer 50 loop could be spread across a number of CPUs, and the inner 60 and 70 loops could execute in entirety within a single CPU.

In Chapter 11, I discussed loop interchange—a technique for trading one of the outer loops of a loop nest with one of the inner ones. Sometimes you want to interchange loops so that you can improve the memory access patterns. Other times it's good for moving the meatier calculations into the inner loop. For instance, with matrix multiplication, loop interchange can move a dot product into the center and cut down on the memory traffic.

Loop interchange can also help expose larger chunks of code for distribution across a multiprocessor. For instance, if the inner loop is only a few iterations long, yet the outer loop goes around several thousand times, loop interchange can change the nest so that long vector operations are in the center (provided dependencies allow for interchange). However, some other challenging problems come in to play. The code below shows an exaggerated example of a loop nest that (at first glance) appears as though it could benefit from loop interchange:

```
n = 400000;
m = 10;
...
for (i=0; i<n; i++) {
    for (j=0; j<m; j++) {
        a[i][j] = a[i][j] + b[i][j] * c[i][j];
        .....
    }
}
```

The inner loop has a trip count of only ten, while the outer loop goes around many times. Suppose you have four processors at your disposal. Rather than have each run the outer loop 100,000 times, you could interchange the nest so that the outer loop goes around only ten times. However, with only four processors, there is now a load balancing problem. Each can run two outer loop iterations and keep the machine totally occupied. But that leaves two outer loop iterations left over, meaning two of the processors will go idle for a time. Perhaps the loop would be better left alone!

Manual Parallelism

Multiprocessor parallelizing compilers, both C and FORTRAN, feature a number of directives for describing where to place synchronization points (barriers), how many threads to run, what variables are shared, etc. You can do most of the same kinds of manual programming we did in the "Multiprocessor Software Concepts" section, under a parallelizing compiler—just by placing your own directives in the code. This is convenient because you can specify how a loop is to be parallelized without diving into the index calculations. And though automatic parallelizing compilers come at a premium, you might consider the consequences of coding parallel control constructs manually, with forks and spin-locks: portability and readability will suffer.

The code below is a mythical loop with directives in place of lower level calls and declarations. A parallelizing compiler can produce parallel code from these without hurting the ability to compile and run on a sequential machine, if desired.

```
      subroutine freck
      integer i

C$ <directive for declaring shared vars: a,b,c,result>
C$ <directive specifying number of processes>
C$ <directive specifying parallel do-loop>

      do 10 i=1,m

C$ <directive for overlapping subroutine calls>

      do 20 j=1,n
        call xnerx (a(1,j),b(1,j),c(i,1),n)
20      continue

C$ <barrier>

      do 30 j=1,n
        call gznz (a(1,j),b(1,j),result(i))
30      continue
10    continue
```

Closing Notes

When single processor performance increases get harder to come by (as they are now—clocking general purpose machines at 200-plus MHz isn't going to be easy), multiprocessors will creep in to fill the gaps. Today you can choose from symmetric multiprocessors from a number of workstation and PC vendors. And you will be seeing single chip multiprocessors in a few years. Intel is already talking about the Intel 2000, a 200 MHz, 4 CPU multiprocessor with vector units on one chip. (Whether they will be able to feed the beast with enough memory is anyone's guess.)

Exercises

1. The program below uses the parallel programming primitives discussed in this chapter. The parent creates a single child and goes to sleep for one second. This will almost guarantee that the child prints its *itid* first. Under what circumstances might the parent report first?

   ```
   program main
   implicit none
   local integer itid
   itid   = pfork(1)
   if (itid .eq. 0) then
     call sleep (1)
   endif
   write (*,*) itid
   end
   ```

2. Explain how the following code segment could cause deadlock—two or more processes waiting for a resource that can't be relinquished.

   ```
        ...
   call lock    (lword1)
   call lock    (lword2)
        ...
   call unlock (lword1)
   call unlock (lword2)
        .

        .

        .
   call lock    (lword2)
   call lock    (lword1)
        ...
   call unlock (lword2)
   call unlock (lword1)
        ...
   ```

3. If you were to code the functionality of a spin-lock in C, it might look like this:

```
while (!lockword);
lockword = !lockword;
```

As you know from the first sections of the book, the same statements would be compiled into explicit loads and stores, a comparison, and a branch. There's a danger that two processes could each load `lockword`, find it unset, and continue on as if they owned the lock (we have a race condition). This suggests that spin-locks are implemented differently—that they're not merely the two lines of C above. How do you suppose they are implemented?

A

Processor Overview

Table A-1 summarizes the CPU architecture and instruction execution characteristics of some common processors.

Table A-1: CPU Characteristics

Processor and Architecture	CPU Characteristics
DEC AXP 21064 superscalar/superpipelined	3 operations per clock; 1 integer, 1 floating point, 1 memory.
TI SuperSPARC superscalar	3 operations per clock; 2 integer, 1 floating point. Integer operations may include 1 branch and 1 memory reference.
Motorola 88110 superscalar	2 operations per clock; 1 or 2 integer, floating point multiply or add, memory, divide, bit field manipulation, 1 or 2 graphics ops.
IBM RIOS (RS/6000) superscalar	4 operations per clock; 1 floating point, 1 integer or memory, 1 branch, 1 condition code.
Intel i860XP long instruction word	2 operations per clock; 1 floating point and 1 integer or memory. Can operate at single instruction/clock.
Intel Pentium CISC superscalar	2 80X86 operations per clock. Pipelined floating point (1 per clock). Can overlap memory operations.
Hewlett-Packard PA 7100 superscalar	2 operations per clock; 1 floating point, 1 integer or memory.
MIPS (SGI) R4000 superpipelined	1 operation per clock. Any combination.

Table A-2 summarizes the cache architecture and branching characteristics of some common processors.

Table A-2: Cache and Branch Architecture

Processor	Caches	Branch Prediction
DEC AXP 21064	*ICache:* 8 KB, 32b lines direct-mapped *DCache:* 8 KB, 32b lines direct-mapped	Early resolution or static, based on forward/backward branch displacement.
TI SuperSPARC	*ICache:* 20 KB, 8b lines 5-way set associative *DCache:* 16 KB, 4b lines 4-way set associative	Static with ability to cancel instructions if mispredicted.
Motorola 88110	*ICache:* 8 KB, 32b lines 2-way set associative *DCache:* 8 KB, 32b lines 2-way set associative_	Static forward/backward prediction backed by target instruction cache. Instructions can be canceled on mispredict.
IBM RIOS (RS/6000)	*ICache:* 8 KB, 64b lines 2-way set associative *DCache:* 64 KB, 128b lines 4-way set associative	Early branch resolution or static forward predicted with ability to cancel.
Intel i860XP	*ICache:* 16 KB, 32b lines 2-way set associative *DCache:* 16 KB, 32b lines 2-way set associative	Static with ability to cancel instruction in branch delay slot.

Table A-2: Cache and Branch Architecture (continued)

Processor	Caches	Branch Prediction
Intel Pentium	*ICache:* 8 KB 2-way set associative *DCache:* 8 KB Dual access 2-way set associative	Dynamic with support of a branch target buffer.
Hewlett-Packard PA 7100	*ICache:* External, 4KB to 1MB, 8b lines direct-mapped. *Dcache:* External, 4KB to 2MB, 8b lines direct-mapped.	Static prediction based on forward/backward displacement. Instructions can be canceled when mispredicted.
MIPS (SGI) R4000	*ICache:* 8 KB, 32b or 64b lines direct-mapped. *DCache:* 8 KB, 32b or 64b lines	Static with branch delay slot.

B

How to Tell When Loops Can Be Interchanged

It is easy to demonstrate loop reversal on loops you know can be interchanged, but sometimes you are staring at an ugly mess, and it isn't at all clear that interchanged loops will produce the right answer. The easiest way to tell, of course, is to try it. Unfortunately, there will be a few codes out there where reversal works for the test case, but not in production, and someone will get mad at me.

This section describes a graphical method for getting a picture of how data is moving within a loop nest. The method is based on a description of an *iteration space* by Michael Joseph Wolfe in his thesis "Optimizing Supercompilers for Supercomputers." I have extended his method slightly to handle repeated access to the same array element. I will demostrate with some straightforward cases—you can extend them to others as needed. Basically what we will do is draw a picture, and from the picture decide how we can iterate differently through the nest.

What we care about is dependencies. A loop nest with no dependencies is not a problem because it Example B-1, the calculation for the elements of **A** can be all jumbled around, but the final values of **A** will still be the same.

Example B-1: Each iteration is independent

```
        DO 10 I=1,N
          DO 20 J=1,N
            A(J,I) = B(I,J) + C(I) * D(J)
    20      CONTINUE
    10    CONTINUE
```

However, when you look at a nest as in Example B-2, it isn't clear whether you can interchange the loops. This is because one or more variables—**A** in this case—appear on both the left and right hand side of assignment statements with different subscript expressions. **B** also appears in the loop, but no assignments are made to **B**, so the order in which you use the elements doesn't matter. Likewise with **C**: elements are assigned, but none are used. The array **A** is the only one presenting a problem. Therefore, we can consider **A** independently of all the other variables. If there were two or more arrays, both assigned and used in the nest, we could consider them separately too.

Example B-2: Can we interchange these loops?

```
      DO 10 I=1,N-1
        DO 20 J=2,N
          A(I,J) = A(I+1,J-1) * B(I,J)
          C(I,J) = B(J,I)
 20      CONTINUE
 10    CONTINUE
```

Draw a box with just enough room in it to represent a handful of columns and rows of the array **A**. For the above loop, a box that holds a four by four matrix would be enough.

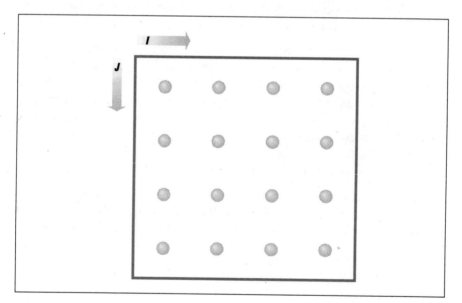

Figure B-1: 4x4 matrix

Note the inner loop index variable. Iterate through the space in your box, drawing dots, circles and arrows according to the following rules:

- Locate the position of the element being "sourced"—A(I+1,J-1). The first time through, when I=1, and J=2, this corresponds to A(1+1,2-1) = A(2,1) at column 2, row 1. If the location is empty, draw a dot.

- Locate the position of the element being assigned. The first time through this is A(1,2). If the location is empty, draw a dot. Otherwise, draw a circle around whatever is there; it may be a dot, a circle or a dot surrounded by one or more circles.

- Connect the two locations with an arrow proceeding from the source dot or circle to the new circle at the assigned location. If the sourced and assigned locations are the same, loop the arrow back from inside of the circle to the outside.

- Proceed to the next iteration until finished.

After the first step, your box should look like Figure B-2. When you have finished all iterations, it should look like Figure B-3.

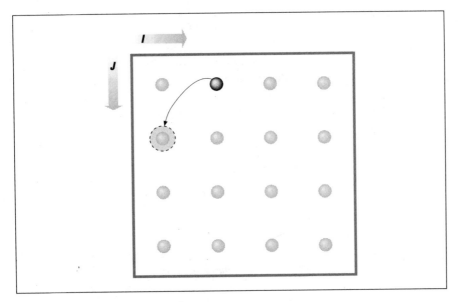

Figure B-2: One iteration complete

Now we have a picture of how data moves in the **A** array during execution. From this picture, we can determine whether the loops can be interchanged, or even run backwards, if desired. The governing rule is that dots

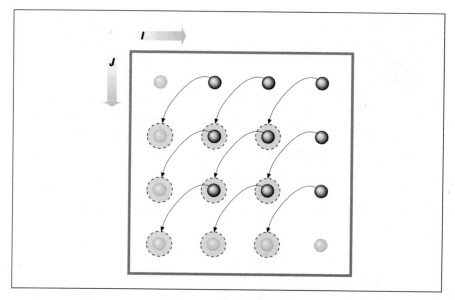

Figure B-3: All iterations completed

and circles must be consumed in the same order as they were in the original loop nest. For instance, the dot at position 2,2 must not be overwritten before it gets sourced. What freedom does this give us? If you drag your finger across the matrix in in both directions and along both axes, you will find that there are eight permutations you can choose from. Four of them preserve the original order of operand consumption. The rest are not legal transformations of the loop nest.

Example B-3: Legal alternate loop nests

```
      DO 10 I=1,N-1        (original)
        DO 20 J=2,N

      DO 10 I=1,N-1
        DO 20 J=N,2,-1

      DO 20 J=N,2,-1
        DO 10 I=1,N-1     ← gives positive unit stride

      DO 20 J=N,2,-1
        DO 10 I=N-1,1,-1
```

You can see we are *not* able to interchange the inner and outer loops to ease the stride on **A**. This would have been our first choice. However, there are two other combinations that *will* allow is to have unit strides (positive and negative) on the inner loop. They are direct replacements for the loop nest currently in use.

Here's another, more complicated loop nest. It contains strided and non-strided references to the array **A**. The question is: what choices do we have for changing the way the loop nest iterates through **A**?

Example B-4: More complicated references

```
      DO 10 I=1,N
        DO 20 J=1,N
          A(J,I) = B(I,J) + A(I,J)
 20      CONTINUE
 10      CONTINUE
```

The picture of data movement looks like Figure B-4.

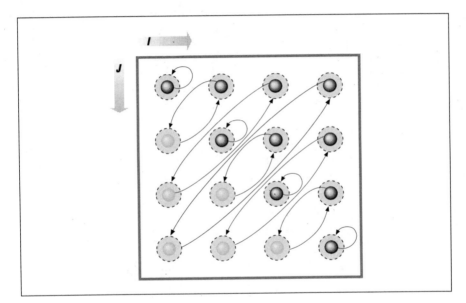

Figure B-4: Movement of data in array A

Again, interchanging the loops is not legal because it changes the results. You can see this by running your finger across the top row of **A**. In the second column you encounter an operation that consumes an element in row 2, column 1, which has not yet been written. However, there are some alternatives that allow us to swap strides for references to **A** on the left and right hand sides of the assignment (if this is what we want to do). For instance, if you are willing to run the J loop backwards, you *can* move it to the outside to obtain the loop nest in Example B-5.

Example B-5: More complicated references

```
        DO 20 J=N,1,-1
          DO 10 I=1,N
            A(J,I) = B(I,J) + A(I,J)
10        CONTINUE
20      CONTINUE
```

The question that may have crept into your mind is: "What happens to the performance of loops with negative strides?" Frankly, negative unit strides aren't as good as positive unit strides. But if the loop with the negative stride is on the outside, as in the figure above, you won't notice it too much, And even at that, negative unit strides are going to be preferable to extremely large, non-unit strides on most machines.

C
Obtaining Sample Programs and Problem Set Answers

Some of the examples in this book, and a set of answers to the "problems" posed at the end of most chapters, are available electronically in a number of ways: by ftp, ftpmail, bitftp, and uucp. The cheapest, fastest, and easiest ways are listed first. If you read from the top down, the first one that works for you is probably the best. Use *ftp* if you are directly on the Internet. Use ftpmail if you are not on the Internet but can send and receive electronic mail to internet sites (this includes CompuServe users). Use BITFTP if you send electronic mail via BITNET. Use UUCP if none of the above works.

FTP

To use FTP, you need a machine with direct access to the Internet. A sample session is shown, with what you should type in boldface.

```
% ftp ftp.uu.net
Connected to ftp.uu.net.
220 FTP server (Version 6.21 Tue Mar 10 22:09:55 EST 1992) ready.
Name (ftp.uu.net:kismet): anonymous
331 Guest login OK, send domain style e-mail address as password.
Password: kismet@ora.com (use your user name and host here)
230 Guest login OK, access restrictions apply.
ftp> cd /published/oreilly/nutshell/hpc
250 CWD command successful.
ftp> binary (Very important! You must specify binary transfer for compressed files.)
200 Type set to I.
ftp> get hpc.jun93.tar.Z
200 PORT command successful.
150 Opening BINARY mode data connection for hpc.jun93.tar.Z.
226 Transfer complete.
ftp> quit
221 Goodbye.
%
```

If the file is a compressed tar archive, extract the files from the archive by typing:

```
% zcat hpc.jun93.tar.Z | tar xf -
```

System V systems require the following tar command instead:

```
% zcat hpc.jun93.tar.Z | tar xof -
```

If *zcat* is not available on your system, use separate uncompress and tar commands.

FTPMAIL

FTPMAIL is a mail server available to anyone who can send and receive electronic mail to and from Internet sites. This includes most workstations that have an e-mail connection to the outside world, and CompuServe users. You do not need to be directly on the Internet. Here's how to do it.

You send mail to *ftpmail@decwrl.dec.com*. In the message body, give the name of the anonymous ftp host and the ftp commands you want to run. The server will run anonymous ftp for you and mail the files back to you. To get a complete help file, send a message with no subject and the single word "help" in the body. The following is an example mail session that should get you the examples. This command sends you a listing of the files in the selected directory, and the requested examples file. The listing is useful in case there's a later version of the examples you're interested in.

```
% mail ftpmail@decwrl.dec.com
Subject:
reply alan@ora.com              (where you want files mailed)
connect ftp.uu.net
chdir /published/oreilly/nutshell/hpc
dir
binary
uuencode                        (or btoa if you have it)
get hpc.jun93.tar.Z
quit
%
```

A signature at the end of the message is acceptable as long as it appears after "quit."

All retrieved files will be split into 60KB chunks and mailed to you. You then remove the mail headers and concatenate them into one file, and then *uudecode* or *atob* it. Once you've got the desired file, follow the directions under FTP to extract the files from the archive.

VMS, DOS, and Mac versions of *uudecode, atob, uncompress,* and *tar* are available. The VMS versions are on *gatekeeper.dec.com in /archive/pub/VMS.*

BITFTP

BITFTP is a mail server for BITNET users. You send it electronic mail messages requesting files, and it sends you back the files by electronic mail. BITFTP currently serves only users who send it mail from nodes that are directly on BITNET, EARN, or NetNorth. BITFTP is a public service of Princeton University. Here's how it works.

To use BITFTP, send mail containing your ftp commands to *BITFTP@PUCC.* For a complete help file, send HELP as the message body.

The following is the message body you should send to BITFTP:

```
FTP   ftp.uu.net   NETDATA
USER  anonymous
PASS your Internet email address (not your bitnet address)
CD   /published/oreilly/nutshell/hpc
DIR
BINARY
GET  hpc.jun93.tar.Z
QUIT
```

Once you've got the desired file, follow the directions under FTP to extract the files from the archive. Since you are probably not on a UNIX system, you may need to get versions of *uudecode, uncompress, atob,* and *tar* for your system. VMS, DOS, and Mac versions are available. The VMS versions are on *gatekeeper.dec.com* in */archive/pub/VMS.*

Questions about BITFTP can be directed to Melinda Varian, *MAINT@PUCC* on BITNET.

UUCP

UUCP is standard on virtually all UNIX systems, and is available for IBM-compatible PCs and Apple Macintoshes. The examples are available by UUCP via modem from UUNET; UUNET's connect-time charges apply.

You can get the examples from UUNET whether you have an account or not. If you or your company has an account with UUNET, you will have a system with a direct UUCP connection to UUNET. Find that system, and type:

```
uucp uunet\!~/published/oreilly/nutshell/hpc/hpc.jun93.tar.Z
     yourhost\!~/yourname/
```

The backslashes can be omitted if you use the Bourne shell (*sh*) instead of *csh*. The file should appear some time later (up to a day or more) in the directory */usr/spool/uucppublic/yourname.* If you don't have an account but would like one so that you can get electronic mail, then contact UUNET at 703-204-8000.

If you don't have a UUNET account, you can set up a UUCP connection to UUNET using the phone number 1-900-468-7727. As of this writing, the cost is 50 cents per minute. The charges will appear on your next telephone bill. The login name is "uucp" with no password. For example, an *L.sys/Systems* entry might look like:

```
uunet Any ACU 19200 1-900-468-7727 ogin:--ogin: uucp
```

Your entry may vary depending on your UUCP configuration. If you have a PEP-capable modem, make sure s50=255s111=30 is set before calling.

Try to get the file */published/oreilly/nutshell/hpc/ls-lR.Z* as a short test file containing the filenames and sizes of all the files in the directory.

Once you've got the desired file, follow the directions under FTP to extract the files from the archive.

Index

Books That Help People Get More Out of Computers

Please send me the following:

❑ A free catalog of titles.

❑ A list of Bookstores in my area that carry your books (U.S. and Canada only).

❑ A list of book distributors outside the U.S. and Canada.

❑ Information about consulting services for documentation or programming.

❑ Information about bundling books with my product.

❑ On-line descriptions of your books.

Name _____

Address _____

_____

City _____

State, ZIP _____

Country _____

Phone _____

Email Address _____
(Internet or Uunet)

Books That Help People Get More Out of Computers

Please send me the following:

❑ A free catalog of titles.

❑ A list of Bookstores in my area that carry your books (U.S. and Canada only).

❑ A list of book distributors outside the U.S. and Canada.

❑ Information about consulting services for documentation or programming.

❑ Information about bundling books with my product.

❑ On-line descriptions of your books.

Name _____

Address _____

_____

City _____

State, ZIP _____

Country _____

Phone _____

Email Address _____
(Internet or Uunet)

NAME_____

COMPANY_____

ADDRESS_____

CITY_____ STATE_____ ZIP_____

BUSINESS REPLY MAIL

FIRST CLASS MAIL PERMIT NO. 80 SEBASTOPOL, CA

POSTAGE WILL BE PAID BY ADDRESSEE

O'REILLY & ASSOCIATES, INC.

103 Morris Street Suite A
Sebastopol CA 95472-9902

NAME_____

COMPANY_____

ADDRESS_____

CITY_____ STATE_____ ZIP_____

BUSINESS REPLY MAIL

FIRST CLASS MAIL PERMIT NO. 80 SEBASTOPOL, CA

POSTAGE WILL BE PAID BY ADDRESSEE

O'REILLY & ASSOCIATES, INC.

103 Morris Street Suite A
Sebastopol CA 95472-9902

About the Author

Kevin Dowd is a consultant to the Aerospace and Commercial industries, specializing in performance computing and information infrastructures. He is a veteran of two computer companies (which no longer make computers), and the nuclear power plant business (not many more of those have been made either). Kevin is a principal in the Atlantic Computing Technology Corporation, located in Wethersfield, Connecticut. He can be reached at dowd@atlantic.com.

Colophon

Our look is the result of reader comments, our own experimentation, and distribution channels.

Distinctive covers complement our distinctive approach to technical topics, breathing personality and life into potentially dry subjects. UNIX and its attendant programs can be unruly beasts. Nutshell Handbooks help you tame them.

The animal featured on the cover of *High Performance Computing* is the Northern harrier (also known as the hen harrier or marsh hawk). Unlike most other hawks, this harrier likes to hunt exclusively on the wing—cruising up to 100 miles a day—and prefers roosting and nesting on the ground. Hunting forays over field and marsh consist of long, low glides powered by intermittent flaps, with an occasional pause to hover briefly. The Harrier aircraft is named for this characteristic.

This species is one of the most acrobatic and agile of raptors. During courtship, males perform spectacular aerobatics, marked by tumbling, drifting upside down, 200-foot spiral dives, stalls and wingovers.

Northern harriers prey on a variety of animals—predominately small mammals, birds and reptiles—which they detect with their keen sense of hearing (they are considered the diurnal counterpart of the short-eared owl). An owl-like facial ruff helps reflect sound (such as squeaking mice) to the harrier's sensitive ears. This bird of prey ranges over most temperate regions of the Northern Hemisphere.

Edie Freedman designed this cover and the entire UNIX bestiary that appears on other Nutshell Handbooks. The beasts themselves are adapted from 19th-century engravings from the Dover Pictorial Archive. The cover layout was produced with Quark XPress 3.1 using the ITC Garamond font.

The inside layout was formatted in sqtroff by Lenny Muellner and Kismet McDonough using ITC Garamond Light and ITC Garamond Book fonts, and was designed by Edie Freedman. The figures were created in Aldus Freehand 3.1 by Chris Reilley.

System Performance Tuning

By Mike Loukides

System Performance Tuning answers one of the most fundamental questions you can ask about your computer: "How can I get it to do more work without buying more hardware?" Anyone who has ever used a computer has wished that the system was faster, particularly at times when it was under heavy load.

If your system gets sluggish when you start a big job, if it feels as if you spend hours waiting for remote file access to complete, if your system stops dead when several users are active at the same time, you need to read this book. Some performance problems do require you to buy a bigger or faster computer, but many can be solved simply by making better use of the resources you already have.

336 pages, ISBN 0-937175-60-9

Essential System Administration

By Æleen Frisch

Like any other multi-user system, UNIX requires some care and feeding. *Essential System Administration* tells you how. This book strips away the myth and confusion surrounding this important topic and provides a compact, manageable introduction to the tasks faced by anyone responsible for a UNIX system.

If you use a stand-alone UNIX system, whether it's a PC or a workstation, you know how much you need this book: on these systems the fine line between a user and an administrator has vanished. Either you're both or you're in trouble. If you routinely provide administrative support for a larger shared system or a network of workstations, you will find this book indispensable. Even if you aren't directly responsible for system administration, you will find that understanding basic administrative functions greatly increases your ability to use UNIX effectively.

466 pages
ISBN 0-937175-80-3

Practical UNIX Security

By Simson Garfinkel & Gene Spafford

If you are a UNIX system administrator or user who needs to deal with security, you need this book.

Practical UNIX Security describes the issues, approaches, and methods for implementing security measures—spelling out what the varying approaches cost and require in the way of equipment. After presenting UNIX security basics and network security, this guide goes on to suggest how to keep intruders out, how to tell if they've gotten in, how to clean up after them, and even how to prosecute them. Filled with practical scripts, tricks and warnings, *Practical UNIX Security* tells you what you need to know to make your UNIX system as secure as it can be.

"Worried about who's in your Unix system? Losing sleep because someone might be messing with your computer? Having headaches from obscure computer manuals? Then *Practical Unix Security* is for you. This handy book tells you where the holes are and how to cork'em up.

"Moreover, you'll learn about how Unix security really works. Spafford and Garfinkel show you how to tighten up your Unix system without pain. No secrets here—just solid computing advice.

"Buy this book and save on aspirin."—Cliff Stoll
512 pages, ISBN 0-937175-72-2

Computer Security Basics

By Deborah Russell & G.T. Gangemi Sr.

There's a lot more consciousness of security today, but not a lot of understanding of what it means and how far it should go. This handbook describes complicated concepts like trusted systems, encryption and mandatory access control in simple terms.

For example, most U.S. government equipment acquisitions now require "Orange Book" (Trusted Computer System Evaluation Criteria) certification. A lot of people have a vague feeling that they ought to know about the Orange Book, but few make the effort to track it down and read it. *Computer Security Basics* contains a more readable introduction to the Orange Book—why it exists, what it contains, and what the different security levels are all about—than any other book or government publication.

464 pages, ISBN 0-937175-71-4

Computer Security

COMPUTER
SECURITY
BASICS

Deborah Russell and G. T. Gangemi Sr.
O'Reilly & Associates, Inc.

Managing UUCP and Usenet

10th Edition
By Tim O'Reilly & Grace Todino

For all its widespread use, UUCP is one of the most difficult UNIX utilities to master. Poor documentation, cryptic messages, and differences between various implementations make setting up UUCP links a nightmare for many a system administrator.

This handbook is meant for system administrators who want to install and manage the UUCP and Usenet software. It covers HoneyDanBer UUCP as well as standard Version 2 UUCP, with special notes on Xenix. As one reader noted over the Net, "Don't even TRY to install UUCP without it!"

368 pages, ISBN 0-937175-93-5

Using UUCP and Usenet

By Grace Todino & Dale Dougherty

Using UUCP shows how to communicate with both UNIX and non-UNIX systems using UUCP and *cu* or *tip*. It also shows how to read news and post your own articles and mail to other Usenet members. This handbook assumes that UUCP and Usenet links to other computer systems have already been established by your system administrator.

While clear enough for a novice, this book is packed with information that even experienced users will find indispensable. Take the mystery out of questions such as why files sent via UUCP don't always end up where you want them, how to find out the status of your file transfer requests, and how to execute programs remotely with *uux*.

210 pages, ISBN 0-937175-10-2

Understanding DCE

By Ward Rosenberry, David Kenney, and Gerry Fisher

Understanding DCE is a technical and conceptual overview of OSF's Distributed Computing Environment for programmers and technical managers, marketing and sales people. Unlike many O'Reilly & Associates books, *Understanding DCE* has no hands-on programming elements. Instead, the book focuses on how DCE can be used to accomplish typical programming tasks and provides explanations to help the reader understand all the parts of DCE.

266 pages (estimated), ISBN 1-56592-005-8

Guide to Writing DCE Applications

By John Shirley

A hands-on programming guide to OSF's Distributed Computing Environment (DCE) for first-time DCE application programmers. This book is designed to help new DCE users make the transition from conventional, nondistributed applications programming to distributed DCE programming. Covers the IDL and ACF files, essential RPC calls, binding methods and the name service, server initialization, memory management, and selected advanced topics. Includes practical programming examples.

282 pages, ISBN 1-56592-004-X

Learning GNU Emacs

By Deb Cameron & Bill Rosenblatt

GNU Emacs is the most popular and widespread of the Emacs family of editors. It is also the most powerful and flexible. (Unlike all other text editors, GNU Emacs is a complete working environment—you can stay within Emacs all day without leaving.) This book tells you how to get started with the GNU Emacs editor. It will also "grow" with you: as you become more proficient, this book will help you learn how to use Emacs more effectively. It will take you from basic Emacs usage (simple text editing) to moderately complicated customization and programming.

The book is aimed at new Emacs users, whether or not they are programmers. Also useful for readers switching from other Emacs implementations to GNU Emacs.

442 pages, ISBN 0-937175-84-6

Learning the vi Editor

5th Edition
By Linda Lamb

For many users, working in the UNIX environment means using *vi*, a full-screen text editor available on most UNIX systems. Even those who know *vi* often make use of only a small number of its features. This is the complete guide to text editing with *vi*. Early chapters cover the basics; later chapters explain more advanced editing tools, such as *ex* commands and global search and replacement.

192 pages, ISBN 0-937175-67-6

Learning the UNIX Operating System

2nd Edition
By Grace Todino & John Strang

If you are new to UNIX, this concise introduction will tell you just what you need to get started, and no more. Why wade through a 600-page book when you can begin working productively in a matter of minutes?

Topics covered include:

- Logging in and logging out
- Managing UNIX files and directories
- Sending and receiving mail
- Redirecting input/output
- Pipes and filters
- Background processing
- Customizing your account

"If you have someone on your site who has never worked on a UNIX system and who needs a quick how-to, Nutshell has the right booklet. *Learning the UNIX Operating System* can get a newcomer rolling in a single session."—;login

84 pages, ISBN 0-937175-16-1

MH & xmh:
E-mail for Users and Programmers

2nd Edition
By Jerry Peek

Customizing your e-mail environment can save you time and make communicating more enjoyable. *MH & xmh: E-mail for Users and Programmers* explains how to use, customize, and program with the MH electronic mail commands, available on virtually any UNIX system. The handbook also covers *xmh*, an X Window System client that runs MH programs.

The basics are easy. But MH lets you do much more than what most people expect an e-mail system to be able to do. This handbook is packed with explanations and useful examples of MH features, some of which the standard MH documentation only hints at.

728 pages, ISBN 1-56592-027-9

UNIX Text Processing

Learning

GNU Emacs

Debra Cameron and Bill Rosenblatt
O'Reilly & Associates, Inc.

Guide to OSF/1: A Technical Synopsis

By O'Reilly & Associates Staff

OSF/1, Mach, POSIX, SVID, SVR4, X/Open, 4.4BSD, XPG, B-1 security, parallelization, threads, virtual file systems, shared libraries, streams, extensible loader, internationalization.... Need help sorting it all out? If so, then this technically competent introduction to the mysteries of the OSF/1 operating system is a book for you. In addition to its exposition of OSF/1, it offers a list of differences between OSF/1 and System V, Release 4 and a look ahead at what is coming in DCE.

This is not the usual O'Reilly how-to book. It will not lead you through detailed programming examples under OSF/1. Instead, it asks the prior question, What is the nature of the beast? It helps you figure out how to approach the programming task by giving you a comprehensive technical overview of the operating system's features and services, and by showing how they work together.

304 pages, ISBN 0-937175-78-1

POSIX Programmer's Guide

By Donald Lewine

Most UNIX systems today are POSIX-compliant because the Federal government requires it. Even OSF and UI agree on support for POSIX. However, given the manufacturer's documentation, it can be difficult to distinguish system-specific features from those features defined by POSIX.

The *POSIX Programmer's Guide*, intended as an explanation of the POSIX standard and as a reference for the POSIX.1 programming library, will help you write more portable programs. This guide is especially helpful if you are writing programs that must run on multiple UNIX platforms. This guide will also help you convert existing UNIX programs for POSIX-compliance.

640 pages
ISBN 0-937175-73-0

Managing NFS and NIS

By Hal Stern

A modern computer system that is not part of a network is an anomaly. But managing a network and getting it to perform well can be a problem. This book describes two tools that are absolutely essential to distributed computing environments: the Network Filesystem (NFS) and the Network Information System (formerly called the "yellow pages" or YP).

As popular as NFS is, it is a black box for most users and administrators. This book provides a comprehensive discussion of how to plan, set up, and debug an NFS network. It is the only book we're aware of that discusses NFS and network performance tuning. This book also covers the NFS automounter, network security issues, diskless workstations, and PC/NFS. It also tells you how to use NIS to manage your own database applications, ranging from a simple telephone list to controlling access to network services. If you are managing a network of UNIX systems, or are thinking of setting up a UNIX network, you can't afford to overlook this book.

436 pages, ISBN 0-937175-75-7

Power Programming with RPC

By John Bloomer

A distributed application is designed to access resources across a network. In a broad sense, these resources could be user input, a central database, configuration files, etc., that are distributed on various computers across the network rather than found on a single computer. RPC, or remote procedure calling, is the ability to distribute the execution of functions on remote computers outside of the application's current address space. This allows you to break large or complex programming problems into routines that can be executed independently of one another to take advantage of multiple computers. Thus, RPC makes it possible to attack a problem using a form of parallel or multi-processing.

Written from a programmer's perspective, this book shows what you can do with RPC and presents a framework for learning it.

494 pages, ISBN 0-937175-77-3